The
Successful
Creative
Secretary

The
Successful

Creative Secretary

Carolyn Kristt

Parker Publishing Company, Inc.   West Nyack, N.Y.

THE SUCCESSFUL CREATIVE SECRETARY
by Carolyn Kristt

©1979, *by*

PARKER PUBLISHING COMPANY, INC.
West Nyack, New York

Library of Congress Cataloging in Publication Data

Kristt, Carolyn
    The successful creative secretary.

    Includes index.
    1. Secretaries--Handbooks, manuals, etc. 2. Office
practice--Handbooks, manuals, etc. I. Title.
HF5547.5.K74   651'.3741   78-13732
ISBN 0-13-860486-X

Printed in the United States of America

why this book offers extraordinary value to secretaries

This unique collection of practical reference data provides the Secretary with On-The-Job *Answers*. Here are the "tricks of the trade" so vital for effortless efficiency, packed with essential facts you'll be able to use, all organized for easiest reference and understanding; the "how-to," "what-to," "where-to-find" information, all detailed and further clarified with hundreds of illustrations, maps, diagrams, charts, and sample forms you can quickly and easily adapt to your needs.

This is a book to help the secretary function—a "right arm" with fingertip information. The simplified grammar review and basic spelling rules provide fast solutions to daily office correspondence problems. The illustrated ledger pages, bank deposit slips, checkbook stubs, receipts, and related information will be invaluable in filling *any* secretarial bookkeeping need. The memory, reading and comprehension aids will help the secretary function more efficiently, with less effort. And the practical application of procedures from all parts of the book forms the basis of finding shortcuts and *saving time*.

This is a problem solver book where the secretary will learn invaluable tips such as how to take quicker shorthand notes, more easily and efficiently transcribed belts and cassettes, keep a "short-list" for ordering supplies, color code a Rolidex, set up a numerical or alphabetical filing system, design a document to fit a situation, form a system to meet a new need.

It is a workbook showing how to properly type minutes of a meeting, a script and other passages of dialogue, a manuscript, a thesis, business letters in different styles, with lots of shortcut form letters and memos.

It is a "shop talk" book with handy suggestions for using tools such as a magnifying glass ruler, a translucent triangle for copy typing, a magnet to hold paper clips, a razor blade to scrape carbon copies, double sided tape, colored pencils, a kneaded eraser for cleaning key bar typewriters and adding machines, marking pens for notes, and crayons for package labeling.

It is a creative ideas book. Many times a spur of the moment situation is a "react now" situation—a brand new problem to be solved at once. What to do? Create something—innovate by learning from this book—use a 3 × 5 card instead of a postcard—print the billing form on colored paper—make a ruler on scissors with nailpolish—mail a post card requesting a telephone call from the client who works—staple an envelope inside the front cover of a file folder for small papers—paste repair telephone numbers on all office machines—keep emergency phone numbers all in one place labeled in red—reuse the large manilla envelope from the morning mail for the papers that must go out immediately by blacklining the writing or covering it altogether with 2 inch strips of wrapping tape and printing the address on that—type that rough draft on 8½ × 13 inch paper, with 2 inch margins on each side, 4 inch margins top and bottom (white space for notes) with carbon copies to each participant so ideas and changes can be noted before the meeting and, when necessary,—call the main office of the copy machine company to find out the location of a pay copier in your vicinity to use while waiting for the repairman.

It is a valuable collection of information such as an easy way to proofread, common abbreviations, the fact that matte carbon paper rarely smudges, the use of "Pending," "Current Work," "Mail," "For Signature," "Rush," "Urgent," folders, and the suggestion that if long distance telephone calls are logged, the log could be a small hard cover notebook kept under or next to the telephone.

This is an answer book where the secretary can find tricks for composing letters, ways to keep everything in its place, how to work with a telephone answering service, international time zones (for telephoning or trips), a listing of weights and measures (English and Metric with conversions), arabic numerals and their roman numeral equivalents, a list of widely used abbreviations, cable and telegram information, type faces in common use, a list of signs and symbols, postal regulations, and instructions for preparation of an original for black and white as well as color copying.

And this is a source book where the secretary can find out where to go to get the boss varied and unusual information such as the price of a stock over a certain period of time, biographical information on a famous person, a recent Supreme Court decision, licensing requirements for a particular profession, the translation of foreign words and phrases, information from a newspaper of 10 years ago, the nearest notary public, today's prime interest rate, the cost of an advertisement in (and the circulation of) a magazine, the function of various branches of government on a local, national or international level, the weather halfway around the world, the current price of gold, and the main office of a company.

The precious moments saved by the use of the shortcuts and timesavers in this treasury are priceless in themselves, but take on even greater value when viewed in the context of the secretary's role as fact finder, efficiency expert, and *the* person the boss turns to for a superior job performance and reliable information . . . quickly. To sum up, this treasurehouse of essential business data will enhance your reputation as a "successful and creative" secretary.

Carolyn Kristt

acknowledgments

With thanks to the participants:

Ingrid Anderson of White Collar Personnel Agency, Elsa Allen Fertig of Elsa Allen Personnel Agency, Copy Copia, Inc., IBD Graphics; all of San Francisco, California.

Peter Bessol, Helen Cortes, Audrey J. Gill, Josephine Danziger, Jack Emmetts, Dr. Samuel Esterkyn, Kenneth and Cherie Fehrman, Gil and Mickie Gillespie, Kip Goldman, Dr. Alan Green, Arlene Greenstein, Joseph and Zeevia Jaffa, R. Laniado Junas, Julius Kamp, Lewis Kimler, the Kristts, Bess Nemet Melinkoff, Isabel Moskow, Howard Ullman, Ruth Wiesner and Richard Wilson.

contents

8 **how to save time and money in postal matters......... 117**

9 **ideas for telephone efficiency and economy 137**

10 **time-saving knowledge about mailgrams, telegrams, telex and twx, radio, news and computer communications—what each is and how each is used 153**

11 **secretarial billing, banking, and bookkeeping made effortless 171**

1

how to organize your time . . . supplies . . . work . . . desk— and how to stay organized

Knowing the essential skills to do a job is only half the battle. The other half is getting it done, and it is organizing that is the key.

In order to handle an emergency, a priority, and/or a routine task, you first have to know what each one is and then how to work your way through one. Included here are daily situations and their solutions under each category. Once you have the formula, apply it to your own office.

Not only do you have to handle situations, you have to handle supplies. A way to keep track of what you already have in stock is illustrated in **10 Tips From A Stationer** and **Ideas From A Mail Order Catalog**.

You also have to record happenings, sales, dates, payments, holidays, vacations, meetings and deadlines; and what better way to record than with calendars? There are desk calendars in book style, single page and petite; and wall calendars showing one week, one month, two months (with the months of the current year for reference) and a year (with the first three months of the following year on the reverse side). Use what is easiest for you to write things down on as you find out about them. The value of lists speaks for itself.

A place for everything and everything in its place is the only way to stay organized. Included to help you get ideas are pictures of a pencil holder, pen stands, list finders, a card file, a stationery tray, a note rack, a copyholder, stackable trays and super-stackable trays, an add-a-file, desk top organizers, a hanging folder frame, an in-out message board, a wire organizer, book and catalog racks, bookends, stationery holders, cash and file boxes, posting tubs, a canceled check file, roll-about files, drawer files and carry files.

Finally, a word about innovation. Folders marked "Pending," "Current Work," "Mail," "For Signature," "Rush" and "Urgent" are very helpful.

HANDLING EMERGENCIES, PRIORITIES AND ROUTINE TASKS

An **emergency** situation requires immediate attention and is handled in two parts:

1. The groundwork that gives INSTANT ACCESSIBILITY TO NECESSARY INFORMATION:
   a. Know ahead of time the location of fire exits, alarms and extinguishers.
   b. Keep emergency phone numbers where they can be instantly found.
   c. Keep repair phone numbers taped to office machines.
   d. Make duplicate keys.
   e. Keep the first aid box properly stocked.

2. REACT CALMLY AND RATIONALLY, and if you cannot handle a particular situation ask a neighboring office for help or call either "Operator" or local emergency (911 most places).

Priorities come ahead of something else in time, importance and order and are twofold:

1. *Anticipated* (around which work is scheduled)—monthly billings, payroll, tax reports, sales meetings and the like. The important thing is to calendar ahead and begin to compile data as you go along.
2. *Unanticipated*—on-the-spot work which must be done

immediately, such as letters, sales orders and court papers.

Tips: 1. If you must stop someone else's work to get out a priority item and their expected deadline will be missed, TELL THEM AS FAR IN ADVANCE AS POSSIBLE.
2. Take the few extra minutes each time to keep supplies organized as you use them.
3. Work step by step under pressure—DON'T PANIC—DON'T TENSE UP. The result will be better work.

Routine work is work that is ongoing and important.

1. Try to set aside a certain time each day for the "regulars" (on-going projects)—sort filing at the end of the day instead of after each letter; do the same kinds of things together (see what is needed from the supply room and bring many items in one trip—copy as much each time as you can).
2. Fill-in. Use extra minutes here and there to sort and straighten supplies; sharpen many pencils at the same time.

THE VALUE OF INVENTORY

Knowing at a glance how much stock you have of a particular item enables you to put together an order list quickly and accurately. It also gives you a picture of how fast you are using certain things by showing the previous purchase date, quantity and price. The use of inventory sheets is a good cross-check against stock and is a good "short list" (items running low). Paste it on the inside of a file cabinet door or in a stock room.

---

10 TIPS FROM A STATIONER

Schwabacher-Frey Office Supply Company of San Francisco suggests:

1. Set up a charge.
2. Go in and browse.

INVENTORY

Sheet No._____

Page No._____

_____19_____

Department_____Priced by_____Checked by_____

Location_____Extended by_____Checked by_____

Called by_____Entered by_____Footed by_____Examined by_____

QUANTITY	UNIT	DESCRIPTION	PRICE	UNIT	EXTENSION	TOTAL	✓

Rediform 3G 477

Courtesy of Rediform office products, Paramus, New Jersey

3. Request to be put on the mailing list so you will know about new products, store specials and sales.

4. Talk to the clerks. They know their stock and their field. Tell them the type of job to be done and if you are not sure about how to do it, ask what supplies are needed.

5. Keep an open mind. New products are being invented all the time.

6. If you intend to purchase a specific item, always bring the brand name and the model number.

7. If you do not see the item you want, ask if it can be special ordered.

8. The best price is a bulk price—dozen(s), ream(s), and, of course, a sale price.

9. At the time of purchase, ask the clerk about anything special you should know about maintenance of the article.

10. Ask for a catalog and take it back to your office. Let the other people in the office, whose jobs and needs might differ from yours, look through it. Ask to browse through catalogs of office products not regularly stocked.

IDEAS FROM A MAIL ORDER CATALOG

One of the many mail order firms specializing in office supplies is

the drawing board, inc.®

OFFICES: 256 REGAL ROW • P. O. BOX 505 • DALLAS, TEXAS 75221 • (214) 637-0390

They offer a money-back guarantee and can be reached by calling Toll Free 1-800-527-2666 in the continental United States; except for calls originating in Texas, where the number is 1-800-5134 for information or for their full color, approximately 100-page catalog containing the following illustrations:

GENERAL INDEX

ORGANIZING YOUR WORK WITH CALENDARS

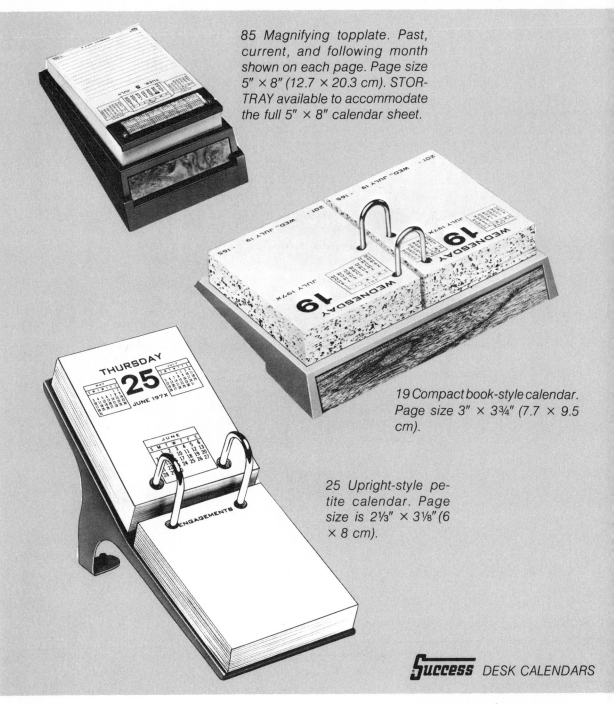

85 *Magnifying topplate. Past, current, and following month shown on each page. Page size 5" × 8" (12.7 × 20.3 cm). STOR-TRAY available to accommodate the full 5" × 8" calendar sheet.*

19 *Compact book-style calendar. Page size 3" × 3¾" (7.7 × 9.5 cm).*

25 *Upright-style petite calendar. Page size is 2⅓" × 3⅛" (6 × 8 cm).*

Success *DESK CALENDARS*

COLUMBIAN *Art* **WORKS, INC.**
5700 W. BENDER COURT • MILWAUKEE, WISCONSIN 53218
MADE IN U.S.A.

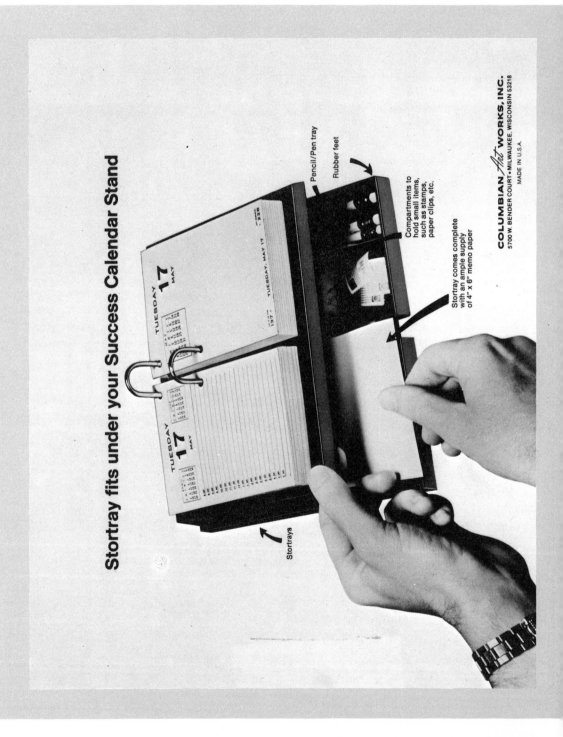

Stortray fits under your Success Calendar Stand

Pencil/Pen tray

Rubber feet

Compartments to hold small items, such as stamps, paper clips, etc.

Stortray comes complete with an ample supply of 4" x 6" memo paper

Stortrays

COLUMBIAN *Art* WORKS, INC.
5700 W. BENDER COURT • MILWAUKEE, WISCONSIN 53218
MADE IN U.S.A.

JANUARY

SUNDAY 2		
MONDAY 3		
TUESDAY 4		
WEDNESDAY 5		
THURSDAY 6		
FRIDAY 7		
SATURDAY 8		

JANUARY

Weekly Calendar

Appointments and notations for an entire week can be handily made with this 5" × 8" planning calendar. Wire-O-Bound and one hole center punched for wall or desk use, heavy tagboard backing, the metric converter and 400 + year perpetual calendar.

JANUARY

SUN	MON	TUE	WED	THU	FRI	SAT
DECEMBER 5	6	7	1	2	3	4
12	13	14	8	9	10	11
19	20	21	15	16	17	18
26	27	28	22	23	24	25
			29	30	31	1
2	3	4	5	6	7	8
9	10	11	12	13	14	15
16	17	18	19	20	21	22
23	24	25	26	27	28	29
30	31	FEBRUARY				
		1	2	3	4	5
6	7	8	9	10	11	12
13	14	15	16	17	18	19
20	21	22	23	24	25	26
27	28					
SUN	MON	TUE	WED	THU	FRI	SAT

Three Month Wall Planners

Note space is provided in both current and future; six months before and twelve months after each three month display is shown at top of the calendar page.

Available in two sizes:
1032-0—8" × 13½" Wire-O-Bound
1034-0—12 ¼"× 22½" Wire-O-Bound

SUCCESS WALL CALENDARS

EASY WAYS TO KEEP EVERYTHING IN ITS PLACE

50177

Courtesy Hunt/Lit-Ning Products, Desk Top Organizers, Filing Supplies
Division of Hunt Manufacturing Company,
7435 Industrial Highway, Florence, Kentucky 41042 and
2496 S. Cherry, Fresno, California 93706.

Courtesy Hunt/Lit-Ning Products, Desk Top Organizers, Filing Supplies
Division of Hunt Manufacturing Company
7435 Industrial Highway, Florence, Kentucky 41042 and
2496 S. Cherry, Fresno, California 93706.

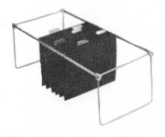

Courtesy Hunt/Lit-Ning Products, Desk Top Organizers, Filing Supplies
Division of Hunt Manufacturing Company
7435 Industrial Highway, Florence, Kentucky 41042 and
2496 S. Cherry, Fresno, California 93706.

HOW TO USE SPACE EFFICIENTLY

Eldon® Reflection 2000™ *Penstand,
a product of Eldon Office Products, Inc.*

Eldon® Reflection 2000™ *Pencil Cup,
a product of Eldon Office Products, Inc.*

Eldon® Card File,
a product of Eldon Office Products, Inc.

Eldon® Stationery Tray,
a product of Eldon Office Products, Inc.

Eldon® Note Rack,
a product of Eldon Office Products, Inc.

Eldon® List Finders,
a product of Eldon Office Products, Inc.

Eldon® Add-A-File®,
a product of Eldon Office Products, Inc.

Eldon® Copyholder,
a product of Eldon Office Products, Inc.

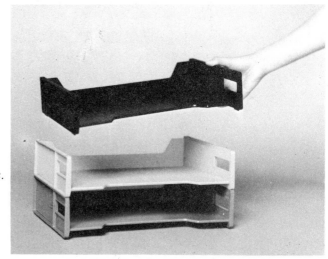

Eldon® Stackables®,
a product of Eldon Office Products, Inc.

ELDON®OFFICE PRODUCTS
1130 East 230th St | Carson. Calif 90745 | (213) 518-1600
Division of Eldon Industries Inc

Eldon® Super Stackables®,
a product of Eldon Office Products, Inc.

2

taking and transcribing
letters more easily

Along with a solid working knowledge of your particular type of shorthand and the efficient use of your supplies, it is important to have a common sense approach to dictation and transcription.

Keep your notebook in the same place so you can get to it quickly for spur-of-the-moment emergencies. Keep a pen or pencil clipped or tied to the spiral and keep it open to a fresh page.

Know your dictation equipment. If you are using tapes, it only takes a moment to erase them. This method is better than dictating over a voice because pauses allow old dictation to filter through and, once a tape is erased, there is never the problem of typing it twice. Rewind it and label it "erased" by taping a note to the plastic when you return it. If a tape or belt is worn and the dictation is fuzzy because of age, alert your boss so that future work and time are not wasted.

Many people know your firm *only* by its letters. You are the "middleman" between your boss's spoken words and the typed, finished copy. It goes without saying that they should be neat and easy to read. That they should be correct does not imply omnipotence—it affirms the use of your dictionary; a thesaurus; this book; city, county, and state maps; and for the answer you can't find, the telephone number of the public library.

Last, but certainly not least, if you compose your own letters or write for someone else, always give it the "acid" test—put yourself in the addressee's place—is the message clear?

EFFICIENT USE OF YOUR NOTEBOOK, PENS AND PENCILS

Shorthand is exactly what it says—a short method of handwriting. Basically, there are three shorthand systems:

Gregg—a system of symbols representing words and phrases.
Pittman—a system of symbols and light and dark strokes representing words and phrases.
Speedwriting—a system of letters of the alph⸱⸱⸱ ⸱⸱⸱arks of punctuation to represent words an⸱ ⸱⸱⸱

Proficiency and speed in notetaking in any form of shorthand come from the total concentration on the spoken sound, the use of as many brief forms (single symbols representing many words or particular long phrases) as possible, the pinpointing of special instructions without loss of text, and the coordination of notes to correspondence being answered. The *efficient* use of your tools frees you to concentrate.

1. Use separate notebooks for each dictator.
2. Date and number each page.
3. Keep a rubber band around transcribed pages.
4. Use only half the page:
   a. if the dictator makes many changes;
   b. if there are many special instructions;
   c. to use for longhand spelling of names or for notes to yourself about context when the dictator is interrupted.
5. If the dictator works from correspondence, take a file folder to dictation so their order will be proper.
6. Use the dictator's pause to turn the page if there are only one or two lines left.
7. Use colored pens or pencils for special instructions.
8. Make sure the major writing instrument is comfortable.
9. If you use lead pencils rather than a mechanical pencil, bring extras (sharpened).
10. Paper clips can be used to mark priority items, special

passages in your book, or for small papers; so keep a few around the cover.
11. Skip spaces or draw a line between letters.
12. Save notebooks.

TIPS FOR ROUTINE DICTATION

1. Develop your own "brief forms"—if you are in a secretarial pool where others transcribe your notes, make up a "dictionary" of brief forms and post it so everyone can learn and add new symbols.
2. If the dictator is going too fast, speak up.
3. Check items not specified by the dictator such as letter or memo, addressee, spelling, number of carbon copies ١d/or other special instructions.
4. Check unfamiliar words or names and spell in longhand if necessary.
5. If part of the dictation is to be a passage read from other material, ask for the material instead of taking it all down.

TIPS FOR ON-THE-SPOT DICTATION

1. Ideally, one notebook is kept for routine dictation and one for "other."
2. If you have to use scratch paper, use a small note pad and treat the width of the page as one shorthand column.
3. If you have to use a large sheet, divide the page in half vertically.
4. Date, number and label with the dictator's initials and staple pages together IMMEDIATELY upon completion.
5. Eventually staple pages into shorthand notebook.

TIPS FOR VERBATIM DICTATION

1. Use a cassette tape recorder as back-up if possible.
2. When circumstances permit, obtain the agenda first.
3. If it is to be an all day session, see if one stenographer can take the morning and one the afternoon.
4. If you do it all, rest during breaks and eat a good lunch.
5. Keep extra, sharpened pencils as well as pens.
6. Stop the speaker if you miss something important.

TIPS FOR CONTEXT DICTATION
AND EDITING

1. For part of a meeting—instead of pacing yourself as during long, routine dictation—work at your top pace for the short time interval. Question if you miss something.
2. If you are to sit through a meeting to take notes that edit the content:
   a. familiarize yourself first with the subject matter and agenda when possible;
   b. ascertain the train of thought you are to follow and whether to indicate names of speakers throughout;
   c. check if the points you pick out should be taken down verbatim or if you should edit completely.

HINTS FOR ERRORLESS SHORTHAND
TRANSCRIPTION

1. Re-read notes during pauses in dictation and write down unusual or problematic words in longhand and in colored pencil.
2. Circle words to check later if there is no time to question.
3. Double check unclear phraseology and punctuation during the dictation.
4. Keep coordinating correspondence from the dictator in the same order as it was dictated.
5. **Before typing:**
   a. Read the letter through.
   b. Correct grammar and punctuation *if this is your responsibility*.
   c. Check spelling, addresses and special instructions.
   d. Pull files.
   e. If you cannot figure out a symbol through context, ask the dictator. If he is out, hold the letter or type as much as you can and wait to ask. (Sometimes another letter on the same subject will clarify the symbol, or just some time away from it may make it clearer.)
   f. Learn to gauge the size of the finished letter by the amount of space of the dictation.
      Generally:
      Short letter—up to 100 words, 50 space line, margins—pica 17 and 67; elite 25 and 75.

Medium—100 to 300 words, 60 space line, margins—
pica 12 and 72; elite 20 and 80.

Long—over 300 words, 65 space line for pica with margins at 10 and 75, and 75 space line for elite with
margins at 12 and 90.

KEYS FOR ERRORLESS
MACHINE TRANSCRIPTION

1. **Before beginning**, note the kind and length of dictated
   material from the dictation instructions accompanying the
   tape or belt.
2. **Before beginning**, note special instructions such as the
   number of carbon copies, place of inserts or deletions,
   attachments, rough draft and original for printer.
3. **Before beginning**, pull files if necessary.
4. **Listen a phrase ahead for:**
   a. garbled words or phrases,
   b. insertion or deletion,
   c. special instructions (e.g. call Mr. Jones for address),
   d. to punctuate if that is your responsibility.
5. In case of a garbled word or phrase:
   a. If operating the machine on battery, plug it in.
   b. Listen word for word, then phrase for phrase.
   c. Change the tone button and listen again.
   d. Change the speed button and listen again.
   e. Clean the heads of the tape recorder with alcohol on a
      piece of cloth or cotton.
   f. Play the machine without earphones.
   g. Have someone else listen (people hear differently).
   h. Try to identify the word from context.
   i. If the dictator cannot be located, go on to the next
      dictation and check later. Note the location of the prob-
      lem by tape number or by ticket number.

TIPS FROM AT&T FOR
TELEPHONE DICTATION

Taking dictation by telephone is different from taking dictation in
the usual manner. You hear only the voice and unless you are using
special equipment (headset, speakerphone, etc.), you have only

one hand free to use. The dictator is unable to observe the appropriateness of the dictating speed and rate, and whether or not you understand.

1. Have your notebook and pen or pencil readily accessible.
2. Write well-proportioned characters.
3. Record instructions (do not rely on memory).
4. Verify numbers and names.
5. Be sure you understand instructions and content of material before terminating the call.
6. If the person dictates too rapidly:
   a. Repeat the last word or phrase.
   b. Use an expression such as "I'm sorry. I didn't understand that," to suggest that the person speak more slowly, or ask tactfully that the dictation be slowed down.
7. If the person dictates so slowly that you are unable to grasp the thoughts expressed:
   a. Use such phrases as "Yes," "All right," or "I have that."
8. If you do not understand:
   a. Repeat the word or expression, using a questioning tone.
   b. Request that the word be spelled by using an expression such as "How is that spelled, please?"

These techniques give the person dictating the opportunity to make corrections in the case of misunderstandings, or to speak more distinctly if necessary.

GUIDELINES FOR COMPOSING LETTERS

A letter is a story, a telling of a series of events. It is also a silent conversation.

1. State your business so it will be easily understood.
2. As a guideline, use the journalist's checklist:
   Who —the principal characters involved.
   What —the end result desired.
   Where —any necessary location indication (your other city plant).

> *When* —time sequence of topic (our memo of blank date, our invoice of blank date, necessary answer date).
>
> *How* —the way the end result will materialize (please mail your payment, please call Mr. Blank in the other city office).
>
> *Why* —the reason for writing—the topic

3. If you are writing for someone else or in the name of your company, use the style associated with the writer.
4. If you are writing under your own signature, speak in your own words, but with enough formality to convey that you are speaking on behalf of another entity or person.
5. Avoid run-on sentences, too many pronouns, unnecessary words or phrases and sentences with ambiguous meaning.
6. Use particulars (model numbers, file numbers, invoice numbers, case names, brand names, arrival times, dates, flight numbers, account numbers).
7. As a check, read the letter back as if you were the addressee—does it tell, simply, the reason for writing?

USING THE DICTIONARY AND THESAURUS

For commonly used words, a good paperback dictionary will give you:

1. definitions,
2. spelling and variant spellings,
3. pronunciation,
4. capitalization,
5. syllabication,
6. stress (the spoken amount of loudness of syllables),
7. the plural sense in addition to the listed singular noun,
8. part of speech,
9. usage labels (tells reader a word is used only in some contexts),
10. field labels (specialized sense of the word),
11. etymology (original development of the word from pre-English sources),
12. abbreviations and idioms,
13. regular, present tense verbs,

14. irregular inflections (the change of the form of a word to indicate number, gender, tense, etc. for plurals, principal parts of verbs, comparatives and superlatives).

A desk size dictionary will give you many more words, all of the above and:

1. scientific names of plants and animals,
2. cross reference to words of similar meaning,
3. synonyms (words in the same language with the same or nearly the same meaning),
4. homographs (words of the same spelling but different meaning and origin),
5. prefixes and suffixes,
6. foreign sounds, symbols and words,
7. prepositions generally used with verbs,
8. transitive verbs,
9. language labels (language origin of the word).

An unabridged dictionary, which is said to give the most complete list of words will include all of the above plus:

1. restrictive labels (entries which are all or partially limited to a special time, region, subject or level of usage such as slang),
2. biographical notations,
3. geographical notations,
4. acronyms (a word formed from the first or first few letters of a series of words),
5. blends (parts of two words combined to make one new word),
6. literal translations,
7. indication of unknown etymology.

A thesaurus is a book of synonyms (words and phrases of the same meaning) and antonyms (words and phrases of opposite meaning) arranged by category or by dictionary method and category. Use it to improve vocabulary and when composing letters.

3

time-saving typewriter knowledge

The knowledge of the scope of things which can be done by different typewriters enables you to know that a project is feasible (even if a certain typewriter must be rented or it is necessary to bring the work to a commercial secretarial service having the proper equipment to do the job). It also gives a basis for judgment when new systems are being developed within the office which might require more sophisticated machines.

In addition, it is handy to know that there are keyboards available in foreign languages and special symbol keys that can be substituted.

Covered in this chapter are descriptions, basic specifications and brief discussions of the individual and unique capabilities of some of the different IBM typewriters.

The IBM Model D is the basic typewriter; the IBM Executive is the proportional spacing machine (and beautifully justifies a right hand margin).

The IBM Correcting Selectric has, in addition to the self-correcting tape mechanism, interchangeable elements for different typefaces. To familiarize you with the typefaces available, illustrations show each typeface, its size and suggest its best use. Also included is a chart showing the type styles in relation to the number of carbon copies each will make as well as how each works in relation to offset masters, spirit masters, stencils, diazo and office copier machines.

Not to be forgotten is the IBM Mag Card II—the typewriter with Electronic Memory and Machine Logic.

The IBM Model D Typewriter

The IBM Model D Typewriter is the perfect partner for typists who must do many different typing jobs in any word processing environment...and do them well. With its wide selection of optional features and time-saving attachments, it can be tailored to meet the needs of any typing job...from routine work to highly specialized assignments.

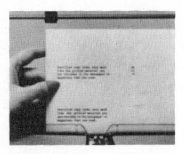

The typing is fast and easy

- Advanced keyboard with sculptured keys provides a more natural typing position...promotes keyboard security.
- Controls are grouped conveniently to minimize hand movements at keyboard level.
- Half Space Lever simplifies error correction, speeds typing to justified right-hand margin.
- Universal Card Holder makes it convenient to type cards and labels.
- Rapid ribbon rewind makes fabric ribbon changes faster and cleaner.
- Typamatic Keys provide rapid, automatic repeat action for carriage return, space bar, backspace, underscore, hyphen, period, and "x".
- Zero Center Copy Guide Scale speeds and simplifies centering.

Quality is assured

- Adjustable Impression Control allows typist to vary striking force of type bars for different applications.
- Center Basket Underscore assures even lines across the page.
- Dual Impression Control automatically shifts striking force of uppercase and lowercase characters to provide uniform color and density.
- Individually aligned Type Bars insure even typing lines.
- Individually regulated striking force of Type Bars assures consistently uniform impressions.
- Quiet-Glide Carriage eliminates distracting jolts and noises that can affect typing accuracy.
- Strong box frame construction provides the stable base necessary for uniformity...assures longer carriage life.

Typists can handle special work with speed and ease

- Changeable Type Bars
- Special Type and Line Spacing
- Interchangeable Platens
- Attachments for Continuous Forms and Index Cards
- Carbon or Fabric Ribbon Models
- Variety of Keyboard Arrangements
- Wide Selection of Type Styles
- 88 Character Keyboard
- Choice of 2 Carriage Sizes

Specifications

Dimensions: Height 236.2 mm (9.3"), Depth 429.3 mm (16.9"), Case Width (base) 421.6 mm (16.6"). (Standard for all IBM Model D Typewriters.)

Carriage Sizes	Models with 16" Carriage	Models with 19" Carriage
Writing Line:	403.9 mm (15.9")	480.1 mm (18.9")
Maximum Paper Accommodation:	406.4 mm (16.0")	482.6 mm (19.0")
Outside Width (Carriage Centered):	561.3 mm (22.1")	635.0 mm (25.0")
Weight:	22.7 kg (50 lbs.)	23.6 kg (52 lbs.)

IBM

International Business Machines Corporation
Office Products Division
For additional information, consult the nearest IBM Branch Office.

The IBM Executive. Typewriter

Everything typed on it is distinctively different. Proportional lettering is why. Each typed character uses as much space as it needs to produce that fine print-like quality so easy to distinguish from conventionally typed material. Impressions that identify the sender . . . invite response from the recipient. When it comes to more effective communications, the IBM "Executive" Typewriter delivers the competitive edge.

Standard typing.
A single space for each character.

communications

IBM Proportional typing.
A single space for each character *unit*.

communications

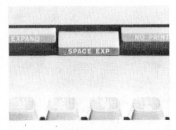

Proportional typing . . . for more effective communication

The unique typing action of the IBM "Executive" Typewriter gives each character the space it requires by using four different letter widths. Wide characters typed next to each other are never crowded; gaps between narrow letters are eliminated. This typographic balance makes your message easier to read, pleases the eye and encourages prompt consideration.

Refined impression controls create a uniform appearance

- Adjustable Impression Control regulates striking force of type bars simply by turning a dial.
- Dual Impression Control allows individual adjustment of upper- and lower-case characters.
- Exclusive Secondary Impression Control prevents embossing of punctuation marks and other normally penetrating characters.
- Multiple Copy Control maintains quality by adjusting platen for varying quantities.

New ease of operation for increased typing productivity

- Repositioning Indicator Control at keyboard level permits corrections with absolute precision.
- Zero Center-Point Scale and No-Print Control permit rapid, accurate centering.
- Contoured keyboard encourages natural typing position, greater comfort.
- Keyboard functions are located conveniently to eliminate wasted motion . . . reduce typing fatigue.
- Seven Typamatic keys provide rapid, automatic repeat action.
- Instant Line Finder returns the platen to original typing line after typing above or below it.

Versatility for maximum contribution to your typing needs

- Space Expand Lever adds one unit to the two-unit space bar for rapid statistical typing.
- Expand Lever adds a unit of space to space bars and characters for open headings.
- Select from variety of type styles for distinctive appearance, perfect reproduction masters, special requirements.
- Changeable type bars permit insertion of special characters.
- Choose carbon ribbons for perfect impressions, quality and durability.
- 88-character keyboard is available in a variety of keyboard arrangements, with unit escapements of 1/32", or 1/36".

Specifications

Dimensions: Height 9¼", Depth 16⅞". Case Width (base) 16⅝"

Carriage Sizes	Models with 16" Carriage	Models with 19" Carriage
Writing Line	15.9"	18.9"
Maximum Paper Accommodation	16.0"	19.0"
Outside Width (Carriage Centered)	22⅛"	25⅛"
Weight	52 lbs.	54 lbs.

IBM
Word Processing

International Business Machines Corporation
Office Products Division
For additional information, consult the nearest IBM Branch Office

The IBM Correcting Selectric® Typewriter

A typewriter that does just about everything.
Featuring the IBM correcting capability that corrects typing errors as simply as striking a keyboard button for each incorrectly typed character.

An Innovation in Error Correction
The correcting capability is within the typewriter and is controlled by a conveniently located Correcting Key positioned on the keyboard. This means that original copies can now be corrected as a normal part of the typing function.

New Ribbon/Tape System
IBM has developed a new ribbon/tape system especially for this new typewriter. IBM Correctable Film Ribbon and IBM Lift-off Tape work in tandem to assure the complete removal of the typed image on original copies when a mistake is made.

Although carbon copies still have to be erased in the usual way, corrected errors on the original document look flawless. This means that you can now use letterheads and envelopes that might ordinarily have to be discarded because of the poor appearance caused by typing corrections. Moreover, the clean appearance of the corrected originals provides you with a better document for your copy machine needs.

The Correctable Film Ribbon has been developed for all general correspondence applications. When typing negotiable instruments, the IBM Tech III Ribbon should be used.

Alternate System
The typewriter is also designed to accept an alternate correcting capability: an IBM Tech III Ribbon with IBM Tech III Cover-up Tape. IBM Tech III Ribbon offers many proven benefits — extra long life and sharp, easy-to-read impressions. It is virtually impossible to decipher any information on the IBM Tech III Ribbon after its use. The advanced fluid ink technology enables the ribbon to be struck several times in the same area…without reducing the clarity of the typewritten page. The IBM Tech III Cover-up Tape provides a quality white formulation for masking typing errors.

Easy to Use
Both correcting systems are color coded for easy identification: yellow spools for IBM Correctable Film Ribbon and IBM Lift-off Tape and blue spools for IBM Tech III Ribbon and IBM Tech III Cover-up Tape. And both systems can be installed in the typewriter as easily as an ordinary ribbon.

Dual Pitch
This feature enables the IBM Correcting "Selectric" Typewriter to type either 10 or 12 characters per inch.

Stroke Storage System prevents crowded or missing characters.

Interchangeable Elements
These typing elements can be snapped on and off, in seconds. They offer interchangeable typefaces — to give new freshness and distinction to correspondence, reports, bulletins and other documents.

Half Backspace
When a character has been left out of a word, the Half Backspace Lever allows the typist to insert the character without affecting the rest of the typed line. When used with the typewriter's new correcting capability, insertions are easier to make. (Dual Pitch models only.)

Sound Reduction Option
Some noise-sensitive areas — hospitals, libraries, executive floors — may require extra-quiet typing stations. The new Sound Reduction Option is designed for just such locations. The sound dampening features are an integral part of the typewriter.

Specifications:
Operates on 115 volt, 60 Hertz, 1.2 amperes AC current.

Single Pitch Models	Model 853	Model 855
Dual Pitch Models	**Model 893**	**Model 895**
Writing Line	11.0"	13.0"
Maximum Paper Accommodation	13.5"	15.5"
Case Width	18.5"	20.5"
Outside Width (Including Platen Knobs)	20.0"	22.0"
Depth (Front to Back)	15.6"	15.6"
Height	7.6"	7.6"
Weight	36 lbs.	38 lbs.

Typewriter Colors Available: Emerald Green, Classic Blue, Sandstone Beige, Willow Green, Topaz Bronze, Garnet Rose, Pearl White and Raven Black.

IBM
International Business Machines Corporation
Office Products Division
For additional information, consult the nearest IBM Branch Office.

TYPING ELEMENTS

The IBM Correcting "Selectric" Typewriter and the IBM "Selectric" II Typewriter incorporate interchangeable Element technology for the greatest versatility and flexibility in typing. When changing typing applications, simply change the typing Element. They snap in and out in seconds.

On top of each Element is the following:

- The name of the type style; example, Courier 72.
- A 10 or 12 indicating pitch.
- The black Element Release Lever (except on Elements with a specially requested character which have a white Lever).
- A three-digit part number under the Element Release Lever.

The wide range of type styles available from IBM cover virtually every typing application. From general correspondence to specialized formats. You'll find one right for every typing job. You can even order type Elements applicable to specific industries and foreign languages—with special characters, punctuation marks, and symbols.

If you don't find the typing Elements just right for you among the standard keyboard arrangements, ask your IBM Representative about Custom Typing Elements.

Note: Using a typing Element of one pitch when the typewriter is set for the other pitch will alter only the amount of space between each character.

SUGGESTED ELEMENT SETS

Accounting:
Advocate
Letter Gothic
Manifold (006)
Scribe
Prestige Pica 72
Bookface
   Academic 72

Correspondence:
Artisan 12
Courier 12
Courier 72
Prestige Elite 72

Engineering and Scientific:
Delegate
Dual Gothic
Light Italic
Symbol 10 or 12

Executive:
Courier 12
Light Italic
Orator
Script
Bookface
   Academic 72

Forms:
Artisan 12
Courier 12
Dual Gothic
Manifold 72 (010)

General Typing:
Advocate
Courier 12
Letter Gothic
Prestige Elite 72
Prestige Pica 72
Bookface
   Academic 72

Legal:
Large Elite
Light Italic
Pica 72 (legal)*
Prestige Elite 72
Prestige Pica 72
Bookface
   Academic 72

Library:
Delegate
Elite 72 (library)
Orator
Script

Medical:
Advocate
Courier 12
Courier 12 italic
Letter Gothic

Personnel:
Advocate
Artisan 12
Letter Gothic
Orator

Sales:
Courier 72
Dual Gothic
Orator
Prestige Elite 72

Statistical:
Artisan 12
Light Italic
Manifold 72 (019)
Prestige Elite 72
Prestige Pica 72

*A specialized keyboard arrangement is available for this element.

10 Pitch Type Styles and Their Applications

Advocate 1167130	10 Pitch, 12 Point	**Bookface Academic 72*** 1167158	10 Pitch, 10 Point
IBM ADVOCATE type is well suited for all general correspondence applications. Note the easy reading of its open-spaced, square-serif design.		IBM BOOKFACE ACADEMIC 72 Type is ideal for executive correspondence, offset reproduction and statistical reports, with its large, bold serif design.	

Delegate 1167135 10 Pitch, 12 Point	**Pica 72** 1167142 10 Pitch, 12 Point
IBM DELEGATE Type is recommended for text copy and similar jobs, where a weighted type conveying the feeling of printed material is used.	IBM PICA 72 Type is used for general correspondence, stencils and manifolding. It is also available in legal, court reporter and chemical versions.
Prestige Pica 72* 1167123 10 Pitch, 12 Point	**Courier 72** 1167134 10 Pitch, 10 Point
IBM PRESTIGE PICA 72 Type is ideal for legal correspondence, offset reproduction, statistical reports and manifolding. There is also an accounting version.	IBM COURIER 72 Type finds wide use in general correspondence, offset reproduction and manifolding. It is a square-serif design in the Pica family.

Special Typing Applications

Orator** 1167141   10 Pitch, 14 and 8 Point
IBM ORATOR TYPE IS RECOMMENDED FOR SPEECHES, CHARTS, LABELS AND VISUALS. ITS BOLD, LEGIBLE CHARACTERS PROVIDE IMPACT AND COMMAND ATTENTION.

12 Pitch Type Styles and Their Applications

Adjutant 1167129 12 Pitch, 9 Point	**Artisan 12** (72) 1167131 12 Pitch, 10 Point
IBM ADJUTANT Type is recommended for the preparation of text copy and other similar typing applications. A weighted serif type design, it conveys the feeling of printed material.	IBM ARTISAN 12 (72) Type is well suited for general correspondence and offset reproduction requiring the maximum utilization of space. Type is a clean, easy-to-read sans-serif design.

Courier 12 **12 Pitch, 8 Point** **Italic** **1167133** *IBM COURIER 12 ITALIC Type* *is also widely used for gen-* *eral correspondence, offset* *reproduction and other appli-* *cations requiring the maximum* *utilization of space.*	**Scribe*** **12 Pitch, 10 Point** **1167144** IBM SCRIBE Type is ideally suit- ed for the preparation of reports and correspondence, where the user desires a modern square- serif design in the Elite family of type styles.
Prestige Elite **12 Pitch, 10 Point** **(72)** **1167143** IBM PRESTIGE ELITE 72 Type is available for general, legal, chemical and French/English correspondence, offset repro- duction, statistical reports, text material of high density.	**Courier 12** **12 Pitch, 8 Point** **1167132** IBM COURIER 12 Type is ideal for general correspondence, offset reproduction and a wide variety of general applications which require the maximum use of typing space.
Prestige Elite **12 Pitch, 10 Point** **(72)** **1167143** **Typed in 10 pitch mode**** This is an example of the 12 pitch Prestige Elite 72 type style, illustrating how it appears when typed on a typewriter set for 10 pitch.	**Elite 72*** **12 Pitch, 10 Point** **1167137** IBM ELITE 72 Type is used for correspondence, offset reproduc- tion, statistical reports and text material of high density. Special characters are available for library or tri-lingual work.

Letter Gothic   **12 Pitch, 12 Point**
1167138

IBM LETTER GOTHIC Type is an
ideal selection for invoices,
statements and other typing
applications where boldness is
desired. It is a distinctive
sans-serif type.

*Recommended for use with stencils.

†Not compatible for use on the IBM Mag Card
"Selectric" Typewriter, the Magnetic Tape
"Selectric" Typewriter, Memory Typewriters,
and the Model 721 "Selectric" Typewriter.

**Special Typing Applications
for 12 Pitch Type Styles**

Light Italic **12 Pitch** **1167139** *IBM LIGHT ITALIC Type is recommended for use alone or in combination with Pica or Elite type styles to add impact and emphasis to a wide variety of typing applications.*	**Script** **12 Pitch, 12 Point** **1167145** *IBM SCRIPT Type is widely used for correspondence and other typing applications to simulate handwriting, and to provide the look of a personal note and a change of emphasis.*

**Special Type Styles
and Their Applications**

	Manifold 72 **10 Pitch, 10 Point** **1167140** IBM MANIFOLD 72 TYPE IS RECOMMENDED FOR BILLING AND FORM PREPARATION. IT IS ALSO AVAILABLE IN PICA NUMERAL AND CANCELLED ZERO VERSIONS.
108 OCR† **10 Pitch, 10 Point** **1167108** IBM 108 OCR TYPE FINDS WIDE USE IN THE PREPARATION OF MATERIAL TO BE READ BY OCR EQUIPMENT. IT IS AVAILABLE WITH A KEYPUNCH SIMULATOR KEYBOARD.	**Printing and** **10 Pitch, 10 Point** **Publishing 1** **ANSI-OCR†** **1167170** IBM ANSI Type is ideal for the preparation of computer-readable documents. It is available in correspondence or keypunch simulator keyboard arrangements.
Symbol 10 **10 Pitch, 12 Point** **1167061**	**Symbol 12** **12 Pitch, 10 Point** **1167004**

Custom-made for your special applications

Typographical

. period
, comma
: colon
; semi-colon
– dash
_ underscore
= double underscore
? question mark
! exclamation
(left parenthesis
) right parenthesis
[left bracket
] right bracket
† dagger
‡ double dagger
§ section
¶ paragraph
' apostrophe
" quotation
& ampersand
* asterisk
~ tilde
^ circumflex
¯ macron
˘ breve
¨ dieresis
↓ cedilla
´ acute
` grave
| vertical line
— through score

Language

¡ inverted exclamation
¿ inverted question
Ñ n ya
Æ ligature U.C.
æ ligature L.C.
Å angstron
Ä umlaut A
Ö umlaut O
Ü umlaut U

Currency

$ dollar
¢ cent
£ pound sterling
¥ yen

Technical

+ plus
× multiplication
÷ division
= equals
> greater than
≥ greater than or equal to
< less than
≤ less than or equal to
∞ infinity
√ radical
∫ integral
π pi
° degree

α alpha
β beta
Δ delta
γ gamma
· multiplication
↑ arrow up
↓ arrow down
← arrow left
→ arrow right
± plus or minus
Ω ohm
μ mu
∇ inverted delta
∅ cancelled zero
1234567890
  Subscripts
1234567890
  Exponents
$\frac{1}{4}$ fraction
$\frac{1}{2}$ fraction
$\frac{3}{4}$ fraction
ℓ script L — laplace

Legal

Q̣ q period
Ạ a period
𝕏 plaintiff

OCR

∫ hook
ᴪ fork
⌐ chair
| vertical line
– minus
█ blob

Miscellaneous

@ commercial A
# number
% percent
® registry
© copyright
™ trademark
● circle
■ square
◆ diamond
🝳 beaker
/ slash
♀ female
♂ male
∩ logical product
∪ logical sum
⊂ contained in
⊃ excluded from
≢ group mark
≠ record mark
⧻ segment mark
◊ lozenge
♭ substituted
¬ logical not
≡ identical with
\ reverse slant

NOTE: Since certain symbols match the type styles, the ones shown are not representative of typewritten material and should be used as a guide to type and symbol selection only. Special symbols not shown may be provided for an extra charge.

This list of characters and their most common description is intended as an aid to describing and ordering special symbols.

Type codes are compatible with the 101 American Standard Keyboard.

The gray areas on this keyboard chart indicate the positions where you can substitute custom characters for standard characters.

CUSTOM ELEMENTS, FOR SPECIAL APPLICATIONS, ADD SPEED AND VERSATILITY

Simplify Specialized Typing

With an IBM Custom Element, there's no need to interrupt typing to change elements or to insert special characters by hand. The symbols you use repeatedly are incorporated on your Custom Element—so they're always at your typist's fingertips.

Substitute Custom Characters Where You Need Them

IBM Custom Elements let you choose from 128 characters designed for virtually every kind of specialized typing—subscript and superscript, numerals, medical, scientific, legal and OCR symbols, accent marks for foreign languages, and many more. The examples at right show the range of custom symbols which can be substituted for regular characters on the typing element.

Up to 26 Positions to Choose From

Simply substitute the symbols your industry or application requires for those you don't need. You can use the same element for your regular correspondence as well as your specialized work. Even your logo or trademark can be furnished on your own Custom Element at additional cost.

Select from Eight Type Styles

Now you can harmonize the appearance of your symbols with the type style of the rest of the document. IBM Custom Elements are available in eight styles—six for correspondence and two for specialized use.

IBM Custom Elements Increase Typing Output

When your typist uses an IBM Custom Element, specialized applications can be completed without wasting time. This is particularly true when magnetic media are used since there is no slow-up in playback speed. Moreover, every symbol typed will have the same neat and professional appearance you have come to expect from IBM word processing equipment.

Compatible with nine different type styles

Prestige Elite 72
12 Pitch

ABCDEFGHIJKLMNOPQRSTUVWXYZ
abcdefghijklmnopqrstuvwxyz
1234567890$.,'":;?*$\frac{1}{4}\frac{1}{2}$-()_+=&¢%#@/!

Elite 72
12 Pitch

ABCDEFGHIJKLMNOPQRSTUVWXYZ
abcdefghijklmnopqrstuvwxyz
1234567890$.,'":;?*$\frac{1}{4}\frac{1}{2}$-()_+=&¢%#@/!

Letter Gothic
12 Pitch

ABCDEFGHIJKLMNOPQRSTUVWXYZ
abcdefghijklmnopqrstuvwxyz
1234567890$.,'":;?*¼½-()_+=&¢%#@/!

Pica 72
10 Pitch

ABCDEFGHIJKLMNOPQRSTUVWXYZ
abcdefghijklmnopqrstuvwxyz
1234567890$.,'":;?*¼½-()_+=&¢%#@/!

Courier 72
10 Pitch

ABCDEFGHIJKLMNOPQRSTUVWXYZ
abcdefghijklmnopqrstuvwxyz
1234567890$.,'":;?*¼½-()_+=&¢%#@/!

Delegate
10 Pitch

ABCDEFGHIJKLMNOPQRSTUVWXYZ
abcdefghijklmnopqrstuvwxyz
1234567890$.,'":;?*¼½-()_+=&¢%#@/!

Manifold 72
10 Pitch

ABCDEFGHIJKLMNOPQRSTUVWXYZ
1234567890$.,'":;?∷¼½-()_+=&¢%#@/!

ANSI OCR
10 Pitch

ABCDEFGHIJKLMNOPQRSTUVWXYZ
abcdefghijklmnopqrstuvwxyz
1234567890$.⌐'":;?*■■-{}—+=&|%⊣♪/Ɏ

Data #1
10 Pitch

ABCDEFGHIJKLMNOPQRSTUVWXYZ
abcdefghijklmnopqrstuvwxyz
1234567890$.,'":;?*¬()_-+=&¢%#><!

Element Application Rating*

Type Style	Maximum Carbon Copies	Offset Masters	Spirit Masters	Stencils	Diazo	Office Copier Machines
Adjutant	B	A	B	B	A	A
Advocate	A	B	A	A	B	A
Artisan 12 (72)	B	B	B	B	B	A
Bookface Academic 72	B	A	B	B	B	A
Courier 12	B	A	B	B	B	A
Courier 12 Italic	B	A	B	B	B	A
Courier 72	B	A	B	B	B	A
Delegate	B	A	B	C	A	A
Elite 72	A	A	A	A	A	A
Letter Gothic	A	A	B	B	B	A
Light Italic	A	A	A	A	A	A
Manifold 72	A	B	B	B	A	A
Orator	C	C	C	C	C	A
Pica 72	A	A	A	A	A	A
Prestige Elite 72	A	A	A	A	A	A
Prestige Pica 72	B	A	B	B	B	A
Scribe	A	B	A	A	A	A
Script	C	B	C	C	B	A

10 and 12 Pitch Similarities

In many cases, the same type design is available in different sizes under different names. For example:

10 Pitch	12 Pitch
Delegate	Adjutant
Advocate	Scribe
Pica 72	Elite 72
Prestige Pica 72	Prestige Elite 72
Courier 72	Courier 12
	Courier 12 Italic

*Ratings:
A—Good; B—Fair; C—Marginal

Assumptions:
1. Typewriters are equipped with Impression Selector and Automatic Impression Equalizer.
2. Proper selection of ribbon, carbon paper, stencils, etc.

Note:
Symbol and OCR elements are special application type styles.

The IBM Mag Card II Typewriter

Combines convenience and capability right at the keyboard. A combination of typing technologies does much of the work the operator would normally do. For the first time in an IBM Typewriter, we've combined an electronic memory with an electronic keyboard and the convenience of magnetic cards. These capabilities give you unlimited revision power...with no loss in output efficiency.

Electronic Memory & Machine Logic. The IBM Mag Card II Typewriter incorporates advanced machine logic with an electronic memory that cuts manual motions to a minimum. The operator can't see the memory, but it's there; recording, remembering and reacting to everything the operator types—copy as well as instructions. It enables the typist to type into memory, record copy out of memory, read copy into memory, revise copy in memory, play out copy in memory and create final copy in memory. The memory, which is one of the latest innovations in electronic solid state memories, has a storage capacity of 8,000 characters—just about equal to 2½ pages of typed copy.

Immediate Accessibility. Turn it on, and the IBM Mag Card II Typewriter is ready to type. No intermediate time-consuming steps are required. Tabs and margins are pre-set for typing convenience and are easily changed for specific applications.

Copy Correction Capability. This mechanism uses IBM's correcting technology to actually lift off or cover up each incorrect character with a *single* key stroke at the same time it's being corrected in memory. Avoids the need for extra playout to gain clean, error-free draft copy.

Selective Ribbon System. Accepts either an IBM Correctable Film Ribbon with IBM Lift-off Tape or an IBM Tech III Ribbon with IBM Tech III Cover-up Tape. Both are as easy to install as an ordinary ribbon.

The Correctable Film ribbon has been developed for all general correspondence applications. When typing negotiable instruments, the IBM Tech III ribbon should be used.

Mag Card Compatibility. Magnetic cards created on the IBM Mag Card II Typewriter can be played out on any IBM Mag Card Typewriter...including the IBM Mag Card Executive® Typewriter when the ultimate in quality and appearance are essential. And to help you realize the full benefit of this typewriter, any magnetic cards created on other IBM Mag Card Typewriters can be revised and updated on the IBM Mag Card II Typewriter.

Media Duplication. IBM magnetic cards can be reproduced automatically in seconds on the IBM Mag Card II Typewriter. Additional sets of cards can be duplicated for other locations.

Acoustical Filter Hood. Designed for sound-sensitive work areas. The translucent filter hood significantly reduces sound levels—especially on automatic playout when the typewriter is operating at rapid speed.

Specifications: System Model #6616. Operates on 115 Volt, 60 Hertz, 3.0 Amperes, AC current. Console dimensions: 12" wide, 19" deep, 26½" high. Typewriter: Model 545 Input/Output Writer, 22¼" wide, 15⅝" deep, 7⅝" high. 15⅛" paper capacity, 12-5/6" writing line, nominal operating speed of 15.5 characters per second. Net weights: Console, 65 lbs; Model 545 Typewriter, 50 lbs. Total shipping weight: 158 lbs. Console color: Charcoal Black with Pearl White face plate. Typewriter color: Charcoal Black with Charcoal Black key buttons and platen knobs.

IBM

International Business Machines Corporation
Office Products Division
For additional information, consult the nearest IBM Branch Office.

4

guidelines for format typing

This chapter covers letters and other typewritten forms, stressing the visual coordination of type style and letterhead, placement on page and message which makes each a complete picture.

The *Long Form Promissory Note* covers the involved transaction and has a schedule for payments on the back.

The *Short Form Promissory Note* takes care of less complicated transactions.

The *Minutes Of A Corporate Meeting* show the variables, the proper order of business, language, spacing, and paragraphing (notice that the names of the directors are alphabetized and there is space left at the end to paste the bank resolution). Each page of each set of minutes is numbered beginning with page 1, and the number is centered at the bottom of the page.

The *Press Release* can begin

TO:	FOR RELEASE:
FROM:	PERSONAL CONTACT:

but the general use is letterhead with information under and/or a cover letter. Always double space. If there are many pages, end all but the last with -MORE- alone on a line 1 inch from the bottom and number each page. Always indicate the end of the release—the usual end is # # # alone on the line below the last line of typing.

The *Block Style Letter* indents the date and the complimentary close at the same tab. All else is flush left.

The *Indented Style Letter* indents the date and complimentary close at the same tab, and indents each paragraph.

The *Official Style Letter* indents the date line and the complimentary close at the same tab, but has the inside address flush left under the complimentary close. (Notice the omission of dictation initials.) This is one of the most formal letter styles.

The *Advertising Style Letter* omits the inside address and is shown here as a full block style (everything flush left), though style is optional.

Not shown are:

The Thesis—each educational institution has different requirements, so go directly to the source.

The Manuscript—Use 8½ x 11 inch white bond paper approximately 16-20 lb. bond, one inch margins all around, double space and type on only one side of the page.

The *Script* must be typed to indicate what will be seen on the screen and how it will be seen. This can be done by the indented paragraph style (generally used for "story" type scripts) or by the column style (generally used for training and documentary films) which gives the scene description on the left in a column and the narration on the right in a column. The formats can be interchanged so check for preference.

Poetry—check with author or library.

Speeches—use the largest typewriter type available and triple space (on 8½ x 14 inch paper, if possible).

LONG FORM PROMISSORY INSTALLMENT NOTE

$.................................   ....19..........

𝔉𝔬𝔯 𝔙𝔞𝔩𝔲𝔢 𝔕𝔢𝔠𝔢𝔦𝔳𝔢𝔡..

promise to pay to..

....*or order, at*

....*the sum of*

....*dollars,*

together with interest on the unpaid portion thereof from date until paid at the rate

....................................*per cent per*... *both principal and interest payable in*

lawful money of the United States, in installments, and at the times hereinafter stated, to wit:

    Said principal and interest shall be payable in..*installments of*

....*dollars*

each, the first of said installments to be paid, in said lawful money, on the...................................

day of..........................., 19.........., *and a like installment, in said lawful money, on the*

....*day of each and every*....................................... *thereafter until*

....

....

....

the said principal sum and interest shall be fully paid. As each payment is made it shall be

applied first, in payment of the interest then due, and the remainder on account of the principal

sum, and thereupon interest shall cease upon the amount so paid on the principal sum.

    And ....*agree......that in case any*

one of said installments, or any part thereof, is not paid as it becomes due, then such unpaid

installment shall bear interest from the date of its maturity until paid at the rate of

.............................*per cent per*...*and in case any one of said installments,*

or any part thereof, is not paid within.....................................*days after the same becomes due and*

payable, or in case any change is made in the title to all or any part of the property described in

the instrument securing this note, then the whole of said principal sum then remaining unpaid,

together with all interest unpaid thereon, shall forthwith become due and payable at the election

of the holder of this note, of which election notice is hereby waived. If action be instituted on

this note ....*promise to pay such sum as the court*

may fix as attorney's fees.

    This note is secured by a..*bearing even date herewith.*

....

Patrick Form No. LB 1072—PROMISSORY INSTALLMENT NOTE—Installments Include Interest
Courtesy Patrick & Company, 560 Market Street,
San Francisco, California 94104.

PROMISSORY INSTALLMENT NOTE

PAYMENTS

DATE PAID M D Y	DATE DUE M D Y	AMOUNT PAID	CREDITED ON INTEREST	PRINCIPAL	BALANCE OF PRIN. UNPAID	TO WHOM PAID

Reverse of Patrick Form No. LB 1072
PROMISSORY INSTALLMENT NOTE—Installments Include Interest
Courtesy Patrick & Company, 560 Market Street,
San Francisco, California 94104.

SHORT FORM PROMISSORY NOTE

No. _____   *Due* _____

$ _____   _____ , 19 _____

_____ *after date, for value received,*

_____ *promise to pay to*

_____ , *or order,*

at _____

the sum of _____ *dollars*

in lawful money of the United States of America, with interest thereon, payable in like lawful money

_____ , *at the rate of* _____ *per cent per* _____ *from date*

until paid.

Patrick Form No. LB 1074—SHORT FORM PROMISSORY NOTE

Courtesy Patrick & Company, 560 Market Street,
San Francisco, California 94104.

MINUTES OF A CORPORATE MEETING

MINUTES OF _____ MEETING OF

BOARD OF DIRECTORS OF

ABC CORPORATION

July __, 19--

The meeting of the Board of Directors of ABC CORPORATION was held at its offices, City, State, on Wednesday, July __, 19--, at   .m. The meeting was called to order by James R. Cartwright, Chairman of the Board, who presided at the meeting.

The following Directors were present:

John D. Boyer
James R. Cartwright
Frederick Grenn
Robert Merridith
Warren Pritchard
Arnold Wellsely

The following Director was absent:

Kenneth Harding

Also present was Alan Blane, Vice President of Blank Bank.

Robert Merridith, Secretary of the Board, acted as Secretary of the meeting.

The Secretary stated that notice of the meeting had been given to each of the Directors by letter on Wednesday, July __, 19--. It was moved by Director Boyer, seconded by Director Pritchard, and unanimously carried, to accept this method as the official notice of the meeting.

The Secretary announced that the minutes of the Special Board Meeting Held on June __, 19-- were mailed to individual members of the Board. On motion duly made, seconded, and unanimously carried, these minutes were approved.

The Chairman then presented to the Board for its approval a proposed new form of share certificate to be used by the corporation for its common shares. On motion duly made, duly seconded, and unanimously carried, the following resolution was adopted:

-1-

RESOLVED that the proposed form of common
share certificate presented to this meeting
is adopted for use by the corporation for
its common shares, and the Secretary is
directed to insert a copy of this certificate
in the minute book following the minutes of
this meeting.

The Treasurer presented to the meeting a standard form of

resolution for an additional corporate account with Blank Bank,

completed to show the type of account and the persons

authorized to draw on the account. On motion duly made,

seconded, and unanimously carried, the following resolution,

introduced by Director Boyer, was approved:

WHEREAS, business has expanded for the
corporation, and it is deemed in the best
interests of this corporation and its
shareholders;

IT IS THEREFORE RESOLVED that the standard
form of corporate resolution required by
Blank Bank for opening a corporate account,
as presented to this meeting, showing the
persons authorized to draw on this account,
is adopted as the resolution of the Board
of Directors, and the Secretary is directed
to make it a part of the minutes of this
meeting by inserting it immediately
following this resolution, and to execute
the Certificate of Secretary included on
this standard form.

There being no further business to come before this meeting,

on motion duly made, seconded, and unanimously carried, the

meeting was adjourned at   .m.

Robert Merridith
Secretary of the Board

-2-

Courtesy Richard A. Schindler, Esq.
San Francisco, California

PRESS RELEASE

2206union st., san francisco, ca., 94123
tel. (415) 563·2200 cable: discoverer

SERENDIPITY travel service, inc.
ser'·en·dip'·i·ty, n., an apparent aptitude for making fortunate discoveries....

FOR IMMEDIATE RELEASE

THE TRAVEL AGENT -- THE SECRETARY'S BEST TRAVEL HELP

      Secretaries often have to work out detailed
trips for their employers. They can make separate
arrangements or depend on one telephone call to a good
travel agent who will accomplish the necessary results.
It generally does not cost the employer a penny more,
gets the job done efficiently, and saves the secretary
time.

      The travel agent works with all airlines,
railroads, ships, cruises, tours, car rentals and
coordinates connections, ticketing and accommodations.
This specialist is familiar with lower fare and lodging
"packages," has many brochures available, knows many
time and money saving "travel tips," and in most cases
will arrange for delivery of tickets in the local area.
A detailed file is kept on each trip.

      All it takes is one phone call - a travel
agent will be delighted to help.

            # # #

Courtesy Richard A. Schindler, Esq.
San Francisco, California

BLOCK STYLE

LonginesWittnauer

Longines-Wittnauer Watch Company, Longines-Wittnauer World Headquarters, New Rochelle, New York 10810 (914) 576-1000

September 26, 19--

Mr. Karl Baker
265 Main Street
Bellevue, New York 12306

Dear Mr. Baker:

Many thanks for sending us your letter and comments pertaining to our TV commercial.

We regret that the concept of the vignette has been somewhat misconstrued. As you noted correctly, the young man does turn to a confidante, possibly his mother or an aunt, after looking at the watch given to him and states, "I was kind of hoping for a Longines."

If the older individual were indeed the person who had given the young man the watch, then it would be an ungrateful and crude statement to make. However, we had hoped that the viewing audience would understand that the lady is not the donor or giver of the gift, but rather someone who has observed the young man's reaction. Naturally, if she had purchased the gift and given it to the young man his reaction would be uncouth and boorish. However, to repeat, she is simply a confidante or friend and his statement, "I was kind of hoping for a Longines," is simply a comment to her at that moment.

Very frankly Mr. Baker, all of us in the course of our lifetime, have had a similar reaction. Many of us have had the occasion to receive fine gifts which simply may not have been precisely what we had been looking for. Therefore, the matter of verbalizing a minor disappointment (so long as it is not done to the person thoughtful enough to give the gift) is something that is a natural reaction. Thus, we felt if the vignette is properly interpreted, then it is not in bad taste or does not contravene the ethics of good behavior.

We certainly agree with you and your kind comments that "we would all like to receive a beautiful watch made by Longines." It is that thought that we have tried to project in this particular commercial.

Most important, Mr. Baker, we appreciate your taking the time to let us have your thoughts and may we too, at this time, wish you and yours, the very best of the season and a Happy New Year to all.

Cordially,

LONGINES-WITTNAUER WATCH COMPANY

Max S. Beschloss
Advertising Director

MSB:hb

Mailing Address: Longines-Wittnauer Watch Company, P.O. Box 2500, New Rochelle, New York 10810

INDENTED STYLE

HALLMARK CARDS INCORPORATED
KANSAS CITY, MISSOURI 64141

June 27, 19--

Mr. John Doe
The ABC Company
123 Main Street
San Francisco, CA   94108

Dear Mr. Doe:

We appreciate your very kind comments regarding the Hallmark Hall of Fame series.

It has always been our intention to sponsor quality television entertainment of lasting value. Your vote of confidence will help guide our future efforts.

Please accept our thanks for having taken the time to write.

Cordially,

Jim McDowell
Nat'l. Advertising Mgr.

JMcD:jac

OFFICIAL STYLE

Sheraton-Palace Hotel
SHERATON HOTELS & INNS, WORLDWIDE

639 MARKET STREET
SAN FRANCISCO, CALIF. 94119
TELEPHONE: (415) 392-8600

October 14, 19-⊥

Dear Mr. Doe:

Thank you for your interest in San Francisco. The fabled Sheraton-Palace Hotel, host to Presidents and Kings for over a century, would be honored to be your choice.

I have learned from our Regional Sales Office in New York that ABC Company is considering June 4-9, 19-- for its annual meeting.

I understand your expected attendance is 100 and the number of bedrooms requested to be 50 Twins. I further understand that you have no exhibits. We are pleased to inform you that your preferred dates are currently available.

Enclosed you will find preliminary information on the Sheraton-Palace Hotel. I look forward to speaking with you in the next couple of days and to eventually meeting you.

Very truly yours,

John Smith
Director of Sales

Mr. John Doe
ABC Company
123 Main Street
New York, New York 10036

ADVERTISING STYLE

U. S. News & World Report
WASHINGTON

2300 N STREET, N W · WASHINGTON, D. C. 20037

September 22, 19--

OFFICE OF THE
PUBLISHER

Dear Advertiser:

Attention.

That's what advertising is out to get. Before anything else.
Without it, no ad -- however brilliantly conceived and
executed -- can begin to do its job.

The best way to get the attention your advertising needs and
deserves is to place it in front of readers, not skimmers.
Like the regular readers you reach each week in U.S.News &
World Report.

There's a usefulness and a vitality about the news in our
magazine that commands and gets real attention. We know that
the median reading time of our subscribers is close to
two hours an issue. More than nine in 10 of them say they
read something in each quarter of the magazine. Eight in 10
of our subscribers report they don't read Time or Newsweek or
Sports Illustrated.

Research also shows that the upscale men and women who prefer
U.S.News & World Report number among the advertiser's best
customers and prospects. Your message in our pages gets the
right kind of attention from the right kind of people because:

> We spare our readers unimportant news.
> We spare our advertisers unimportant readers.

Sincerely,

John H. Sweet

John H. Sweet
Publisher

JHS:sgs

5

the art of designing forms, form letters and envelopes

The easiest way to put a project together is to learn about mechanics, organize the message and construct the finished product to do its particular task. Covered here are the basic elements of design, printing, color and paper and illustrations which show you how to apply your knowledge to create forms, form letters and envelopes.

Form spacing—Horizontal and vertical space requirements are determined by the amount of fill-in to be entered and the printed matter such as box captions, column and section heads, and text. The writing method (hand, typewriter or a special office machine) determines the amount of space to be allowed for fill-in data; while the number of characters per inch of the typeface used determines the amount of space to be allowed for printed matter.

Horizontal spacing is based on the number of characters written per inch, which is controlled by the writing method used to enter the data. There are 12 characters of elite type to the inch and 10 characters of pica type on standard typewriters. Accordingly, when counting horizontal spaces allow $1/12$ inch for elite or $1/10$ inch for pica type. An allowance of $1/10$ inch accommodates either elite or pica type and allows maximum entry space. Wherever possible,

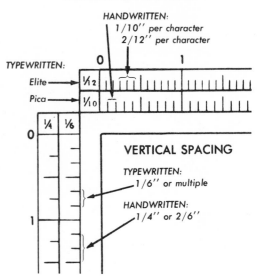

WRITING METHOD	SPACE PER CHARACTER
Elite Typewriter	1/12″
Pica Typewriter	1/10″
Handwriting	1/10″ to 1/6″
Space per character determines	Horizontal space between vertical rules

WRITING METHOD	SPACE PER LINE
Typewriter	1/6″ or multiple
Handwriting	1/4″
Handwriting and typing	1/3″
Space per line determines	Vertical spacing between horizontal rules

add a minimum of one extra space to the required number of characters to prevent crowding.

Vertical spacing is based on the number of writing lines that can be written per inch. There are 6 vertical lines per inch on the standard typewriter—elite or pica. Accordingly, allow 1/6 inch or its multiple for each line of typing. By measuring spacing in this way, a form may be adjusted in the machine for the first line of typing with no further adjustment needed.

Composition for letterpress printing is set in metal type. Reproduction is accomplished by direct printing from raised type.

Printing measurement—The standard for type measurement is the point system. The point is used to measure the thickness of a piece of type. 12 points equal one pica, 6 picas equal one inch, 72 points equal one inch.

Offset—Any copy which can be photographed may be reproduced by the offset method.

If you want people to read letters and read them easily, use short sentences averaging not more than 21 words, short words (not more than 165 syllables per 100 words) and use only about four personal references per 100 words.

A form letter is appropriate if it is about a routine business or informational matter or if it is not a personal letter. On the basis of a three-month supply, a form letter is economical if

Line count is:	Monthly usage is:
5	30 or more
10	20 or more
15	15 or more
20 or more	10 or more

Color—the warm and stimulating colors of red, orange and yellow suggest action since they have a tendency to come forward. They should not be used in large masses as a background color for printed type, as they would over-dominate. The cool or sedate colors of blue, green and purple imply prestige, dignity and relaxation. Since they tend to recede, they can make small areas appear larger. Tints suggest lightness and airiness while darker tones imply stability and weight—although sometimes to the point of being depressing. Color responses can be keyed to geography— warm colors in winter, cool colors in summer. Generally, men prefer shades and cool hues while women prefer tints and warm hues, with grey being neutral. There are three ways to use color in envelopes—colored ink, colored paper stock and color seen through a die-cut window.

The direction of the grain of the paper on which a form is printed may be an important factor since there is greater strength in this direction than in the other. This is true particularly of heavy paper such as index or ledger. Paper bends, folds or stands upright more easily with the grain than against it. Some practical applications of grain direction for forms printed on index or ledger paper are:

a. Forms to be filled in by typewriter or other business machines should have the grain in the paper running parallel to the platen of the machine so that the form will wrap around the platen more easily.

b. Forms to be filed vertically in a box, drawer, tray, etc., should have the grain running vertically to lend added stiffness so that the forms will stand up in the file without additional support.

c. Ledger sheets to be filed in binders should have the grain running parallel to the binding edge to provide flexibility when the pages are turned.

PAPER SELECTION GUIDE FOR FORMS

Kinds of paper	Grades of paper	Substance (Weight) 1000 sheets Gov't	Substance (Weight) 500 sheets Commercial	Opacity (For front and back printing) One side only	Opacity Pre-fer one side	Opacity One or two sides
• Acceptable in appearance • All erase well • Long-lasting qualities • Good for pencil, pen, or machine writing • Suitable for offset or letterpress printing						
Writing: Close, uniform formation; smooth, flat surface.	Chemical wood	24	12	X		
		32	16		X	
		40	20			X
Bond: Smooth, flat surface. Good folding qualities.	Chemical wood	40	20			X
	25 percent rag (watermark of U.S. seal—one star)	24	12	X		
		32	16		X	
		40	20			X
Bond: Dense, hard formation; smooth surface, great strength, exceptionally good folding and erasing qualities, and resistance to discoloration from age and exposure to light.	50 percent rag (watermark of U.S. seal—two stars)	32	16		X	
	100 percent rag (watermark of U.S. seal—four stars)	32	16		X	

GENERAL USE FORMS

		Material				
GENERAL USE AND BOOKKEEPING FORMS	Manifold: Lightweight; slight bulk; smooth surface.	Chemical wood	18	9	X	
		25 percent rag	18	9	X	
	Ledger: Semistiffness, strength, flexibility, durability; smooth surface. Good folding qualities.	Chemical wood	48	24		X
			64	32		X
			88	44		X
		25 percent rag (watermark of U.S. seal—one star)	48	24		X
			64	32		X
			88	44		X
		100 percent rag (watermark of U.S. seal—four stars)	48	24		X
			64	32		X
			88	44		X
CARD FORMS	Index: Semistiffness, strength, flexibility, durability, smooth surface. Good folding qualities.	Chemical wood	220	110		X
			280	140		X
			340	170		X
		25 percent rag	220	110		X
		100 percent rag	250	125		X

Compiled from "Standard Paper Samples and Their Principal Uses for the Government Printing and Binding."

WHEN TO USE GOTHIC TYPE

HARD TO READ

7. SEX	8. CLAIM NO.
☐ MALE ☐ FEMALE	C-

RECEIVING STATION ONLY		
9. DATE OF RECEIPT	10. DATE SCHED. OR AUTH.	11. DATE COMPLETED

12. PLACE OF EXAMINATION *(Check one)*
☐ CLINIC   ☐ FEE   ☐ OTHER STATION
13. NAME OF FEE EXAMINER OR OTHER STATION

14. EXAMINATION SCHEDULED
☐ AT ONCE   ☐ OTHER *(Specify date)*
15. PURPOSE OF EXAMINATION *(Check appropriate boxes)*

☐ TERMINAL   ☐ ORIGINAL (S. C.)   ☐ REOPENED

☐ POW   ☐ ORIGINAL (N. S. C.)   ☐ INCREASE

☐ COMBAT INITIAL   ☐ CONVALESCENT   ☐ REVIEW

EASIER TO READ

16. REQUIRE MEDICA
☐ COMPETENCY
17. SIGNATURE OF A *(Ch., Clm. Div.)*

7. SEX	8. CLAIM NO.
☐ MALE ☐ FEMALE	C-

RECEIVING STATION ONLY		
9. DATE OF RECEIPT	10. DATE SCHED. OR AUTH.	11. DATE COMPLETED

12. PLACE OF EXAMINATION *(Check one)*
☐ CLINIC   ☐ FEE   ☐ OTHER STATION
13. NAME OF FEE EXAMINER OR OTHER STATION

14. EXAMINATION SCHEDULED
☐ AT ONCE   ☐ OTHER *(Specify date)*
15. PURPOSE OF EXAMINATION *(Check appropriate boxes)*

☐ TERMINAL   ☐ ORIGINAL (S. C.)   ☐ REOPENED

☐ POW   ☐ ORIGINAL (N. S. C.)   ☐ INCREASE

☐ COMBAT INITIAL   ☐ CONVALESCENT   ☐ REVIEW

☐ OTHER *(Specify)*

16. REQUIRE MEDICAL DETERMINATION OF *(Check one)*
☐ COMPETENCY   ☐ NEED FOR AID AND ATTENDANCE *(Provide VA Form 10–2680)*
17. SIGNATURE OF ADJ. OFFICER OR ASST. *(Ch., Clm. Div.)*   18. SYMBOL

From U. S. Government Records Management Handbook: Forms Design

WHEN NOT TO USE GOTHIC TYPE

HARD TO READ

ITEM 13.—ANALYSIS OF SALES BY COMMODITY LINES

REPORT THE DOLLAR VOLUME OF SALES
ON RECORDS ARE NOT AVAILABLE, GIVE

	4	Code
TOTAL SALES—(TOTAL OF SALES BY COMMODITY LINES SHOULD BE SAME AS TOTAL SALES 1958, ITEM 7a)................................... $		0
ELECTRICAL APPARATUS AND SUPPLIES		
1. ELECTRICAL RESIDENTIAL SPACE HEATING EQUIPMENT (EXCEPT PORTABLE)..... $		704220
2. ELECTRICAL WIRING SUPPLIES, CONSTRUCTION MATERIALS, TOTAL (SUM OF LINES A THROUGH D)................................... $		603100
A. INTERIOR WIRING, CONSTRUCTION MATERIALS..... $		603101
B. OUTSIDE CONSTRUCTION MATERIALS.............. $		603102
C. LIGHTING FIXTURES........................... $		603103
D. ELECTRIC LAMPS (INCANDESCENT AND FLUORESCENT). $		603104
ELECTRICAL APPLIANCES AND COMMERCIAL EQUIPMENT		
EVISION SETS, TOTAL (SUM OF LINES A .... $		604110

EASIER TO READ

A. RADIO SETS, A

B. TELEVISION SE

C. RECORD PLAYER

ITEM 13.—ANALYSIS OF SALES BY COMMODITY LINES

Report the dollar v
on records are not a

	4	Code
Total sales—(Total of sales by commodity lines should be same as Total Sales 1958, Item 7a)................................ $		0
Electrical apparatus and supplies		
1. Electrical residential space heating equipment (except portable) . $		704220
2. Electrical wiring supplies, construction materials, total (sum of lines a through d)................................ $		603100
a. Interior wiring, construction materials .... $		603101
b. Outside construction materials.......... $		603102
c. Lighting fixtures..................... $		603103
d. Electric lamps (incandescent and fluores- cent)............................... $		603104
Electrical appliances and commercial equipment		
5. Electrical appliances, radio and television sets, total (sum of lines a through g)................................ $		604110
a. Radio sets, all types................. $		604111
b. Television sets..................... $		604112
c. Record players, tape recorders.......... $		604113

From U. S. Government Records Management Handbook: Forms Design

WAYS OF PRESENTING INSTRUCTIONS FOR READABILITY

ITEM 5.—PERSONNEL AND PAYROLL

	Dollars
a. Total payroll for the year 19XX, before payroll deductions	

	Number of employees	Payroll (dollars)
b. Paid employees and payroll for the work-week ended nearest November 15, 19XX		

	Number
c. Number of paid employees for workweek ended nearest:	
(1) March 15, 19XX..........................	

(2) May 15, 19XX ...

(3) August 15,
   19XX

d. Proprietors or partners
   ment 15 hours or more
   nearest November 15, 1

e. Number of salesmen

Instructions
keyed to items on
form for easier
reading

ITEM 5.—PERSONNEL AND PAYROLL

Include payments to corporation officers and executives working in this establishment.

Do not include salaries or withdrawals (whether in cash or kind) of proprietors or partners of unincorporated business.

For purposes of this item, the workweek ended nearest the 15th of the month should be one ending in the period of the 12th through 18th inclusive.

Line a.—Report the full amount of salaries, wages, bonuses, vacation allowances, and commissions before deductions for Social Security, income tax withholding, insurance, dues, etc.

Line b.—Include both full- and part-time employees. If your payroll is for a period other than a week, please adjust the figures to a 1-week basis. Commissions paid on other than a weekly basis should also be adjusted to a 1-week basis.

Lines c(1)-(3).—Include both full- and part-time employees.

Line d.—To be reported by proprietorships and partnerships only.

Line e.—Include all persons engaged in making sales.

BEFORE AND

Read the certificate at the end of this questionnaire before completing your answers. *Print* or *Type* all answers. All questions and statements must be completed. If proper answer is "no" or "none" so indicate. Fill out, sign, and return to requesting agency. If more space is required, use remarks section.

AFTER

Outline instruc-
tions easier
to read than
paragraph
instructions

1. Read the certificate at the end of this questionnaire before completing your answers.
2. PRINT or TYPE all answers. All questions and statements, must be completed. If proper answer is "no" or "none," so indicate.
3. Fill out, sign, and return to requesting agency.
4. If more space is required, use remarks section.

From U. S. Government Records Management Handbook: Forms Design

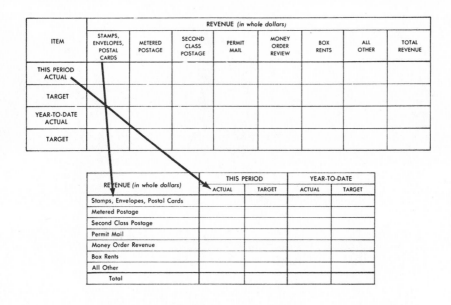

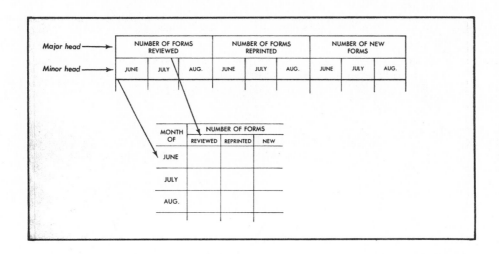

From U. S. Government Records Management Handbook: Forms Design

CHECKLIST

Do typefaces insure good readability and appearance?

Do rule weights and dingbats guide the eye, give emphasis or attract attention to the neighboring parts of a form?

Is the title placed where it can readily be seen but will not interfere with the filing and other data?

Are pages of a multiple-page form numbered?

Is the form a standard size?

Does the horizontal and vertical spacing conform to the writing method—typewritten, handwritten or both?

Is the form designed so that it will not be necessary for the typist to space through captions or roll the typewriter platen up to see the caption and roll it back to make the entry?

Does the typing start from a common left position?

Are vertical rules aligned to reduce tabular stops to a minimum?

Have the various columnar arrangements been considered for using space advantageously and for reading and writing ease?

Are boxes, stub heads, column heads, sections and parts of the form identified by letters and figures?

Are entry spaces which are not to be used blocked out or instructions supplied?

Have the different ways of placing **X**-boxes been considered to insure the best arrangement?

Has sufficient space been allowed for certifications, signatures, titles or dates?

Are "To" and "From" boxes used to make the form self-routing?

Are copies in a set of forms identified to make them self-routing?

Has a form to be mailed been designed to fit into a window envelope?

Has a form requiring a reply been designed for return mailing in a window envelope?

Does a self-mailer form meet postal regulations, and is the address area in the proper position?

Does the form request the respondent to give a change in address to keep the mailing list up to date?

Have binding margins been allowed on a form which is to be punched for filing in a binder?

Is filing information placed on the form so it can be filed and found readily?

Has consideration been given to folding a large form to standard size to fit into standard equipment, binders, or folders?

Have the correct weight, grade, and color of paper been chosen to perform the particular job efficiently?

Is there sufficient contrast between the paper and ink to insure good readability?

Have the use of the form and the method of filing or binding been considered in determining whether a two-sided form is to be printed head to head, head to foot or head to side?

If printed on both sides, have margins been properly specified for each side?

From U. S. Government Records Management Handbook: Forms Design

PERSONALIZED FORM LETTER

Designed to resemble a personal letter, this form does not require any additions to the text. Shaded areas show the only typed additions required.

Printed dot (.) guides typist on where to begin the address.

Typed salutation adds personal touch.

October 4, 19xx

Miss Elizabeth C. Piper
1730 Locust Lane
Meadowtown, Minnesota 55400

Dear Miss Piper:

Your interest in employment with our agency is appreciated, and we are sorry that we cannot be very encouraging about the immediate prospects. There are no openings here just now that would be suitable for a person with the background and experience shown on your application.

Our present clerical requirements are for persons who have had some schooling or practical work experience as keypunch operators, typists, file clerks, telephone operators and stock clerks. Examination for eligibility and certification by the Civil Service Commission are an essential requirement in filling these jobs.

Perhaps you will be interested in the enclosed announcement of Civil Service examinations. Upon your request, the Civil Service Commission here in Washington or in its local office nearest you will gladly send you an announcement of other upcoming examinations.

Again, thank you for thinking of us and all good wishes for success in your employment career.

Sincerely yours,

Charles L. Stewart
Personnel Director

Encl

FL Pers 192

From U.S. Government Records Management Handbook: Managing Correspondence Form and Guide Letters

ALIGNED FILL-IN COMBINED WITH CHECKLIST

February 27, 19xx

Mrs. Dorothy Mortenson
111 Brookdale Drive
Crystal Bay, Nevada 89402

> Space between window-envelope address and salutation is adjusted to give letter the appearance of being framed on the page.

> By leaving the blank space at the end of the line and the paragraph it is easy to vary the length of the fill-in.

Dear Applicant:

Your application for benefits was considered by a review panel, in accordance with the regulations governing this procedure. It is the decision of this panel that your application be approved as filed.

The proceedings of the panel and its decisions relati
have been reviewed and approved by the Chief of the

> The following paragraph is applicable only when checked

☐ Your claim for benefits needs further clarification. Please complete the attached form and mail it in the enclosed envelope at your earliest convenience.

Sincerely yours,

Manager
Records Processing Center

Keep Freedom in Your Future With U.S. Savings Bonds

CHAIN LETTERS

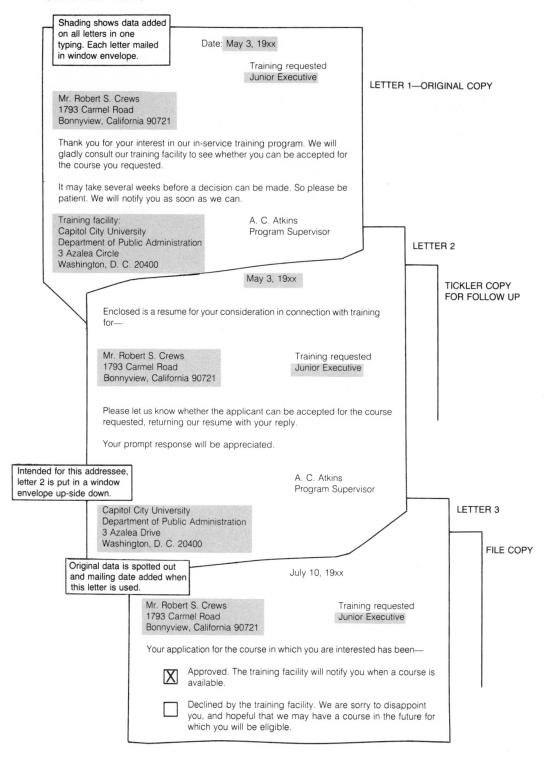

Shading shows data added on all letters in one typing. Each letter mailed in window envelope.

LETTER 1—ORIGINAL COPY

Date: May 3, 19xx

Training requested
Junior Executive

Mr. Robert S. Crews
1793 Carmel Road
Bonnyview, California 90721

Thank you for your interest in our in-service training program. We will gladly consult our training facility to see whether you can be accepted for the course you requested.

It may take several weeks before a decision can be made. So please be patient. We will notify you as soon as we can.

Training facility:
Capitol City University
Department of Public Administration
3 Azalea Circle
Washington, D. C. 20400

A. C. Atkins
Program Supervisor

LETTER 2

TICKLER COPY FOR FOLLOW UP

May 3, 19xx

Enclosed is a resume for your consideration in connection with training for—

Mr. Robert S. Crews
1793 Carmel Road
Bonnyview, California 90721

Training requested
Junior Executive

Please let us know whether the applicant can be accepted for the course requested, returning our resume with your reply.

Your prompt response will be appreciated.

Intended for this addressee, letter 2 is put in a window envelope up-side down.

A. C. Atkins
Program Supervisor

LETTER 3

FILE COPY

Capitol City University
Department of Public Administration
3 Azalea Drive
Washington, D. C. 20400

Original data is spotted out and mailing date added when this letter is used.

July 10, 19xx

Mr. Robert S. Crews
1793 Carmel Road
Bonnyview, California 90721

Training requested
Junior Executive

Your application for the course in which you are interested has been—

[X] Approved. The training facility will notify you when a course is available.

[ ] Declined by the training facility. We are sorry to disappoint you, and hopeful that we may have a course in the future for which you will be eligible.

From U. S. Government Records Management Handbook: Managing Correspondence

Form and Guide Letters

FORM LETTER RESTYLED FOR EASY TYPING AND READING

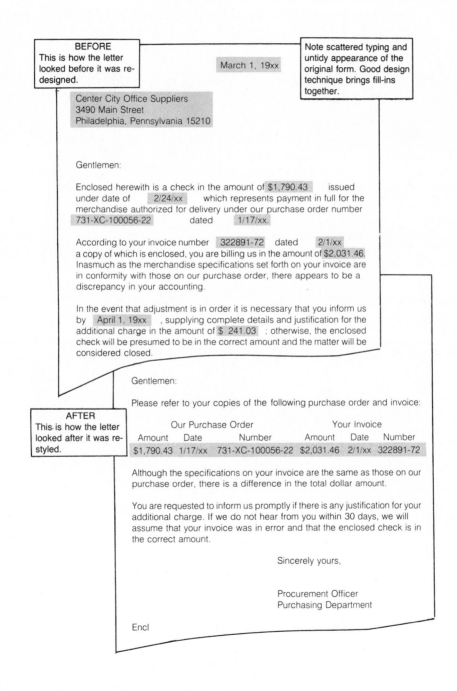

BEFORE
This is how the letter looked before it was re-designed.

March 1, 19xx

Note scattered typing and untidy appearance of the original form. Good design technique brings fill-ins together.

Center City Office Suppliers
3490 Main Street
Philadelphia, Pennsylvania 15210

Gentlemen:

Enclosed herewith is a check in the amount of $1,790.43   issued under date of   2/24/xx   which represents payment in full for the merchandise authorized for delivery under our purchase order number 731-XC-100056-22   dated   1/17/xx.

According to your invoice number   322891-72   dated   2/1/xx a copy of which is enclosed, you are billing us in the amount of $2,031.46. Inasmuch as the merchandise specifications set forth on your invoice are in conformity with those on our purchase order, there appears to be a discrepancy in your accounting.

In the event that adjustment is in order it is necessary that you inform us by   April 1, 19xx   , supplying complete details and justification for the additional charge in the amount of $ 241.03   ; otherwise, the enclosed check will be presumed to be in the correct amount and the matter will be considered closed.

Gentlemen:

Please refer to your copies of the following purchase order and invoice:

AFTER
This is how the letter looked after it was re-styled.

Our Purchase Order			Your Invoice		
Amount	Date	Number	Amount	Date	Number
$1,790.43	1/17/xx	731-XC-100056-22	$2,031.46	2/1/xx	322891-72

Although the specifications on your invoice are the same as those on our purchase order, there is a difference in the total dollar amount.

You are requested to inform us promptly if there is any justification for your additional charge. If we do not hear from you within 30 days, we will assume that your invoice was in error and that the enclosed check is in the correct amount.

Sincerely yours,

Procurement Officer
Purchasing Department

Encl

From U. S. Government Records Management Handbook:
Managing Correspondence Form and Guide Letters

A major program of the post office is the reading of information on envelopes through optical means which increase the sorting rate.

A refinement of this technique now being developed is to convert the address into a series of vertical bars (called a bar code) which are then printed on the face of an envelope.

The Optical Character Recognition equipment then scans these bars rather than the full address, and directs each piece of mail to its proper sorting bin.

Bar codes may be preprinted on envelopes or printed by an operator after he first reads the address and converts it into a bar code.

In order to make systems such as these work effectively, attention must be paid as to what information is printed on the face of the envelope, where it is printed and what types of envelopes it is printed on.

These guidelines are for reference for general situations. Your local postmaster or Customer Service representative will be glad to supply more detailed facts.

Courtesy U.S. Postal Service

GENERAL ENVELOPE DESIGN GUIDELINES

Size The minimum size of the envelope acceptable for machine processing is 3½" high by 5" wide. The maximum size is 6⅛" high by 11½" wide.

Thickness The minimum thickness acceptable for machine processing is 0.010". The maximum thickness is 0.250" evenly distributed.

Color When using colored paper stocks, there should be as much contrast as possible between the paper stock and the ink used to print the address. Generally, pastel-colored or white paper stocks are best. The paper should maintain a reflectivity of greater than 50% when measured on a reflectometer. Paper inks should be carbon-base flexographic inks.

OCR Address Area The placement of an address on an envelope should be within an area no more than 2⅜" high and 8" wide. This area begins 1" from the left edge of the envelope and ⅝" up from the bottom edge. No printing should appear to the right of this area.

Windows A window should appear within the address area defined above. It should be large enough so that there is at least a ¼" clearance between an address on an insert and the edges of the window.

Bar Code Area Bar codes will be printed in an area in the lower right corner of an envelope. An area ⅝" high by 4¼" long should be kept free of all printing and symbols.

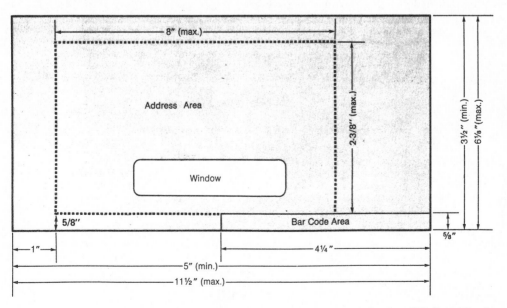

Courtesy U.S. Postal Service

GUIDE TO STANDARD SIZE ENVELOPES

OPEN SIDE ENVELOPES			OPEN END ENVELOPES		
Official &	#6¼	3½″ × 6″	Coin	#1	2¼″ × 3½″
Commercial	#6½	3½″ × 6¼″		#3	2½″ × 4¼″
	#6¾	3⅝″ × 6½″		#4	3″ × 4½″
	#7	3¾″ × 6¾″		#4½	3″ × 4⅞″
	#7¾	3⅞″ × 7½″		#5	2⅞″ × 5¼″
	#8 Monarch	3⅞″ × 7½″		#5½	3⅛″ × 5½″
	#8⅝	3⅝″ × 8⅝″		#6	3⅜″ × 6″
	#9	3⅞″ × 8⅞″		#7	3½″ × 6½″
	#10	4⅛″ × 9½″	Open end	#1	4⅝″ × 6¾″
	#10½	4½″ × 9½″		#3	5″ × 7½″
	#11	4½″ × 10⅜″		#4¼	5½″ × 7½″
	#12	4¾″ × 11″		#6	5½″ × 8¼″
	#14	5″ × 11½″		#7	4″ × 6⅜″
Remittance	#6¼	3½″ × 6″		#8	3⅞″ × 7½″
	#6½	3½″ × 6¼″	Policy	#10	4⅛″ × 9½″
Baronials	#4	3⅝″ × 4⅝″		#11	4½″ × 10⅜″
	#5	4⅛″ × 5⅛″		#14	5″ × 11½″
	#5½	4⅜″ × 5⅝″	Catalog	#1	6″ × 9″
	#6	5″ × 6″		#1¾	6½″ × 9½″
Booklet	#2½	4½″ × 5⅞″		#3	7″ × 10″
	#3	4¾″ × 6½″		#6	7½″ × 10½″
	#5	5½″ × 8½″		#8	8¼″ × 11¼″
	#6	5¾″ × 8⅞″		#9¾	8¾″ × 11¼″
	#6½	6″ × 9″		#10½	9″ × 12″
	#7	6¼″ × 9⅝″		#12½	9½″ × 12½″
	#7½	7½″ × 10½″		#13½	10″ × 13″
	#9	8¾″ × 11½″		#14½	11½″ × 14½″
	#9½	9″ × 12″			
	#10	9½″ × 12⅝″			

Courtesy U. S. Postal Service

6

tricks and tips for photocopying, duplicating and printing

In order for you to be able to successfully put together any project which involves "printing," here is the basic knowledge you will need.

How To Prepare Camera Ready Copy advises you to use a carbon or mylar ribbon, keep the typewriter keys clean, reverse a piece of carbon paper in order to get two images (one in front, one in back) in case your typewriter does not give a clear image and to use double stick tape for paste-ups.

It follows that in order to get good copies certain rules apply for the kind of originals used, for the handling of the paper, the paste-up and the copy itself. All the tips are included, such as— 20-80 lb. paper for originals working best; yellow highlighter appearing very dark on the copies; and if possible, avoiding erasable bond for originals. Tricks for using special originals—oversize originals, colored originals, three-dimensional originals and bound volumes are also included. Unusual end results such as printing on mixed weights of paper, printing dividers on colored paper, two-sided copying and fan folding are described.

There are many special applications such as copy machines which operate either off-line from magnetic tape or on-line directly from computers; machines which can print overlays; a microfiche printer; and engineering print systems which reproduce bulky drawings and reduce them, restore old drawings and create completely new drawings from paste-up originals.

With the advent of the color copying machine by Xerox, a whole new world has opened up and it is necessary not only to know how to use the machine itself, but how to use color. Included are some tips on applying color to text, to tables, to graphics; and speaking of graphics, tips on how to improve the graphics themselves.

Another color-associated medium is the world of transparencies. Some background knowledge on the slides themselves is discussed—a bit of information about the mounts, how to add dimension by using two transparencies together, how to use the transparencies for overhead projection (first, how to prepare them, then how to present them—step by step), making prints from them, using them in coordination with a color copier, and some tips for prepackaged title and art slides.

Stencils are a form of reproduction different from anything else, so if the need arises, you'll find step by step instructions for their preparation.

Also in this chapter is a glossary which will give you the basic information you will need to speak the language of "printing" and the "art" which goes along with it. You will find defined terms such as acetate, binding, carbro, collage, copy, crop marks, deckle edge, dry brush, duotone, em, flap, format, four-color, glossy, halftone, imposition, jacket, key, leader, letterpress, matrix, monotype, montage, offset, opaque, pica, proof, rough, sans serif, silkscreen, stat, tint block, trim and watermark.

HOW TO PREPARE CAMERA READY COPY . . .

If you use a typewriter to prepare your copy, make sure you get a *dark, even* impression on white paper. *A carbon or mylar ribbon will give the best results.* A new, or relatively new ink type ribbon will also produce a good job.

Typewriter keys *must* be clean. However, if your typewriter still does not give you a sharp image, *reverse* a piece of *carbon paper* in order to get two images: one in front and the other in back of the sheet of paper.

When original copy is made from paste-ups, position the paste-up onto a white sheet of paper. If guide lines are used to position paste-ups, use a very light green, blue or yellow pencil as these colors drop out of the picture and do not show on the printed copy.

Rubber cement, glue stick or cellophane type *"double stick tape"* should be used when pasting up. A small amount of cement, or a small piece of tape under ·the paste-up is sufficient and facilitates repositioning of paste-up if needed. It is not necessary to seal edges down.

Copy in *black* or *red* will photograph and *print best.* All other colors, when deep and dark enough, will reproduce with good results.

Newspaper clippings: Although not ideal, will *give satisfactory results.* The paper from these clippings may cause a *slight background* to appear on the printed copies. *Magazine clippings give better results.*

Quality in reproducing *black and white* photographs clipped from newspapers, magazines, etc., will depend on their density or contrast. Avoid colors which are too *deep* if using preprinted color photos from these two sources.

Unscreened photographs, *not* previously broken into *dots,* either black and white, or color, will *give very poor results.* A screened print, *velox,* must be made from the original before attempting to print it.

Use a white correction fluid, available at most graphic arts supply shops or stationery stores, *to get rid of unwanted marks, smears, smudges and shadow lines.*

If still in doubt . . . ask your printer BEFORE preparing your material.

Courtesy PIP—Postal Instant Press of San Francisco, California.

FOR BEST REPRODUCTION, USE:

Smooth Bond Paper. Rough paper may produce shadows on the copies. (Avoid erasable bond.)

20-80 lb. originals.

Originals which are not wrinkled, torn or folded, do not have bent corners and which are undamaged from staples.

Clean Corrections. If you use correction fluid, be sure it is completely dry before typing over it. Add thinner to the liquid if it does not spread easily.

Used with permission of Xerox Corporation.

Non-Reproducible Blue Pencil. For notes on your originals which you don't want to appear on your copies. Avoid yellow highlighter; it will appear very dark on your copies.

Correction tape with beveled edges.

Uniform Page Numbering. Each page should be numbered in the same place. And always number your two-sided originals so that the fronts are odd-numbered and the backs are even.

Adequate Margins. At least ¼" on all sides. If you will place your copies in a binder, leave 1¼" margins.

Originals all the same size if the machine feeds automatically.

RUNNING SPECIAL ORIGINALS

Copies can be made from colored originals (except goldenrod).

Light pencil copy, color-on-color materials, carbonless blue impressions and weak carbon copies can be reproduced to make good, legible copies.

Three-dimensional objects can be copied.

Bound volumes can be copied.

Oversize Originals—Reduce/duplicate large bulky documents down to a more easily handled size (charts, diagrams, computer printouts, ledger sheets).

Any original up to 14" × 18"—one big original, a grouping of smaller originals, or a 14" × 18" segment of an any-size original.

Type lengthy documents on oversize paper—11" × 14" instead of 8½" × 11"—then reduce/duplicate down to standard 8½" × 11"; giving more data on fewer sheets (a 100-page report becomes 64 pages).

Use overlays to add, delete or change information on your originals.

Documents with printing to the edge of the page (Request "98% Reduction").

Use blank paper for originals which will be copied on letterhead.

POSSIBLE END RESULTS

Position of writing on copies can be raised or lowered.

Preprinted forms.

Any paper stock between 16-110 lbs. and *between 5" × 8" and 8½" × 14".*

Mixed weights (card stock can be used *for durable covers).*

Colored Paper (dividers can be copied on colored paper).

Documents (charts, forms, etc.) can be copied onto oversized paper and added to your job.

Two-sided copying (be sure to run the second side within one half hour after running first side to avoid wrinkles).

Your job can be run on paper that is punched, perforated, reinforced and on gummed labels.

Your job can be perforated to your specifications after being printed.

Your job can be made into tear-aways to your specifications after being printed.

There is available a *copy sorter* that *will automatically collate up to 50 sets of multi-page reports* that are ready for binding and distribution.

Documents can be fan folded by machine.

The *finished copies can be stapled* and *stacked by machine.*

SPECIAL APPLICATIONS

There are *copy machines which operate* either *off-line from magnetic tape* or *on-line directly from computers.*

Computer output can be produced on ordinary 8½" × 11" paper.

Overlay capability is available permitting simultaneous printing of the output data and the form on which it appears. An overlay providing any type of fixed-format information—headings, logos, vertical and horizontal lines—solves the problem of maintaining an expensive inventory of pre-printed forms.

There is a *microfiche printer which copies and enlarges directly from standard 4" × 6" microfiche onto ordinary paper* at the rate of nearly a page a second. *The microfiche film sheets each contain up to 98 images and any number of the images can be selected for copying.*

There is an *engineering print system* which *automatically reproduces bulky engineering drawings and other technical information directly from originals, reduces* them *to easy-to-handle sizes* and *folds* and *sorts* them *into complete packages* ready for immediate distribution.

There is a *printer* which fills a variety of engineering needs from *engineering drawing reproduction* and *old drawing restoration* to the *creation of completely new drawings from paste-up originals.*

There is a *microfilm enlarger printer* which was designed primarily *to enlarge and print engineering drawings automatically from aperture cards.*

There is also *a printer* used for engineering *which accepts originals* as large as *24" × 36", reduces* the size of *copies* by either *50% or 60%* and *reproduces same size copies up to 14" × 18".*

There is *another printer* used for engineering which *can take any original as wide as 36", as long as 120" or more and up to ⅛" thick. Originals can be single sheets or board mounted. Copies can be made on paper up to 18" × 60"* and it *reproduces copies same size by dialing in a choice of reduction ratios ranging from 95% down to 45%* of the *original size.*

And a *companion* engineering product—a *printer* which *accepts all types of microfilmed originals as intermediates for producing prints.*

UNDERSTANDING COLOR COPYING

Applying Color to Text

Highlight priority information with color by using:

- Color Graphic Film
- Color Fine Line Pen
- Color Highlighter Pen
- Color Typing Film
- Color Tape

Used with permission of Xerox Corporation.

Visually Identify Text Drafts with Color

Seven different colors can be produced from a black-and-white original document on the Xerox 6500 color copier.

Indicate Changes with Color to Conserve Review Time

Use Informal Color for Quick Response or Last-Minute Changes

Applying Color to Tables

Accentuate Critical Variances in Exception Reports with Color

Achieve Selective Highlighting with Color

Speed Retrieval of Related Information in Supporting Text with Color

Achieve Selective Deletion and Preserve Confidentiality with Color

Applying Color to Graphics

You should be familiar with the principal types of graphics so that you can choose the one best suited to your needs.

Color can be introduced into graphics as:

- Maps
- Pie Charts
- Bar Charts
- Graphs
- Flowcharts
- Schematics

Emphasize Critical Variances Graphically with Color

Color Key Covers for Quick Identification

Extend Communications Through Use of Patterns and Shadings in Color

Update Periodic Reports Quickly and Economically Using Same Original in Color

Interpretation of Computer-Generated Reports Can Be Rapid, Informal and Effective with Color

Tips on Improving Graphic Design

Figures on Graph Elements are Easier to Understand Than Grids

Used with permission of Xerox Corporation.

Labels Identifying Graph Elements are Easier to Read Than Keys

Grouped Data from a Common Base are Better Than Segmented Data

Bar Charts are Easier to Understand Than Curve Charts (or Line Graphs)

Visibility of Graphics Using Yellow is Improved When Bordered or Framed in a Contrasting Color.

Using Color Transparencies

For continuous projection, transparencies in open mounts last longer than glass mounts because of better cooling. Also, experience has shown that open frames or cardboard or plastic mounts handle more easily than do glass mounts, with less incidence of fingerprinting. A cracked or broken glass mount almost always damages the transparency.

Add Dimension or Show Change With Two Transparencies in Color

More than one color transparency can be overlaid at the same time to illustrate color-coded segments of complex diagrams, schematics, maps and other graphics.

Color copies can also be produced for distribution from the same mechanical art or originals used to prepare 35mm slides.

Add Variable Information to Reports with Color Transparencies

Guide to Using Color Transparencies For Overhead Presentations

Preparation

- Convey one idea per page
- Use variety in subject matter
- Know your charts beforehand
- Put notes on transparency frames
- Practice using charts
- Set up the room so that nobody is behind the charts
- Be sure there is sufficient projection light

Presentation

- Keep charts covered
- Show one at a time

Used with permission of Xerox Corporation.

- Vary introduction to each chart
- Don't read from charts
- Make sure charts can be seen and read
- Explain what each chart shows and why
- Have audience participate
- Use pointer to identify details
- Summarize your presentation
- Distribute copies at the end of the presentation to enhance professionalism and improve retention of information

Color Slides to Color Prints

The common 35mm or 2″ × 2″ color slide is often a dead end in itself. It can only be used for projection and as original art for the four-color printing process. But when it comes to getting prints or color "stats" from the slide, turnaround time and cost can be excessive. Then multiply this by the number of slides under consideration and it becomes a visible cost factor.

Getting prints from slides is as easy as pushing a button. The Xerox Corporation now has a slide adapter with which the color copier can be equipped.

The combination places 35mm slides into another dimension of utility.

- Hardcopy of slides in presentation can be used as handouts or included in reports and other business documents.
- "Stats" generated from slides can be created for comprehensive art and layouts.
- Slide catalogs can be assembled from color copies to maintain file integrity.
- Prints from slides can be used as illustrations in contracts, proposals, photodrawings and presentations.

Capabilities

Here's what you can do with the Slide Adapter and Color Copier:

- Make enlargements of 35mm slides
- Produce size-for-size copies of the large size color transparencies and overhead transparencies
- Knock out background

Used with permission of Xerox Corporation.

- Change color of background
- Superimpose text on slide image
- Backlight transparencies
- Add pictorial or graphic element to color or black and white copies

Used with permission of Xerox Corporation.

PREPACKAGED TITLE AND ART SLIDES

To assist you in producing effective slide shows, there are several sources available for standard titles and art slides which can be applied to general topics. These are usually inexpensive, and in some cases, slide production houses maintain art slides which can be customized to your needs at reasonable costs . . . and substantially less than producing original art.

Your own titles can be produced quickly and easily with color paper and plastic letters available from art or photo supply stores. Titles can also be made by mounting letters on glass and shooting through the glass around scenic backgrounds, or more simply by using pickup art that lends itself to the subject material at your slide show.

Another source for inexpensive charts, graphs and diagrams is computer-generated color slides, now available from General Electric's Genigraphics Division, Syracuse, New York. In most cases, these slides can be produced at less cost than equivalent artwork and the original slide.

From Visual Log, a publication of the Motion Picture and Audiovisual Markets Division, Eastman Kodak Company, Rochester, New York 14650.

HOW TO WORK WITH CRYSTAL (FILM) STENCILS

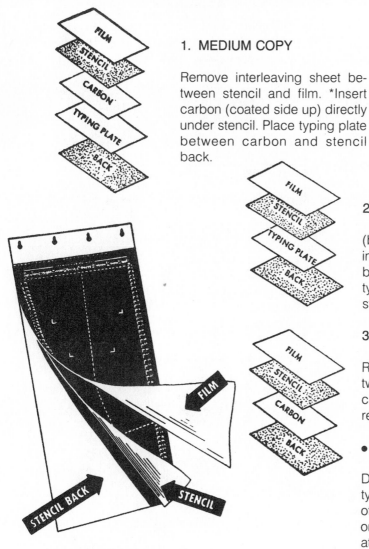

1. MEDIUM COPY

Remove interleaving sheet between stencil and film. *Insert carbon (coated side up) directly under stencil. Place typing plate between carbon and stencil back.

2. LIGHT COPY

(best for bond paper duplicating) Remove interleaving sheet between stencil and film. *Insert typing plate only, directly under stencil.

3. HEAVY COPY

Remove interleaving sheet between stencil and film. *Insert carbon only (coated side up) directly under stencil.

• CORRECTIONS

Do not remove stencil from typewriter. Detach film from top of stencil. Apply correction fluid on stencil and allow to dry. Reattach film to stencil. Then type over corrected spot.

• STYLUS WORK

Remove top film; then insert a drawing plate directly under stencil. Write or draw directly on the stencil itself.

Courtesy Frankel Manufacturing Company, 285 Rio Grande Blvd., Denver, Colorado 80201

**DO NOT REMOVE FILM
FROM STENCIL UNTIL
TYPING IS COMPLETED**

After stencil is cut, tear off along perforation line—the remaining film covers the glue line. This completely eliminates any possibility of glue on operator's hands, glue on mimeograph machine, and sticking together of stencils when filed away.

SPECIAL STENCILS

These three special stencil sheets have special guide marks to show you exactly where to type when you use the 4 page folder stencil, the newspaper stencil, or the addressing stencil. Ask for these stencils by name. We will be glad to send you samples of some with complete instructions.

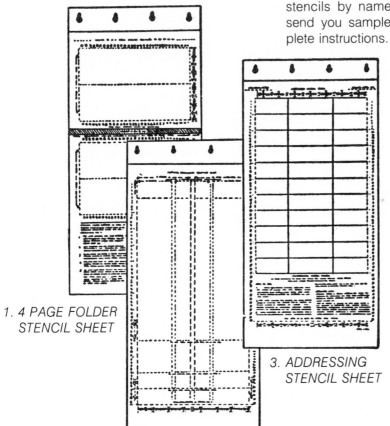

1. 4 PAGE FOLDER STENCIL SHEET

3. ADDRESSING STENCIL SHEET

2. SCHOOL NEWSPAPER STENCIL SHEET

STENCILS FOR ALL MAKES OF DUPLICATORS

In addition to making stencils for all American model machines, we also manufacture stencils for all foreign make machines such as Gestetner, Roneo, and Rex Rotary duplicators.

Courtesy Frankel Manufacturing Company 285 Rio Grande Blvd., Denver, Colorado 80201.

GLOSSARY

Acetate—transparent material used in preparing separations for finished artwork.

Airbrush—the technique of applying paint or dye with an instrument that blows the pigments by air under pressure. Used to emphasize or remove details in photography or artwork.

Alteration—a change made by a client after type has been set. If the typesetter is not at fault, additional charges are legitimate.

Ampersand—the name for the character "&."

Ascender—that part of a lowercase letter that extends above the body of the character.

Author's Alteration (AA)—a correction made by an author, editor or client on typeset material. They are billed to the author or customer.

Basis Weight—a term used to classify papers denoting the actual weight in pounds of 500 sheets of 25″ × 38″ paper.

Benday—the application of dots, lines or other textures to a line plate before etching to produce various tonal and textural effects.

Binding—the method by which papers are held together in a printed piece—stapling, sewing, gluing, etc.

Bleed—printed material that extends to any edge of a page.

Blowup—an enlargement from original size.

Body Type—type used for large amounts of printed material, such as the text of an advertisement, book, or magazine page.

Boldface—heavy, dark type used for emphasis in heads and indexes.

Brochure—a bound and stitched booklet.

Bullet(s)—a dot or series of dots.

Caps—abbreviation for "capitals," the large letters of an alphabet (uppercase) as opposed to the small letters (lowercase).

Caption—description text for an illustration, placed adjacently to it.

Carbro—a process of printing full-color photographs.

Cast Off—to estimate the amount of space required for a given amount of text or copy in a given type size.

Center Spread—the two center pages of a booklet or magazine.

Character—a single printed or typewritten letter.

Character Count—a method of estimating type sizes and space by counting the number of characters in the text or copy.

From Art and Reproduction *by Raymond A. Ballinger, published in 1977 by Van Nostrand Reinhold Company. A division of Litton Educational Publishing, Inc.*

Cold Type—typesetting done by a typewriter-like machine in which a matrix and heat are not used.

Collage—a method of creating a piece of art or a design in which various associated or disassociated materials are pasted together on a flat surface.

Collate—to place pages or forms in proper order or sequence.

Combination Plate—a plate with both line and halftone art.

Composition—typeset material.

Condensed Type—a typeface with narrow characters and vertical design.

Contact Print—a photographic print that is exactly the same size as the negative, made with the film negative and sensitized paper.

Continuous Tone—gradation of tone without halftone dots, as a photograph.

Copy—(a) text for an advertisement, magazine or book (b) an engraver's term for original artwork.

Copyfitting—any of several methods for estimating the space needed for a given amount of text in a given type size.

Cover—the exterior pages of a magazine, catalog, book, referred to as cover 1, cover 2, cover 3 and cover 4; cover 1 indicates the name and sometimes the contents; covers 2, 3, and 4 may contain additional information or advertising.

Crop Marks—indications of where artwork is to be cut or where a bleed page will be cut.

Deadline—the time set for the delivery of work.

Deckle Edge—an edge of paper purposely left untrimmed.

Descender—the part of a lowercase letter that extends below the body of the character.

Die-Cutting—the mechanical process of cutting planned shapes in paper, such as a cover in which a circle is cut so that the first page shows through.

Direct Mail—material designed and prepared for mail distribution.

Display—(a) a very large type size used for headings (b) a design generally prepared for dimensional form (c) the art of show-window design and installation.

Double Spread—a design that spreads across two pages.

Dry Brush—an art technique in which the brush is used with moist—not wet—pigments.

Dry Mount—a method of mounting photographs and artwork by means of a specially prepared tissue and heated instruments.

Dummy—the preparatory facsimile of a booklet, catalog, etc., usually prepared for purposes of approval but useful to typographers, engravers and printers in carrying out the requirements of the designer.

Duotone—the use of a second plate, most often with a second color of ink, to add color or subtlety to a halftone reproduction.

Electrotype—a duplicate engraving plate made from the original.

Em—the square of a type body named after the fact that the letter M is often cast on a square body.

Embossing—printing a design in relief with dies.

En—half the width of an em.

Engraving—a printing plate made by an etching process.

Enlargement—a photographic print that is bigger than the negative.

Extended Type—a typeface that is wide in character and horizontal in design.

Finish—completed artwork.

Flap—protecting paper placed over the surface of finished art, folded over the top and pasted to the back.

Folio—a page number—right hand pages are always odd, left-hand pages, even.

Font—an assortment of type in one size and style.

Format—the general appearance or plan of a printed page.

Four-Color—the exact name for the common term "full-color," denoting the number of plates used in most full-color printing.

Freelance—an independent artist or designer who does work for different organizations.

Full-Color—see four-color.

Galley Proof—proofs of type matter not yet in page form.

Glossy—a photograph or photostat with a very shiny surface.

Gravure—a printing method that utilizes etched intaglio plates.

Gutter—the center of two pages in a book or magazine.

Halftone—(a) a printing plate made by photographing the original through a halftone screen (b) the printed impression from this plate.

Heading—the title on a page, as distinguished from the text material, usually set in larger and/or heavier type.

House Organ—a publication or magazine prepared by a company as opposed to a magazine produced for sale.

From Art and Reproduction *by Raymond A. Ballinger, published in 1977 by Van Nostrand Reinhold Company. A division of Litton Educational Publishing, Inc.*

Imposition—the arrangement of plates in proper order for printing.

Initial Letter—a larger letter in the first word of text.

Insert—a page or signature printed separately, often on different paper or utilizing different printing methods.

Intertype—the trade name for a machine that sets individual type characters (slugs) in a line.

Jacket—originally the dustcover for a book, now utilized as a design area for advertising the book.

Justify—typesetting in which all lines are equally wide, often specified as flush left and flush right.

Key—the identification of positions of copy or art in a dummy or comp, with letters or other symbols.

Key Drawing—a master drawing according to which other drawings in separation art are drawn for correct registration; usually the drawing for black.

Key Plate—the plate according to which other plates are positioned; usually the most detailed plate.

Layout—the composition of the elements in a printed page.

Leader—a dot and/or dash in typographic design, often used in statements and reports.

Leading—space between lines of type achieved by inserting thin lead strips of a specified size in points.

Letterpress—a printing method in which a raised surface such as type or photoengraving is used.

Letterspacing—the allowance of more space between letters in typesetting than normal.

Line—artwork with no tonal variations, used to make linecuts. Line art in pencil or chalk usually requires a halftone screen.

Linotype—trade name for a machine that sets individual type characters (slugs) in a line.

Logotype—a designed signature or trademark used by a company in advertising—often called a logo.

Lowercase—the small letters of the alphabet (as opposed to uppercase, the capital letters).

Ludlow—trade name for a process of casting slugs from handset type.

Makeready—preparation of a press for printing—putting the type form on the press and making the impression even.

Makeup—the arrangement of copy and artwork into page form.

Margin—the space surrounding printed matter on a page.

Mat—(a) a window cut from mat or illustration board to protect and enhance a piece of artwork (b) a papier-mâché matrix in which type is cast.

Matrix—a mold for casting typefaces in monotype and linotype machines.

Measure—the length of a line of type in picas.

Mechanical(s)—finished artwork ready for production.

Monotype—trade name for a machine that automatically casts and assembles individual letters into lines.

Montage—a term applied to a photographic composition in which different elements are superimposed or juxtaposed with each other.

Negative—(a) in photography, the image of an original or film or glass from which a print or positive is taken (b) in a photostat, the image of an original on paper from which a print or positive is taken.

Offset—a printing method in which material is reproduced photographically onto a metal plate.

Opaque—(a) a nontransparent paint or paper (b) in photoengraving, the painting out of areas on the negative that are not desired on the printing plate.

Overlay—any material on which artwork is done and which is transparent enough to show other related art. Drawings for secondary colors are often done on overlays, usually acetate.

Paper—material made from straw, rags, fibers, etc., and usually produced in sheets.

Paste-Up—the term applied to the assembly of artwork for printing, including photographs, headings, logos, etc.

Photocomposition—type set by machine onto photographic paper as opposed to metal type on paper proofs.

Photostat—a photographic method of duplicating originals.

Pica—a typographic measurement—about $1/6$ of an inch.

Plate—the unit, developed from material prepared by designers and processors, from which the printed impression is made.

Point—a unit of measurement denoting the height of a slug on which a type letter is cast—1 point (pt.) is $1/72$ of an inch, or $1/12$ of a pica.

Positive—an image achieved from a photographic negative corresponding in detail to the original.

Press Proof—a proof in one or more colors taken after press makeready.

Primary Colors—red, yellow and blue printing inks, often called process colors.

From Art and Reproduction *by Raymond A. Ballinger, published in 1977 by Van Nostrand Reinhold Company. A division of Litton Educational Publishing, Inc.*

Printer's Error (PE)—a mistake made by a typesetter or printer for which he is responsible and for which the customer is not charged.

Process Plates—the color plates used to print two or more colors; in four-color printing, yellow, red, blue and black.

Progressive Proofs—sets of proofs showing individual colors and combination of colors in process printing. The plates are proofed in proper color rotation using inks and paper specified by the printer.

Proof—printed material furnished by typographers or printers for review, corrections and/or approval. They may be anything from type galleys to proofs of four-color work.

Register—the positioning of reproduction plates for printing.

Reproduction Proofs—final proofs of typographic material ready for reproduction.

Rotogravure—a photographic method of gravure printing.

Rough—a sketch or crude layout.

Runaround—type set to fit around an illustration instead of following a column measure.

Running Head—a title repeated on several consecutive pages.

Sans Serif—a letter or typeface without serifs (see below).

Screen—the number of dots per square inch in a halftone or reproduction.

Separation—a plate of one of the colors used to print color artwork.

Serif—a chisellike ending on the stroke of a letter.

Signature—a section of pages in a book—8, 12, 16 or more—folded from a single sheet.

Silkscreen—a reproduction method in which ink is transferred to the paper through stretched silk.

Small Caps—small capital letters used with many roman typefaces for subheads, etc.

Split Fountain—a method of obtaining several colors in one impression by separating inks in the press.

Stat—a short term for photostat.

Stereotype—a duplicate of a printing plate; a matrix of the original plate is made in papier-mâché, and a cast is taken from it.

Text—the type on a printed page that carries the story or message. In advertising it is often called copy.

Three-Color Process—the reproduction of a full-color original with three colors instead of four. Yellow, red and blue are usually used.

Tint Block—a solid plate used in printing flat colors.

Tip-In—a printed piece that is not bound into a project but inserted separately.

Tissue—a type of paper used in layout work.

Transparency—a transparent black-and-white or color positive.

Transparent—pigment as opposed to opaque paint or paper.

Trim—the place at which a printed page is cut.

Typography—the setting of metal or photographic letterforms (type).

Uppercase—the large letters of the alphabet (as opposed to lowercase, the small letters).

Vignette—an indistinct or soft edge in a drawing, painting, photograph or halftone; a literary sketch.

Wash—a drawing done in a wet medium as opposed to a line drawing.

Watermark—a design or trademark made into paper during manufacture.

Widow—a short line at the end of a paragraph of text, often a single word. Many writers will edit the preceding text to eliminate it.

Work-and-Turn—the printing of both sides of a sheet consecutively. Many modern printing presses print both sides of a sheet simultaneously.

Wraparound—the term applied to a printed piece that wraps around other printed material, such as a label.

Wrong Font—a letter that is the wrong typeface or size.

From Art and Reproduction *by Raymond A. Ballinger, published in 1977 by Van Nostrand Reinhold Company. A division of Litton Educational Publishing, Inc.*

7

how to file it to find it

The basic filing rules are:

    Clarity—logical and understandable choice of categories.

    Simplicity—ease of finding (file drawer "A" above or next to file drawer "B", labeled)

    Workability—the system by which the document can *best* travel smoothly from the file box, through sorting and into the logical folder.

    Consistency—file folders and index cards or rolidex have the same information *and* the same system is used throughout.

A very important area of filing is the follow-up procedure used—and the easiest and most reliable is the Tickler filing system.

Predrafted letters necessitate an individual type of filing system. Paragraphs of letters are organized numerically and by subject on cards in a Correspondex—a desk reference file.

More records and less space have given rise to a number of different forms in which microfilm is made, stored and used—16mm and 35mm reels, microfiche, cartridges, ultrafiche, aperature cards, cassettes, jackets and micro-opaques.

The basic procedures for these areas of filing are set forth here step by step. They can be used directly or adapted to your specific needs.

CHOOSING THE SYSTEM THAT FITS YOUR NEEDS

BASIC ELEMENTS OF FILING BY ALPHABET

Telephone Directory Method—used for volume filing

1. Order of letters of alphabet is used.
2. Key or basic word is first word of name.
3. Second word determines order; if first two words are the same, third word determines order.
4. Disregard -, &, '.
5. Alphabetize numbers as if spelled out.
6. Letters used as words are arranged alphabetically preceding word-names:
   > A-American Cooking School
   > A Barber Shop
   > A-1 Candy Store
   > AA Driving Instruction
   > A & A Gardening Supplies
   > AAA Airlines Company
   > ABC Distributing, Inc.
   > Aames, Joan (Auto Accident)
   > Aames, Joan (Unlawful Detainer)
   > Adams, John C.
   > Air-Lines Ticket Agency
   > Al's Furniture
   > American Bookkeeping Company
   > Artist's Supplies, Inc.
7. Abbreviations are alphabetized as if they were fully spelled-out words:
   > Dane, L. V.
   > D'Angelo, James
   > Dangers, Robert
   > Sail Company, Inc.
   > St. Mary's Church
   > Salo Company
8. Disregard articles, prepositions, conjunctions:
   > *B*est Television Company (The)
   > *D*rapes and Curtains, Inc.
   > *E*dwards & Edwards

9. Disregard titles:
    Adams, James (Doctor)
    Jones, John (Captain)
10. MAC and MC are grouped separately, but alphabetically:
    Mack, John D.
    Mac Bride and Sons, Inc.
    Macchi, James
    Mac Donald, Robert
    Maxwell, Arthur
    Mc Abee, William
    Mc Laughlin, C. L.
    Mc Williams, Jas. T.
    Mead and Sons, Inc.
    Miller, John V.
11. Company Names
    Trade names are alphabetized as full name:
    *E*lizabeth Arden
    *S*ears Roebuck and Co.
    *T*he New Yorker
    All else, surname first:
    *P*enney, J. C. Co. Inc.
    *M*agnin, I. & Co.
    *W*oolworth, F. W. Co. Variety Stores
    Note: Always cross-reference
12. Board of, Bureau of, University of
    File Name, Board of

Dictionary Method of Alphabetizing—used for short lists. Using all words of names, file in strict alphabetical order:
    A Needlepoint Shop
    *B*rooks and Brooks, Inc.
    *J*ones, James
    *J*ones, J. C.
    *T*he Candy Store
    *T*homas and Thomas

Filing by Subject

1. Choose method of alphabetizing and arrange subject and subheadings:
    Business Cards (see PRINTER)
    MAINTENANCE

OFFICE SUPPLIES
PRINTER
Stationery (see OFFICE SUPPLIES)
Typewriter Ribbons (see OFFICE SUPPLIES)
Window Cleaner (see MAINTENANCE)

2. Arrange index cards using identical alphabetizing procedure and cross-index extensively

Filing by Number

1. How to Set Up a Decimal System—main categories are from 000 to 900—for example, a toy company might categorize stuffed animals as 330 and teddy bears as 330.4—cross-index.
2. How to Set Up a Numeral System:
   a. Arrange list in alphabetical order.
   b. Give each folder a number in numerical order.
   c. As new files are opened, assign the next vacant number.
   d. Keep record of next number on card in front of rolidex or index card file.
   e. Sub-divisions are handled by adding either letter or sub-number:
      Jones, John 43
      Jones, John (Insurance) 43a or 43-1
      Jones, John (Lease) 43b or 43-2

Filing by Geographical Location

1. Prepare appropriate classifications and subclassifications.
   a. Generally classified from large to small—country, state or province, county, city.
   b. Can be used with decimal system—for example, 500 could be Western Europe and 510 could be France.
   c. Must be used with cross-reference.
   d. Can be used with either method of alphabetizing, but be *consistent*.

Filing by Date is used for:

1. Extra carbon copies of all outgoing correspondence (usually kept in one folder, most current on top).

2. Newspapers or periodicals.
3. Sequences of certain activities such as semi-annual sales or meetings, contests, holiday promotions.
4. *Be sure to cross-reference.*

Filing by Color using colored labels, colored file folders, colored typewriter ribbons and/or colored stickers in different shapes (circles, squares, rectangles, pasted on label) is a method used as an *additional element* for at-a-glance information such as:

1. Salesman
2. Territory
3. Special Products
4. Credit Rating
5. Department
6. Category

The combinations for visual codes are virtually limitless. *Always key the index or reference card.*

USING AND MAINTAINING A
TICKLER FOLLOW-UP SYSTEM

1. Label 31 folders from 1 and put in front of file drawer; file current month's follow-ups.
2. Label 12 folders January—December and put directly behind folder for days. Put current month's folder behind other monthly folders and use for follow-ups for that month next year.
3. Mark one folder "Future" and place after December.
4. Make one extra carbon copy of each piece of outgoing correspondence requiring follow up, mark follow-up date on copy and file appropriately. If there is no carbon copy, write a memo and file the memo in the proper place.
5. File current month's material behind proper date.
6. Put current day's folder at end of numbered folders after removing material.
7. Be sure to file follow-up material for over a month in proper *monthly* file folder.
8. On first day of month, file material from folder of new month in proper date folder and put current month's folder at the end of the other monthly folders.

9. Reverse folders so tabs show blank for dates throughout month when office is closed.

OTHER FOLLOW-UP METHODS

1. For small amount of correspondence, one folder can be kept chronologically and checked daily.
2. For items other than correspondence, use calendars, appointment books or diaries, but choose a system that *works*.

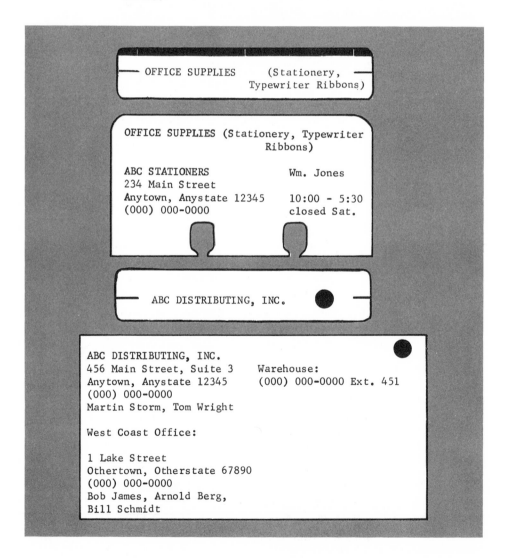

```
┌─────────────────────────────────────────────────────────────────┐
│              LAWDEX®CASE FILE INDEX                               │
│                  INSTRUCTIONS FOR USE                            │
│ FILE FOLDER SHEET (WHITE GUMMED PAPER)   ACCOUNTING SHEET (BLUE GUMMED PAPER) │
│ TOP PORTION: PASTE ON FILE FOLDER.       TOP PORTION: PASTE IN ACCOUNTING LEDGER. │
│ BOTTOM PORTION: PASTE ON FILE TAB.       MIDDLE PORTION: PASTE IN TYPE-OF-CASE INDEX. │
│ ATTORNEY'S SHEET (GOLD PAPER)            BOTTOM PORTION: PASTE IN NUMERICAL OR │
│ FOR ATTORNEY IN CHARGE OF FILE.          TIME LEDGER.             │
│                                          ADVERSE PARTY SHEET (GREEN PAPER) │
│ OUR CLIENT SHEET (WHITE PAPER)           FILE ALPHABETICALLY BY ADVERSE │
│ FILE ALPHABETICALLY BY CLIENT'S NAME.    PARTY'S NAME.           │
│                                                                  │
│ OUR CLIENT              ADVERSE PARTY              FILE NUMBER    │
│ ADDRESS                 ADDRESS                                   │
│                                                                  │
│ PHONE:                  EST. FEE:                                │
│ RE:                                                              │
│ TYPE OF CASE:                       OPEN FILE NO.                │
│ DATE OPENED:                        CLOSED FILE NO.              │
│ REFERRED BY:                                                     │
│ NOTES                   NOTES                                    │
│                                                                  │
│ OUR CLIENT              ADVERSE PARTY              FILE NUMBER    │
│                                                                  │
│            LAWDEX®CASE FILE INDEX                               │
│     © 1970 AND REG. U.S. PAT. OFF. ROSS A. SUSSMAN, ATTORNEY AT LAW │
│ 594846                         ORDER FROM                        │
│                   SHAFER & FELD, INC. — PRINTERS                 │
│              1010 SO. SIXTH ST., MINNEAPOLIS, MINN. 55415        │
│     This sheet IS GUMMED. Moisten and use in regular manner.     │
└─────────────────────────────────────────────────────────────────┘
```

This has an original, four copies and carbon paper.

PROCEDURES TO MAKE DAILY FILING EASIER

1. Keep papers to be filed in one place such as a folder marked "Filing" or a basket or tray.
2. If more than one set of files, categorize filing before sorting.
3. Check all clipped or stapled pages to see if they should be together.
4. Staple paper clipped items.
5. Tape tears.
6. Punch holes.
7. Staple or tape #10 (or smaller) envelope inside front cover of file folder and use for odd-size pieces of paper—label contents.

8. With the Amberg Sort All, papers can be sorted for filing by alphabet, by number, by day of week, by month and by day of month, quickly and neatly.

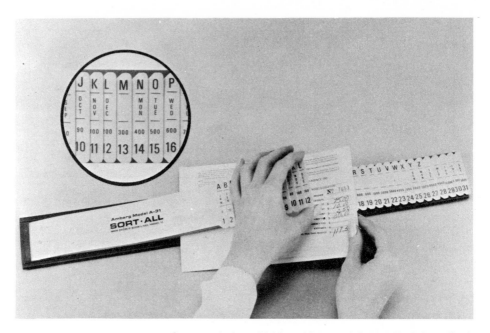

Courtesy Amberg Division of Boorum & Pease, Kankakee, Illinois.

9. Keep substitution card inside front cover with name of document removed, person who removed it and date of removal.
10. Keep sign-out list of files removed—include name of person who removed file and date removed and returned.
11. Take the extra moment to arrange papers within the file and the files within the drawer.
12. To locate lost files:
    a. look for similar names;
    b. look for similar numbers;
    c. look in other sets of files (inactive, dead, etc.);
    d. place "dummy" folder in file indicating date of loss— *reference index card.*

A COLLECTION OF PREDRAFTED LETTERS

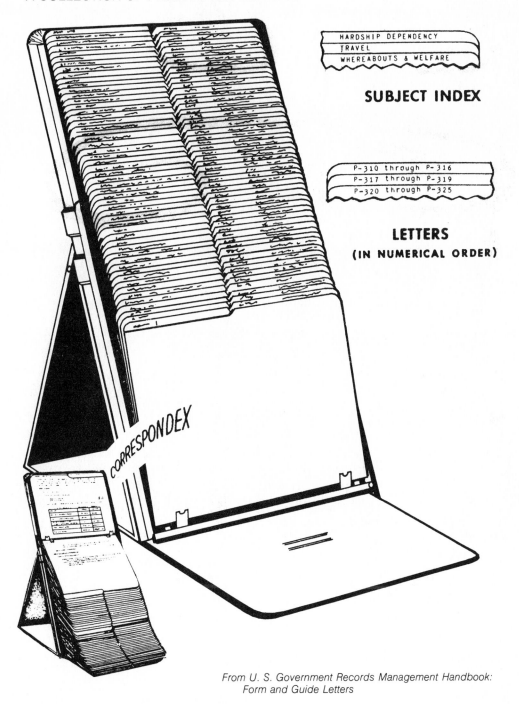

HARDSHIP DEPENDENCY
TRAVEL
WHEREABOUTS & WELFARE

SUBJECT INDEX

P-310 through P-316
P-317 through P-319
P-320 through P-325

LETTERS
(IN NUMERICAL ORDER)

CORRESPONDEX

*From U. S. Government Records Management Handbook:
Form and Guide Letters*

WRITTING LETTERS THE EASY CORRESPONDENCE WAY

LETTERWRITERS LOOK UP LETTERS BY SUBJECT

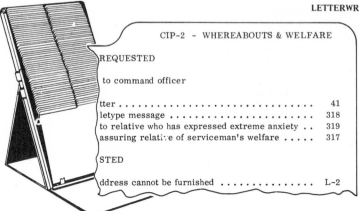

CIP-2 - WHEREABOUTS & WELFARE

REQUESTED

to command officer

tter 41
letype message 318
to relative who has expressed extreme anxiety .. 319
assuring relative of serviceman's welfare 317

STED

ddress cannot be furnished L-2

Letterwriters look in the subject index to get the numbers of letters and paragraphs they want to write. The numbers are then given to typists.

TYPISTS LOOK UP LETTERS BY NUMBER

Predrafted letters and paragraphs are exhibited in numerical order. It takes a typist just a second to find the ones she is asked to prepare.

P-317 through P-319

317 NOTE: Prepare original only; signature, of Hea

The Bureau has received no information disclo
in other than the best of health. In view of
letter has been forwarded to his commanding off
to you

You are assured that in the event of serious
of kin is immediately notified. In the absence
be assumed that your relationship is in good

318 NOTE: Prepare as a message

PEOPLE WHO SIGN LETTERS MAY REFER TO THE CORRESPONDEX TO MAKE SURE THE LETTERS ARE PROPERLY PREPARED

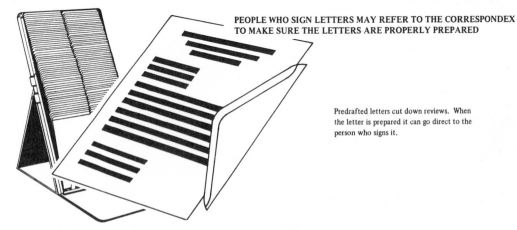

Predrafted letters cut down reviews. When the letter is prepared it can go direct to the person who signs it.

From U. S. Government Records Management Handbook: Form and Guide Letters

AN INTRODUCTION TO THE WORLD OF MICROFILM

microforms

The wide variety of user needs and applications has given rise to a number of different *forms* in which microfilm is made, stored and used. Some of the familiar microforms are shown at the right and described in detail on the following pages.

Each has a range of applications designed to fulfill certain specific user requirements, and the most important planning consideration is to *select the form to match the need*.

Primary factors to consider in selecting the appropriate form of microfilm include type of input, the nature of the information to be stored, and how it is to be used.

There are additional factors. For example:
- Overall system cost;
- Speed and ease of document retrieval;
- Accessibility of information at any desired number of locations;
- Capability and cost of making duplicates, either in large or small quantities and whether they're to be on microfilm or in hard copy blowback form;
- Frequency with which the file is changed or updated;
- Need for file integrity (i.e., the assurance that no document is ever lost or misfiled);
- Storage density;
- Anticipated means of reading and duplication, both at central and/or remote locations;
- Compatibility with other information systems, such as data processing.

Because of the wide variety of individual user requirements, selection of the appropriate microform may be more complex than anticipated. For this reason, a professional microfilm systems expert can provide valuable assistance.

reels, 16mm & 35mm

Microfilm on reels was one of the first microforms. It is still a popular choice because large quantities of information may be stored in very little space, at very low cost. Microfilm on reels provide a high measure of file integrity, are desirable where information is added continuously in sequence and updating is infrequent. 16mm reels are primarily used for alpha and numeric data, such as correspondence, checks, and similar information. 35mm reels are used for graphics and large documents such as engineering drawings, X-rays, newspapers, and maps.

microfiche

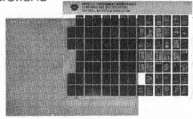

A microfiche, or "fiche," is a sheet of film containing multiple microimages in a grid pattern. It usually contains identification information which can be read without magnification. Available in a variety of styles, microfiche generally permit unitized data storage and updating. They are easily duplicated for mailing, security or reference purposes. Microfiche may contain from a few to several hundred images in a reduction range of 18X to 48X.

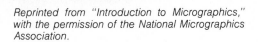

Reprinted from "Introduction to Micrographics," with the permission of the National Micrographics Association.

cartridges

Microfilm cartridges function as "convenience packaging" for rolls of microfilm. Unlike microfilm on reels, which require threading, cartridges can be self threading. Microfilm in cartridges is well protected, and not subject to fingerprints and other possible sources of damage.

ultrafiche

Ultrafiche contain images reduced more than 90X, thus permitting thousands of images per fiche. Ultrafiche offers the advantage of storing more information in less space than a standard microfiche.

aperture cards

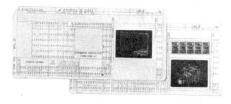

Available in many sizes—with the tab size (82.5mm x 187.25mm or 3¼" x 7⅜") most commonly used - - they combine key punched data and access information with microfilm. Aperture cards may contain a single image, or up to eight page-size images on one 35mm frame.

cassettes

Microfilm in cassettes gives added convenience to the handling of continuous rolls of microfilm. Each cassette contains two film cores—the feed and the take-up. There is no need to rewind a cassette when it is removed from the reader. Any frame may be held in viewing position for further reference at a later time.

jackets

A jacket is a plastic carrier with single or multiple sleeves or channels designed to accept strips of 16mm or 35mm film. Jackets both protect the microfilm and also facilitate organization of material. Images may be copied or read directly from the jacket without removing film. Jackets can be visibly titled for quick, easy file reference.

micro-opaques

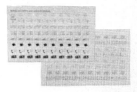

Similar to microfiche in configuration, micro-opaques are, as their name implies, images on opaque stock. Therefore, images may be stored on both sides. Unlike microfiche where transmitted light is used for blowback, opaques use reflected light.

Reprinted from "Introduction to Micrographics," with the permission of the National Micrographics Association.

8

how to save time and money in postal matters

Postal knowledge includes information about the different classes of domestic and international mail, insurance, receipts, registry, special delivery, C.O.D., postal money orders, customs, and proper packaging and addressing.

It also includes keeping up with the latest developments in the postal service in order to take maximum advantage of available services. For instance, if you are rushed you can order stamps by mail for a slight fee, on a special form supplied by the post office. Or, you can mail letters and packages, and buy minimum parcel insurance at a Self Service Center 24 hours a day, seven days a week. Each center even has a direct line telephone which customers can use to obtain mailing information or to request reimbursement (money or stamps) for money lost because of equipment malfunction. All stamps from U. S. Postal Service machines are sold at face value.

One must know that there are things which cannot be mailed such as explosives, poison, all poisonous animals except scorpions, narcotics, illegal documents, certain lottery matter, certain advertisements, certain perishables, certain articles to particular foreign countries, and that a letter or package can be returned because an address is illegible.

Most importantly, you should know that your Post Office Customer Service Representative will supply you with the latest rates, forms, rules, brochures, will answer questions and will take time to help you revamp or set up a new mailing system for greater efficiency—just give him a call.

25 MODERN MAILROOM SECRETS

A postage meter assures you of the correct amount of postage, gives a precise record and allows mail to travel faster at the post office because it is pre-canceled. Always use fluorescent ink so machines can process the mail the first time.

If mail is to be charged back to a department or partner, keep the chart next to the postage meter or postage scale.

Double check your scales—nine pennies weigh exactly one ounce.

Establish a systematic production schedule for lower priority mail to lighten the load of high priority mailings.

For statement mailings, establish a program of cycled billing to eliminate overloads caused by standard first-of-the month mailing patterns.

Borrow sacks, trays, tray labels and tags from the post office if you are a large volume mailer.

Get the most out of an envelope by consolidating all pieces that are going to the same address and mailing them in one envelope. One #10 envelope made of 24-pound stock and five full, typewritten pages weigh less than one ounce.

"FRAGILE" should be marked on all packages containing easily breakable items.

Meter parcels by positioning the meter strip to the corner of the address label.

Piggyback a letter with your package by enclosing a first class letter in a parcel and marking the package "First Class Mail enclosed," then add the first class letter's postage to the parcel's postage. **Or,** tape your first class letter—with its own postage already on it—to the front of the parcel.

Zip code your mail so it can be distributed by high speed mechanical equipment. The first of five digits designates one of ten national areas, the first three digits together designate a large city or sectional center and the last two digits designate a delivery area or a post office within the sectional center. The national Zip Code

Directory is available for a fee and local lists are available from local post offices.

Stamps by mail are available for a small fee.

Non-mailable matter will be refused and returned, so be sure to check first for domestic and international requirements.

Change of address kits are available free from the post office.

Presorting reduces postage price on first class mail of 500 or more identical pieces.

Low rate for bulk mail is available on 200 or more identical pieces mailed at one time.

Update mailing lists by sending your mailing list to any local Postmaster who will check the names against his local address lists for correctness. Names submitted for verification must be on 3 × 5 cards or data processing cards, with only one name and address per card.

Or, print "ADDRESS CORRECTION REQUESTED" on your outgoing envelope. Undeliverable items under two ounces will be returned with a correct address or the reason for non-delivery, for a fee.

Or, borrow and copy computer magnetic tape with Zip Code information from the postal service, free.

Applications for passport are accepted at many post offices. The passport fee must be paid by check or money order made out to the Passport Office. No cash will be accepted.

Personal and business checks will be accepted for payment of stamps (not money orders) at most post offices, with proper identification.

Low cost mailgrams can be sent by calling Western Union. The message is sent electronically to a teleprinter at a post office near its destination and delivered the next business day.

Deposit your mail several times a day, or at a post office **where mail collections** are made **every thirty minutes, or** at branch postal stations at **times listed on collection boxes, or** have **bagged, first class mail ready by 2:00 p.m.**—post offices will pick it up in many cities.

Postal Customer Councils is an organization of mailers and postal officials who meet to discuss matters of mutual concern. Ideas are exchanged through films, lectures, question and answer periods, and various training and orientation sessions.

Post Office Customer Service Representatives are available to help you work out programs for the most efficient and least expensive mail delivery system, as well as details on rates.

DOMESTIC MAIL

	Definition	Weight
First Class	written or recorded communications on a tangible object having the character of actual and personal correspondence including postal cards, personal notes, checks and money orders—up to 13 oz.	may not exceed 70 pounds
Priority	any first class matter weighing more than 13 oz. on which priority rates are paid	
Post Cards		
Business Reply Cards and Envelopes		overage after 2 oz. and 13 oz.
Second Class	* publications which qualify or single copies of newspapers and magazines	
Third Class	* circulars, miscellaneous printed matter, merchandise other than first class	parcels less than 16 oz.
Third Class Bulk	* printed, mimeographed or other processed matter identical in quantities of 200 or more	
Fourth Class	* catalogs	
	* books consisting of 24 or more pages, all reading matter and at least 22 printed pages, 16 mm or narrower width films and catalogs thereof, printed music, printed objective test materials, sound recordings, playscripts and manuscripts for books, periodicals and music, medical information for hospitals, medical schools, educational reference charts	

*Check with post office for additional information.

Dimensions	Endorsement	Additional Information
100″ in length and girth combined	if not letter size, mark "First Class" on letters	given fastest transportation available—may not be opened for inspection
100″ in length and girth combined	use special stickers and/or mark "priority mail" all sides	given fastest transportation available—may not be opened for inspection
minimum 3½ × 5½ or double with reply, maximum 4¼ × 6		sheets of 40 available—reply does not need postage when mailed
		may be printed by sender—first class rate + extra charge when sender receives reply
		must leave post office within 24 hours
		must leave post office within 24 hours—circulars sometimes worked with first class mail—special rates available
	precanceled stamp, printed indicia, or meter stamp	bundled for 10 or more pieces to same state—zip code must be used—annual bulk fee must be paid
	mark "Bound Printed Matter" or "Catalogs"	
	mark "Special 4th Class Rate—Books"—gets economy rate but no specific delivery date	

DOMESTIC MAIL

	Definition	Weight
Fourth Class (continued)	* 16 millimeter or narrower width films, sound recordings, certain museum materials, scientific or mathematical kits (or instruments) and catalogs, guides or scripts relating to these	may not exceed 70 pounds
	* books, periodicals, bound theses, printed music, sound recordings and certain specific library and museum materials	
Parcel Post	* parcels weighing one pound or more	
	* between large U. S. post offices	may not exceed 40 pounds
	* between smaller U. S. post offices and Alaska and Hawaii	may not exceed 70 pounds
	* parcels weighing less than 15 pounds	
Combination	letters may be placed in second, third, or fourth class mail	

*Check with post office for additional information.

Dimensions	Endorsement	Additional Information
	mark "Library Rate"	rate available only when items are mailed by or to schools, colleges, libraries or certain non-profit organizations, and from publishers or dealers to any one of the above
		rate available only when they are loaned or exchanged between schools, colleges, libraries or certain non-profit organizations and libraries and their readers and from publishers or dealers to any one of the above
84″ in length and girth combined		special rate for books, records, materials for the blind, catalogs, gold mailed within Alaska to other states and possessions—postage rate varies with distance—nation is divided into zones
100″ in length and girth combined		
over 84″ but under 100″ in length and girth combined		get minimum rate equal to 15 pound parcel to zone addressed
	mark "First Class Mail Enclosed"	first class postage must be paid

SPECIAL SERVICES	DOMESTIC MAIL	
Express	* on scheduled basis—door to door, door to destination airport, originating airport to addressee, airport to airport—on non-scheduled basis post office to either addressee's post office or door	extra charge—service to over 600 U. S. cities
Special Delivery	* can be purchased on all classes— available at city carrier post offices and within a 1 mile radius of any post office	use stickers or mark "Special Delivery" in large letters— and use plastic bags obtained free from post office
Certificate of Mailing	no insurance coverage, nominal cost, no record at post office	
Certified Mail	mailing receipt and record of delivery at addressee's post office	handled as ordinary mail— not for irreplaceables
Insured Mail	* up to $200 for third class, parcel post, priority mail containing printed matter or merchandise	handled as ordinary parcel post—insurance receipt for articles insured for more than $15
Registered Mail	* can be purchased only at post office—for irreplaceables— insurance protection up to $10,000—receipt given	movement of mail is controlled during complete trip
Return Receipts	available on insured mail over $15, certified, registered and C.O.D.—registered delivery and delivery address available	identifies article by number, shows who signed for it and date delivered
C.O.D.	recipient pays upon delivery— for first class, parcel post and third class mail—insurance protection—maximum of $300	
Postal Money Orders	can be purchased only at post office—in amounts up to $300— replaced if lost or stolen	copies available for 2 years
Special Handling	third and fourth class parcels handled as expeditiously as possible (not special delivery)	mark "Special Handling"

*Check with post office for additional information.

INTERNATIONAL MAIL

* service to United Kingdom, the Netherlands, Japan, Belgium, France, Brazil, Australia

proof of delivery kept at destination post office—items for more than one address may not be combined—same rules as international mail

Postal Union Mail	*Parcel Post*
* available to most countries	* available to some countries
not available	not available
not available	not available
* available to some countries	* available to many countries
available to all countires except Cambodia, North Korea, Vietnam—maximum protection $15.76.	* available to only a few countries
* must be requested at time of mailing	
not available	not available
must be purchased at post office—available to $300	
entitles AO *surface* packages to priority handling	entitles surface parcels to priority handling between mailing point and U. S. point of dispatch

*Check with post office for additional information.

INTERNATIONAL MAIL—Postal Union Mail

	Letters and Letter Packages (LC)	Post Cards (LC)	Matter for the Blind (AO)
Definition	written or recorded communications on a tangible object having the character of actual and personal correspondence	only single cards are acceptable; maximum 6 × 4¼ inches, maximum to Canada and Mexico 5½ × 3¼; all other countries 5½ × 3½	
Weight Limits	Canada 60 lbs.—all others 4 lbs.		
Sealing	registered letters and registered letter packages must be sealed; ordinary letters may be sealed		must be left unsealed
Customs	* if dutiable merchandise is enclosed or if dutiable printed matter, affix form 2976 or if more than $120 valuation, 2976-A		

*Check with post office for additional information.

Small Packets (AO)	Printed Matter (AO)
small items of merchandise and samples, philatetic items Canada only	paper on which letters, words, characters, figures or images, or any combination thereof, not having the character of actual or personal correspondence, have been reproduced in several identical copies by any process other than handwriting or typewriting, manuscripts of literary works or for newspapers and scores and sheets of music in manuscript
	items not acceptable—articles of stationery, stamps of various kinds (whether used or not), framed photographs and certificates, photographic negatives and slides, films, playing cards
	* direct sacks of prints: quantities of 22 lbs. or more to one address may, under certain conditions, be enclosed in mail sacks addressed directly to the addressee
	* surface rates apply separately for (1) regular prints such as greeting cards, circulars and other miscellaneous prints including publications mailed by other than publishers or registered news agents (2) for books having 24 or more pages, at least 22 of which are printed, and containing no advertising other than incidental announcements of other books, printed sheet music (3) certain publications mailed by the publishers or by registered news agents.
	weight limits vary
may be sealed	may be sealed if postage is paid by permit imprint, postage meter stamps, precanceled stamps, second-class or controlled circulation indicias
* if dutiable merchan-dise is enclosed or if dutiable printed matter, affix form 2976; or if more than $120 valuation, 2976-A	

*Check with post office for additional information.

INTERNATIONAL MAIL—Postal Union Mail (continued)

	Letters and Letter Packages (LC)	Post Cards (LC)	Matter for the Blind (AO)
Endorsements	mark "Letter (lettre)" if could be mistaken for another classification		
	airmail articles should be plainly endorsed "Par Avion," or affix "Par Avion" label		
Dimensions	For articles in the form of a roll the maximum is length 36 inches and length plus twice the diameter—43 inches. The minimum length is 4 inches and length plus twice the diameter—6¾ inches.		

INTERNATIONAL PARCEL POST

Definition	*	packages—air and surface to most countries
Weight Limits	*	check with post office
Sealing	*	registered or insured must be sealed
Customs	*	Form 2966, 2966-A and/or 2972
Dimensions		greatest length 3½ feet; greatest length and girth combined, 6 feet
Addressing		address should be on inside and on outside; should be readable from 2 feet away

*Check with post office for additional information.

Small Packets (AO)	Printed Matter (AO)

"Printed Matter" or "Printed Matter-Catalogs" when mailing prints at regular printed matter rates, and "Printed Matter-Books" or "Printed Matter- Sheet Music" if special rates for category

Special Delivery takes red "Express" label, or mark in red "Express (Special Delivery)"

For articles not in the form of a roll the maximum is 36 inches in combined length, breadth and thickness. The minimum is one surface must measure at least 5½ × 3½ inches.

HOW TO PREPARE POSTAL UNION ARTICLES FOR MAILING

Reserve at least the entire right half of the address side for the address of the addressee, the stamps, and the service labels and notations. Address legibly and completely, using Roman letters and Arabic numerals placed lengthwise on one side of the article only. Give house number and street or box number when mail is for towns or cities. Show names of post office and country of destination in capital letters, and include postal code if known. The country name and address should be shown and must be the last item in the address. An address in a foreign language is permissible provided the names of the post office, province, and country are in English, or, if the English form is not known, are in Roman characters. The sender's name and address should be shown in the upper left corner of the address side.

A GUIDE TO PROPER PACKAGING

PROBLEM CATEGORY	EXAMPLE	CONTAINER	CUSHIONING	CLOSURE	SPECIAL REQ.
Soft Goods	shirts, pillows, blankets	self-supporting box or tear-resistant bag		reinforced tape or sealed bag	banding or filament tape
Liquids	shampoo, paint preserves	leakproof	absorbent	sealed	waterproof, secondary container
Powders	soap, dusting powder, detergent	must be sift-proof		sealed by tape	filament tape
Odors	cheese, perfume, fruit	impermeable to contents	absorbent	sealed by tape	
Fragile	clock, china, camera, crystal	fiberboard (min. 275 lb. test)	to distribute shocks and separate from container surfaces with foamed plastic or padding	sealed by tape	banding or filament tape
Shifting Contents	books, plane, nuts, screw	fiberboard (min. 275 lb. test)	interior fiberboard separators or tape reinforcement	reinforced tape	banding or filament tape
High Density Loads	crankshaft, motor saw, electric motor	large enough to distribute weight to 60 lbs. per sq. ft.	block and brace to immobilize with fiberboard pads	reinforced tape	banding or filament tape
Awkward Loads	pipe, globe, pruning shears	fiberboard tubes and boxes with length not over ten times girth	pre-formed fiberboard or foamed plastic shapes	tube/ends equal to side wall strength	banding or filament tape

HOW TO PACK BREAKABLES FOR MAILING

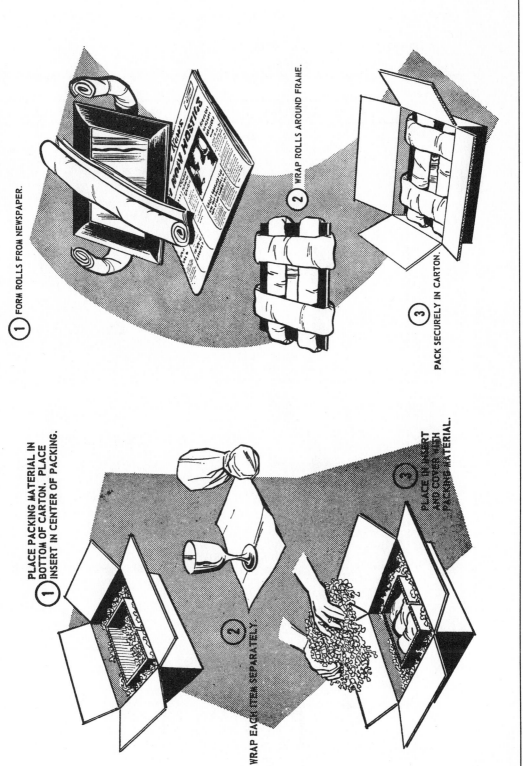

① FORM ROLLS FROM NEWSPAPER.

② WRAP ROLLS AROUND FRAME.

③ PACK SECURELY IN CARTON.

① PLACE PACKING MATERIAL IN BOTTOM OF CARTON. PLACE INSERT IN CENTER OF PACKING.

② WRAP EACH ITEM SEPARATELY.

③ PLACE IN INSERT AND COVER WITH PACKING MATERIAL.

HOW TO PROPERLY CLOSE, REINFORCE, WRAP AND TIE A PACKAGE FOR MAILING

ADEQUATE CLOSURE	INADEQUATE CLOSURE

KRAFT PAPER TAPE

This is a one-thickness tape available in many widths and strengths. It must be correctly applied, both as to positioning and adhesion, and must be graded in use according to the size, shape, and weight of the package. It is not adequate for heavy packages. Of particular importance is the absolute necessity for fully taping down the ends of the package flaps. (✔).

 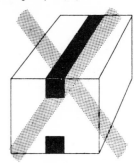

REINFORCED KRAFT PAPER TAPE

This tape is about 3 inches wide and is composed of several laminated layers with filaments running both lengthwise and across. It is extremely break resistant and has excellent adhesive qualities. Reinforced tape is preferred over the plain kraft tape.

 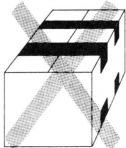

PRESSURE SENSITIVE FILAMENT TAPE

This tape is composed of filaments imbedded in pressure sensitive adhesive. It is extremely strong and only short strips are needed to accomplish effective closure. It is important to tape down the ends of the flaps (✔).

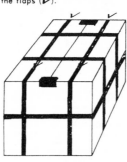 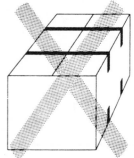

Note: Bursting of corners, especially taped joints, may be a problem for containers under heavy impact.

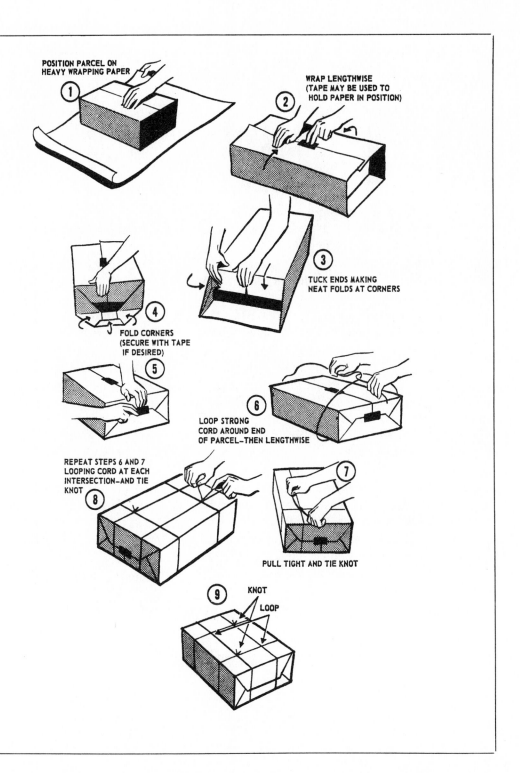

HOW TO ADDRESS YOUR MAIL FOR
FASTEST PROCESSING AND DELIVERY

Basic Format—The address area should be block form (all lines having a uniform left margin). It should be at least one inch from the left edge of the envelope and at least ⅝ inch up from the bottom of the envelope. No print should appear to the right or below it.

GENERAL XYZ CORP
ATTN MR C P JONES
1000 MAIN ST ROOM 4325
DETROIT MI 48217

Type address in upper case letters without punctuation. Try to use fonts other than italic, script or proportional spacing.

City, two-letter state abbreviation and zip code should appear in that order on the bottom line of the address block. This is where the post office automatic sorting equipment is instructed to look for it.

Account numbers, dates, attention lines, etc. can be entered on any line of the address block above the second line from the bottom.

Street address or box number should be placed on the line immediately above the city, state and zip code. When indicating a box number at a particular station, the box number should precede the station name.

The unit number (apartment, room, suite, etc.) should appear immediately after the street address on the same line—never above, below or in front of the street address.

Correct spelling of street names is essential since some post office machines match the names in the address to those like it on the machine's memory.

To use a street location in a mailing address but have mail delivered to a post office box, put the box number on the next-to-last address line. Use the zip code of the box number, not of the street address.

GENERAL XYZ CORP
1000 MAIN ST
PO BOX 3302 JEFFERSON STATION
DETROIT MI 48214

Use rectangular envelopes that will provide good color contrast with the address impression. They should be no smaller than 3½ × 5 inches and no longer than 6⅛ × 11½ inches.

Window envelopes and inserts must be matched so that the address will show through the window no matter how much the insert slides in the envelope. There should be at least ¼ inch between the address and the left, right and bottom edges of the window, whatever the position of the insert.

GEOGRAPHIC ABBREVIATIONS

	In Text	*With Zip Code*		*In Text*	*With Zip Code*
Alabama	Ala.	AL	Oregon	Oreg.	OR
Alaska	Alaska	AK	Pennsylvania	Pa.	PA
Arizona	Ariz.	AZ	Rhode Island	R.I.	RI
Arkansas	Ark.	AR	South Carolina	S.C.	SC
California	Calif.	CA	South Dakota	S.D.	SD
Colorado	Colo.	CO	Tennessee	Tenn.	TN
Connecticut	Conn.	CT	Texas	Tex.	TX
Delaware	Del.	DE	Utah	Utah	UT
Florida	Fla.	FL	Vermont	Vt.	VT
Georgia	Ga.	GA	Virginia	Va.	VA
Hawaii	Hawaii	HI	Washington	Wash.	WA
Idaho	Idaho	ID	West Virginia	W.Va.	WV
Illinois	Ill.	IL	Wisconsin	Wis.	WI
Indiana	Ind.	IN	Wyoming	Wyo.	WY
Iowa	Iowa	IA			
Kansas	Kans.	KS	Canal Zone	C.Z.	CZ
Kentucky	Ky.	KY	District of Columbia	D.C.	DC
Louisiana	La.	LA	Guam	Guam	GU
Maine	Maine	ME	Puerto Rico	P.R.	PR
Maryland	Md.	MD	Virgin Islands	V.I.	VI
Massachusetts	Mass.	MA			
Michigan	Mich.	MI	Canada		
Minnesota	Minn.	MN			
Mississippi	Miss.	MS	Alberta	Alta.	AB
Missouri	Mo.	MO	British Columbia	B.C.	BC
Montana	Mont.	MT	Manitoba	Man.	MB
Nebraska	Nebr.	NE	New Brunswick	N.B.	NB
Nevada	Nev.	NV	Newfoundland	Nfld.	NF
New Hampshire	N.H.	NH	Northwest Territories	N.W.T.	NT
New Jersey	N.J.	NJ	Nova Scotia	N.S.	NS
New Mexico	N.Mex.	NM	Ontario	Ont.	ON
New York	N.Y.	NY	Prince Edward Island	P.E.I.	PE
North Carolina	N.C.	NC	Quebec	Que.	PQ
North Dakota	N.D.	ND	Saskatchewan	Sask.	SK
Ohio	Ohio	OH	Yukon Territory	Y.T.	YT
Oklahoma	Okla.	OK			

9

ideas for telephone efficiency and economy

The telephone is your company's link with the world. Your thorough knowledge of its capabilities and your method of handling calls tell those who may never see your office that your company is efficient and polite. When you are out, those who speak for you—your answering service or your answering machine—should convey the same message.

Prudent use of the telephone can save time and money and Pacific Telephone Company of San Francisco offers the following suggestions:

Dial direct during peak hours.

Dial direct during discount rate periods—evenings, nights, weekends.

If you want to speak to a particular party, schedule your calls so you can direct dial at a time when you are sure the called party will be in.

Plan your conversation—use the special one minute rates—jot down the things you want to say ahead of time.

Special Area Code 800 preceding a number means the company has Inward Wide Area Telephone Service (WATS) and the call is free. You can call 800-555-1212 free to see if the company you want to call offers this service. Toll free numbers are preceded by "Zenith" or "Enterprise" prefixes so check the phone book to see if the business you want has such a number.

Bad connection or cut off—both parties should hang up so the operator can re-establish the call and make an appropriate adjustment.

Coin phone refunds are available by calling "0" (Operator) and reporting the telephone number of the booth where money was lost.

Vacation rates apply if you are going away for over 60 days—you can temporarily suspend your service and pay a lower rate.

Call your local Telephone Company Business Office for extra copies of your local directory or for directories out of area.

TYPES OF TELEPHONES

PRIVATE BRANCH EXCHANGE (PBX) console. A PBX provides for internal communication between telephones in a business as well as facilities for connecting these phones to the telephone network. In businesses where there are many offices or telephone extensions, a full-time attendant uses the PBX console to handle incoming, outgoing and, in some cases, interoffice calls.

Private Branch Exchange

SIX BUTTON TELEPHONE—With this phone, you can handle up to five calls. If a conversation has to be interrupted, a "HOLD" button allows each caller to wait without being cut off. A conversation on one line is not heard by a caller on another line. The phone has light indicators on each of the buttons to show which lines are in use, and it may have either a rotary or a Touchtone dial.

Six-Button Telephone

SPEAKERPHONE—This is a combination loudspeaker and microphone which allows someone to talk on the telephone "hands free" while referring to other material. It also allows several people in the same office to take part in a telephone conversation simultaneously. To make a call from the Speakerphone, you would depress a button on the microphone box and then dial the correct number.

Speakerphone

Courtesy AT&T

MOBILE TELEPHONE SERVICE—This kind of phone can be installed in cars, trucks, trains, planes or boats. A call, whether local or long distance, is placed through a mobile service operator or dialed direct to any other phone, and the conversation is transmitted by conventional telephone circuits and by radio.

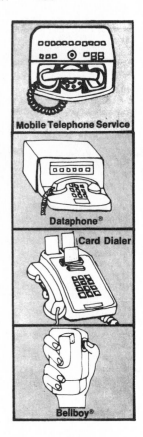

DATAPHONE—This set converts coded information into signal tones which are relayed over telephone lines. In other words, it allows machines to "talk" to one another. With this equipment, you can send payroll, inventories and sales from one location to another at very high speeds. This can also be used as a regular telephone.

CARD DIALERS are automatic dialing telephones which operate by inserting a plastic card. The cards are pre-punched to code them with frequently called numbers. Automatic dialers increase speed and accuracy in dialing calls, and they can also be used as regular telephones.

BELLBOY—this is a pocket signaling set which gives off a beep message tone. It can be dialed from a regular office telephone.

HOW TO PLACE SPECIAL CALLS

DIRECT DISTANCE DIALING is a development which makes it possible for a person to dial station-to-station long distance calls, and in some places person-to-person, collect and credit card calls. To provide for this, the United States and Canada are divided into areas, each having a different three-number Area Code, as shown on the following map. No two telephone numbers within a given area are alike. If this service is available in your community, the introductory pages of the local directory provide complete instructions.

Courtesy AT&T

STATION-TO-STATION CALL—a call to a number at a distant point.

If the caller will talk with anyone who answers the telephone, he places a station-to-station call. The timing of the call for charges begins when the telephone is answered. From most telephones it is now possible to dial most telephone numbers in the United States and Canada.

* Dial the prefix (if one is required), the Area Code (only if different from the Area Code on the telephone you are using) and the telephone number.
* In some areas an operator will ask you for your number. Give her the number of the telephone you are using and you will then hear the ringing signal.

PERSON-TO-PERSON CALL—a call to a particular person, department or extension number at a distant point.

The charge is slightly higher than for a station-to-station call. The timing of the call for charges does not begin until the person, department or extension is on the line. In some communities, person-to-person calls can be dialed directly.

* Dial "0" (Operator), the Area Code (only if different from the Area Code on the telephone you are using) and the telephone number.

* Once the call is dialed, an operator will ask for further instructions.

COLLECT CALL—a call which is charged to the telephone of the person called.

Usually there is no extra charge. There may be a small charge if the regular rate between the two locations is very low.

* Dial "0" (Operator), the Area Code (only if different from the Area Code of the telephone you are using) and the telephone number.

* Once the call is dialed, an operator will ask for further instructions.

CREDIT CARD CALL—a call made from any telephone and billed to the telephone to which the credit card was assigned.

A credit card, which is available from the telephone company for regular subscribers, is similar to a "Charga-Plate."

* Dial "0" (Operator), the Area Code (only if different from the Area Code of the telephone you are using) and the telephone number.

CONFERENCE CALL—a special call involving the interconnection of more than two telephones.

Courtesy AT&T

The telephones may be in the same locality or in several different locations. The arrangements are handled by the operator.

WRONG NUMBER—If you reach a wrong number, dial the operator immediately and relate what happened.

OUT OF TOWN INFORMATION—Dial the prefix (if required), the Area Code (if different from your own) and 555-1212.

INTERNATIONAL DIALING

You can dial your own station calls to the countries shown here. New countries are being added so check with your local telephone office. First, remember that calling Alaska, Hawaii, Canada, Mexico City and certain border points, the Bahamas, Bermuda, the Virgin Islands and Puerto Rico is done by simply dialing the appropriate area code and telephone number. For station calls to all other countries shown here, dialing procedures are:

DIALING INSTRUCTIONS

STATION CALLS—to dial international station calls, dial in sequence:

1. The International Access Code—011—always first.
2. The City Routing Code—a 1 to 5 digit number.
3. The Local Telephone number—a 2 to 9 digit number.
4. The "#" button—(Touchtone telephones).

For example:

To make a call to Germany (country code 49) Frankfurt (Routing Code 611), telephone number 23 06 95 you would dial:

011	+	49	+	611	+	23 06 95	+	(#
International Access Code ·		Country Code		Routing Code		Local Number		button Touchtone equipped)

Allow at least 30 seconds to reach the overseas party before dialing the entire number. Also, because "0" operator is the first digit of the International Access Code (011), remember to dial the second digit within 3 seconds or you will reach the local operator.

OPERATOR ASSISTED CALLS—person-to-person calls, collect calls, credit card calls, third party charge and calls to countries without direct dialing.

Courtesy AT&T

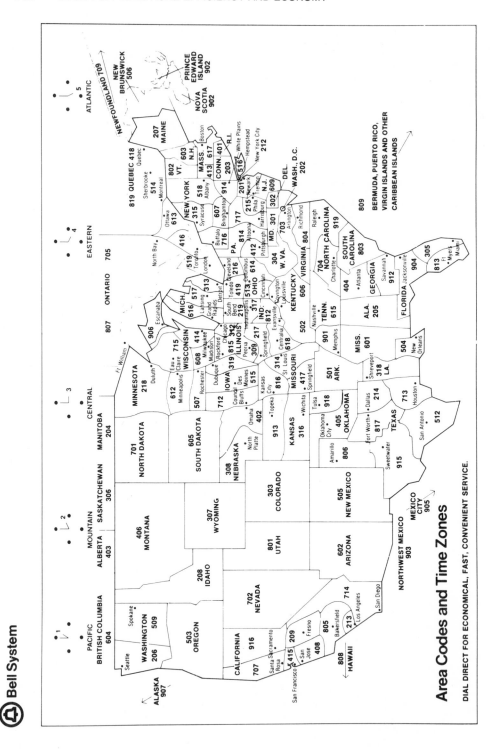

Courtesy AT&T

Bell System

Area Codes and Time Zones

DIAL DIRECT FOR ECONOMICAL, FAST, CONVENIENT SERVICE.

COUNTRY CODE	CITY	ROUTING CODE	LOCAL NUMBER FOREIGN AUDIBLE SIGNAL
39	Bari	80	Local Numbers—4 to 7 digits.
	Bologna	51	Ringing Signal—similar to U.S. (shorter).
	Brindisi	831	Busy Signal—similar to U.S. (faster). Busy signal also indicates all circuits are busy.
	Capri	81	
	Como	31	
	Florence	55	
	Genoa	10	
	Milan	2	
	Naples	81	
	Padua	49	
	Palermo	91	
ITALY	Pisa	50	
	Rome	6	
	Trieste	40	
	Venice	41	
	Verona	45	

COUNTRY CODE	CITY	ROUTING CODE	LOCAL NUMBER FOREIGN AUDIBLE SIGNAL
44	Belfast (n. Ire.)	232	Local Numbers—3 to 7 digits.
	Birmingham	21	Ringing Signal—2 short tones, short pause.
	Bournemouth	202	Busy Signal—similar to U.S. (faster).
	Cardiff (Wales)	222	Other Signals—has different signal for busy circuits. Has special signal for number not in use.
	Durham	385	
	Edinburgh (Scot.)	31	
	Glasgow (Scot.)	41	
	Gloucester	452	
	Ipswich	473	
UNITED KINGDOM	Liverpool	51	
	London	1	
	Manchester	61	
	Nottingham	602	
	Prestwick (Scot.)	292	
	Sheffield	742	
	Southampton	703	

COUNTRY CODE	CITY	ROUTING CODE	LOCAL NUMBER FOREIGN AUDIBLE SIGNAL
33	Aix-En-Provence	91	Local Numbers—6 to 7 digits.
	Bordeaux	56	Ringing Signal—similar to U.S. (longer).
	Cannes	93	Busy Signal—similar to U.S. (faster). Busy signal also indicates all circuits are busy.
	Chauvigny	49	Other Signals—has a transit signal—a rapidly repeated tone while connection being made.
	Cherbourg	33	
	Grenoble	76	
	Le Havre	35	
	Lourdes	62	
	Lyon	78	
	Marseille	91	
FRANCE	Nancy	28	
	Nice	93	
	Paris	1	
	Rouen	35	
	Toulouse	61	
	Tours	47	

COUNTRY CODE	CITY	ROUTING CODE	LOCAL NUMBER FOREIGN AUDIBLE SIGNAL
852	Castle Peak	12	Local Numbers—5 to 7 digits.
	Cheung Chau	5	Ringing Signal—2 short rings, pause.
	Fan Ling	12	Busy Signal—similar to U.S. (slower). Busy signal also indicates all circuits are busy.
	Hong Kong	5	Other Signals—has special signal for number not in use.
	Kowloon	3	
	Kwai Chung	12	
	Lamma	5	
	Ma Wan	5	
	Peng Chau	5	
HONG KONG	Sek Kong	12	
	Sha Tin	12	
	Silvermine Bay	5	
	Tai-o	5	
	Tai Po	12	
	Ting Kau	12	
	Tsun Wan	12	

DIALING INSTRUCTIONS (CONTINUED)

Signals (ringing, number busy, etc.) in other countries differ from what you know. See chart.

When overseas numbers are shown on letterheads or business cards, they are usually preceded by a national access digit and the routing code. For example: (02) 12 34 56. The first digit "0" is a national access digit and is used only when dialing within that foreign country. It should be disregarded. In this case you would dial

011 + (Country Code) + 2 + 12 34 56

ADDITIONAL ASSISTANCE OR INFORMATION—DIAL "0" (OPERATOR) if you need assistance . . .

* to obtain a telephone number you don't know
* to obtain City Routing Codes not listed here
* for help in completing a call
* for credit on a call on which you had difficulty—i.e., reached a wrong number

---

PRONUNCIATION GUIDES

Vowels	Sounded As In	Position Of Mouth
A	FATHER	Open
A	ATE	Half open
A	CALL	Open, lips slightly rounded
A	HAT	Half open
E	HE	Almost closed
E	MET	Slightly open
I	KITE	Open, then closing
I	IT	Slightly open
O	HOT	Open
O	OLD	Open, lips rounded
U	FLUTE	Almost closed, lips rounded
U	HUT	Half open
OI	OIL	Open, then closing
OU	SOUTH	Open, then closing

Courtesy AT&T

Breath	Voice	Nasal	Consonant Formed By
F	V		Lower lip against upper teeth
P	B	M	Lips
	W		Lips
	WH (when)		Lips
T	D		Tip of tongue against upper gums
	L		Tip of tongue against upper gums
TH (three)	TH (then)		Tip of tongue against upper teeth
S	Z (maze)		Tip of tongue almost touching upper gums
SH	Z (azure)		Front of tongue almost touching upper gums
	Y (yet)		Middle of tongue raised close to hard palate
CH	J		Tip and front of tongue against upper gums
K	G (good)	NG	Back of tongue against soft palate
X (axe)	X (exact)		Same as K followed by S
	R (run)		Sides of tongue against back teeth

Number	Pronunciation	Formation of Sound
0	OH	Long O
1	WuN	Strong W and N
2	Too	Strong T and long oo
3	th-R-ee	Strong R and long ee
4	fo-eR	Long 0 and strong R
5	fi-iV	First i long, second i short, strong V
6	SiKS	Strong S and KS
7	SeV-eN	Strong S and V, well-rounded eN
8	aTe	Long a and strong T
9	Ni-eN	First N strong, long i, mild emphasis on eN

Courtesy AT&T

A — Alice	G — George	M — Mary	T — Thomas
B — Bertha	H — Henry	N — Nelly	U — Utah
C — Charles	I — Ida	O — Oliver	V — Victor
D — David	J — James	P — Peter	W — William
E — Edward	K — Kate	Q — Quaker	X — X-ray
F — Frank	L — Louis	R — Robert	Y — Young
		S — Samuel	Z — Zebra

The use of key words is helpful in clarifying spelling.

TACTFUL PHRASEOLOGY FOR TELEPHONE USE

THIS IS BETTER . .	THAN THIS
Answering the Call	
Greeting the Caller	
Good morning, Miss Woods.	Hello (or good morning).
Mr. Moore's office, Mr. Phillips.	Yes, please.
Mr. Gray's office. May I help you?	Extension 4236. What do you want?
Making Sure	
Would you repeat your name for me, please?	What name did you say? I can't hear you.
Would you spell that for me, please?	What did you say? Talk a little louder.
I'm sorry. I didn't get the name of the person.	I can't understand what you're trying to say.
Acknowledging	
Thank you. I'll have her paged for you.	O.K. I'll see if I can get her.
Yes, Mrs. Malloy, I'll be happy to do that for you.	All right. I'll do what I can about it.
I will be glad to give him your message.	I'll tell him what you said when I talk to him.

Courtesy AT&T

THIS IS BETTER . . .	THAN THIS
Assisting the Caller	
Undetermined Party	
Will you wait, please? I'll find who has that information.	I don't know who takes care of that. Who was it you talked to?
Let me transfer you to Personnel (or a certain party). They will be able to help you.	That's another department. Would you want to call back and ask for extension 1234?
Can you recall the name of the person who talked with you?	I don't know. Maybe somebody else can help you.
I'm sorry, we don't carry that product. You might try your Yellow Pages.	We don't handle that product. You must have called the wrong number.
Unusual Delay	
I'm sorry, but he is still on a call. Would you care to wait or may I take a message?	He's been on the telephone all morning. I don't know how long he'll be, maybe a few more minutes.
I'm sorry for the delay. Here's Mr. Adams.	Okay. I can put you through. He's off the phone now.
I'm sorry for the wait, but Mrs. Larson can speak with you now.	Everybody's been calling. I just couldn't get back to you any sooner.
Handling Delayed Calls	
Called Line Is Busy	
Mrs. Simmons is on another call. May I take a message (may someone else help you) (would you care to wait)?	She's busy now. She's talking now. Do you want to call later?
Leaving the Line	
Would you mind waiting while I check, please?	Just a minute. Let me look around for it.
It will take a minute or so. Do you care to wait or shall I call you back? (Wait for acknowledgment).	I'll try to find it.

Hold it. I'll see what I can do. |
Returning to the Line	
Thank you for waiting. I have that information.	The date on that order was June 18.
I'm sorry to have kept you waiting. I can help you now.	Are you still waiting? I can't locate that.

Courtesy AT&T

THIS IS BETTER . . .

Called Party Doesn't Answer

Mr. Cox seems to be away from his desk (out of his office). May I take a message (may someone else help you)?

Called Party Is Not In

(Gone for several days, late in arriving, left early, at lunch, vacation whereabouts unknown, etc.)*

Mrs. Burns is out of the city. We expect her back in the office on Monday.

Mr. Johnson is not in. We expect him within an hour.

I'm sorry, Mr. Smith will be out of the office the rest of the day.

Mrs. Robinson is out of the office. She should be back late this afternoon.

Screening Calls

(Screening calls for an individual is not necessarily the most desirable method of handling calls. However, there are occasions when it is required. In such cases the following procedures are recommended.)

May I say who's calling, please?

He's in a meeting (not at his desk) (out of his office). May I take a message?

Will you wait please while I see if she's in?

After Screening

Here is Mrs. Day, now. Just a moment, please.

Completing the Conversation

Thank you for calling, Mrs. Rogers.

I'm glad I was able to help you. Good-bye.

You're welcome, Mr. Miller, good-bye.

THAN THIS

Mr. Cox isn't answering his phone. I don't know where he went. I could try to find somebody else.

Mrs. Burns isn't here. I don't know when she'll be back, maybe next week.

Mr. Johnson has left for the day. He could call you later.

We haven't heard from Mr. Smith. Why don't you call back tomorrow?

She's gone. Do you want me to take a message for her? Okay. I'll tell her.

He wants to know who's calling.

If you tell me who's calling, I'll see if I can locate him.

Mrs. Long isn't taking calls this morning.

Mrs. Day says she can talk to you now. Hold on a minute.

Bye-bye—O.K.—So long.

That's O.K.—All right now—See you later.

All right, bye.

*In each instance cited here, callers should be asked if someone else can assist them or if they would care to leave a message.

Courtesy AT&T

HOW TO TAKE ACCURATE MESSAGES AND LOG CALLS

Preprinted forms for telephone messages help because the questions for information are already there—all you have to do is fill in the blanks. The person who gets the message can assimilate the data easily because it is logically arranged. These both come four to a page in a spiral notebook with a second sheet that becomes a permanent carbon copy record.

The same theory applies to logging calls—just fill in the blanks and all the points will be covered. These also come in a spiral notebook. An easy place to keep the log is under the telephone.

To_____

Date_____Time_____

WHILE YOU WERE OUT

M_____

of_____

Phone_____

Area Code	Number	Extension
TELEPHONED		PLEASE CALL
CALLED TO SEE YOU		WILL CALL AGAIN
WANTS TO SEE YOU		URGENT
RETURNED YOUR CALL		

Message_____

Operator

EFFICIENCY® LINE NO. 4725 AN **AMPAD** PRODUCT

EFFICIENCY® BUSINESS FORMS by AMERICAN PAD & PAPER CO., Holyoke, Massachusetts 01040

			DATE	TIME	AM PM
TO					
FROM			AREA CODE—TELEPHONE NO.—OR OPER.		
M					
OF			EXTENSION #		

PHONE MEMO

MESSAGE

SIGNED

| Phoned ☐ | Call Back ☐ | Returned Call ☐ | Wants To See You ☐ | Will Call Again ☐ | Was In ☐ | See Operator ☐ |

AICO-UTILITY Line Form No. 50-076—600 CL / 50-036—200 CL

Mfgd. by AICO/UTILITY CO., Chicago, Illinois 60607

LONG DISTANCE TELEPHONE CALL REGISTER

DATE	NUMBER, CITY OR PERSON CALLED	PERSON CALLING	TYPE OF CALL Station	Person to Station	to Person	TIME PLACED	TIME STARTED	TIME FINISHED	ELAPSED TIME (MIN'S)	CHARGES	DATE PAID	MISC. INFORMATION

Manufactured by AICO/UTILITY CO., Chicago, Illinois 60607

HOW TO WORK EFFECTIVELY WITH AN ANSWERING SERVICE

AMONG THE TYPES OF SERVICE an answering service can offer are message taking, paging, cross-connecting (answering your phone, locating you at another number, connecting the caller to you), radio dispatch, wiring messages to you out of town, placing calls for you, taking orders, quoting prices, making appointments, wake up calls, second phone lines as message phones only, elevator phone service.

ONCE YOU DECIDE ON THE TYPE OF SERVICE, work closely with the operators. Tell the answering service exactly how you want your phone answered, what you want to know from everyone calling and what to do in an emergency situation. Change your instructions as your situation changes.

CHECK IN OFTEN ENOUGH—Phone in for messages at regular intervals and frequently enough so calls do not mount up.

BE READY with paper and pencil when you call for messages.

BE PATIENT if your call is interrupted when messages are being given. Remember that the operator may be answering your phone and will get back to you as soon as possible.

IF THERE IS A PROBLEM, call the supervisor. Her job is to see that things run smoothly. Also call if the service has been "above and beyond the call of duty."

Courtesy Artson Answering System San Francisco, California

TELEPHONE ANSWERING MACHINES

These machines are recording devices which plug into standard telephone wall jacks and which are available in both department and specialty stores. When the telephone rings, a pre-recorded cassette is activated and the caller hears instructions such as "Hello, this is Mr. Smith. I am out of my office now and if you will leave a message, I'll return the call. Begin speaking at the sound of the tone."

Different machines have different features such as:

1. Setting so machine will answer on a specific ring
2. Silent monitor—you can hear caller's voice as call comes in and answer if you choose
3. Announce only—gives only your message to caller, then hangs up
4. Dictation capability
5. Two cassette system—one for incoming messages, one for instructional messages
6. Erasing capability
7. Tape rewind and tape forward
8. Fixed caller message time or unlimited caller message time
9. Remote control device which activates the recorder to play messages back and/or allow recording of new instructional messages when you call from an outside telephone
10. Conversion to regular cassette recorder when not being used as answering machine

10

time-saving knowledge about mailgrams, telegrams, telex and twx, radio, news and computer communications—what each is and how each is used

Basically, to communicate means to transmit information. No matter what kind of secretary you are, a knowledge of the means of communication used in the everyday working world is an essential part of your job.

You'll need to know about sending Mailgrams and Telegrams, and a little about teletypewriter networks—Telex and TWX—and a few tips on sending each. Also included is information on the FYI News Service—available by teletype dial-up or subscription, offering fast and concise reports on the latest developments in news, sports, weather, Congress, finance, commodities and more. In addition, available by subscription is News Alert, which automatically delivers to your Telex or TWX major news bulletins which might affect your company's business—all via Western Union.

Along with the things you might personally be called upon to use in the field of communications could be Citizens Band Radio—so it is helpful to know a little about what it is, who uses it and what it is used for.

There are means of communication described in which you may not be directly involved, but which might affect part of your day. Take, for instance, international television, communications

153

to and from ships at sea, the Washington-Moscow Hot Line and the circuits linking Mission Control with the astronauts—all are by ITT.

There is also the printed word—did you know that the *Wall Street Journal* is printed by transmitting electronically a facsimile of each page to a satellite which then relays the page to a production facility where it is received on page-sized photographic film? Dow Jones' New Service—the Broadtape reports all the news that could affect the nation's securities markets and AP-Dow Jones—the International News Service and a companion service AP-Dow Jones Financial Wire get news generated by reporters all over the world via computer and satellite transmission. There is also the AP-DJ Economic Report, the Bankers Report, the Eurofinancial Report and the Petroleum News Service which handle vital information.

SPECIAL SERVICES—DOMESTIC

Originally, all Western Union communications were transmitted over aerial wires, usually running along railroad tracks. Microwave radio transmission gradually replaced the original network of wires and poles. Then, in 1974, Western Union sent into orbit Westar I and Westar II, the first domestic communications satellites, and improved transcontinental transmissions began—via outer space. Westar is monitored by telemetry equipment at Glenwood, New Jersey. Western Union's modern transmission network includes five strategically located Westar earth stations, interconnected with a 9,000 mile microwave system and local cable facilities. These integrated ground-based and space components of the network transmit voice, data, graphic and video signals.

SERVING BUSINESS AND THE PUBLIC—Services range from the basic record Telegram through the Mailgram message, worldwide dial-up teletypewriter communications available through Telex and TWX, electronic funds transfer, money order service, private and shared systems for voice and data transmission, to transmission of television and radio broadcasts.

SERVING GOVERNMENT—Western Union serves eight agencies of the Federal Government with sophisticated private communication systems. Individual private circuits are provided for the Air Force, Army, Navy and the National Aeronautics and Space Administration (NASA). Western Union is building for the Soil Conservation Service a new system using meteor trails for collecting and reporting vital precipitation data. The Department of Defense Autodin data communication network has been provided by Western Union since 1963. Autodin II will be based on new packet switching technology. Western Union received a prime contract to provide NASA with satellite communication services in the 1980's. These services will be provided from the Tracking and Data Relay Satellite System being established by Western Union Space Communications, Inc., which also plans to lease satellite transmission service to The Western Union Telegraph Company to satisfy the latter's needs for Advanced Westar.

SPECIAL SERVICES—INTERNATIONAL

ITT WORLDCOM

CABLE AND SATELLITE FACILITIES offer business and the major press agencies highly versatile international teleprinter channels plus alternate photo, voice and data transmissions simultaneously; high frequency radio, teleprinter and photo broadcasts. A fully equipped technical center for the control of international television programs is maintained at New York headquarters.

MARINE COASTAL STATIONS provide communications service to and from ships at sea, including data on a ship's position, course and estimated time of arrival, warnings of navigational hazards, bulletins on weather conditions and summaries of a day's news developments.

HELPS THE U. S. GOVERNMENT when printed material, data and voice need to be transmitted simultaneously and maintains the Washington-Moscow Hot Line—a direct teleprinter link via both submarine cable and landline and satellite which provides an instant means of written communication.

HELPS THE SPACE PROGRAM with broadband circuits linking NASA's Goddard Space Flight Center in Maryland with world-wide tracking stations. The circuits are used to transmit millions of bits of high-speed data and thousands of voice messages between U.S. astronauts and their Mission Control Center in Houston.

MAILGRAM SERVICE

A Mailgram message is transmitted literally at the speed of light over Western Union's microwave and satellite communications network di-

rectly to a U.S. Post Office near the recipient's address. There, the message is typed by high-speed equipment and inserted into a distinctive blue and white envelope for delivery with the next business day's mail. A Mailgram message entered into the Western Union system by the end of the business day should be on the recipient's desk the next morning.

Among the most important advantages and features of Mailgram service are:

- *A sense of urgency and importance.* Printed in "Telegram format" and delivered in a distinctive envelope, Mailgram messages look urgent and important, and usually get opened first.

- *Preferential treatment by the Postal Service.* Mailgram messages bypass most mail handling and sorting procedures.

- *Ease of sending.* Among the many ways to relay Mailgram messages to Western Union, the most popular are:
  - □ *By telephone.* 24 hours a day, seven days a week.
  - □ *By Telex or TWX.* (See Teletypewriter Networks.)
  - □ *By computer.* For high-volume sending, you can create a magnetic computer tape (or have it done by a computer service bureau) and give it to Western Union to send. Or, your company's computer can be programmed to send directly to Western Union's InfoMaster computer system.
  - □ *By some communicating typewriters, data terminals and facsimile devices.*

- *Stored Mailgram.* To bypass expensive and time-consuming internal processing of frequently used form letters, mailing lists and the like, this service provides computer storage of frequently used letter texts, key paragraphs, mailing lists and sender names and titles. The result: virtually instantaneous access and sending. Stored Mailgram processing is available from any telephone, from your own Mailgram Terminal and may also be available from your company's time-sharing communicating word processing terminal.

- *Multiple address Mailgram messages.* Since Mailgram messages can be sent simultaneously in almost limitless quantities, common-text Mailgrams can be sent to people with different addresses.

- *Business Reply Mailgram messages.* When a written response to your Mailgram is necessary, you can add a reply form at the bottom of your message if you're sending via computer tape or Stored Mailgram. The recipient need only fill it in and fold it into an accompanying business reply envelope for mailing back to you.

- *Certified Mailgram.* When you need to be sure your message was received, this service provides a signed receipt returned to you by the U.S. Postal Service.

WHEN TO CHOOSE:

- When you want to impress the reader with the importance and urgency of the matter.
- When you're not likely to get a busy person's attention with a phone call or letter.
- When saving time and money is important.
- When you need a written record for filing or followup. (A confirmation copy of a message originated by telephone is available at an extra charge.)
- When you want to reach many people at once with the same message.

TELEGRAM SERVICE

Still the fastest type of public message service, the Telegram provides two basic types of delivery—messenger and telephone. Messenger delivery, available in most places, is guaranteed within five hours. Phone delivery is guaranteed within two hours, and a written copy of the message can be sent by mail.

The Telegram is available for sending and phone delivery 24 hours a day, including Sundays and holidays.

Messenger delivery of Telegrams is not available everywhere or at all times. (When calling Western Union with a Telegram to be delivered by messenger, be sure to find out whether it's possible.)

If for any reason a message cannot be delivered, the Western Union office at the destination will notify the sending office, which in turn will notify you.

A variety of special Telegram options are available, at varying costs. They include:

- *Overnight Telegram.* Priced substantially lower than the full rate Telegram, this service offers message delivery by 2 p.m. the following day.

- *Repeat-Back and Valued Message services.* These special services offer financial protection in situations where the Telegram has a monetary value in excess of $500 (for example, the acceptance of an important contract). If the value is $5,000 or less, Repeat-Back service is available. Here, at an additional charge, the receiving office sends the message back to the sending office for verification. If the declared value exceeds $5,000, Valued Message service is available. Here, a repeat-back again is used and the sender pays an additional cost of $1/10$ of one percent of the declared value.

- *Personal delivery only service.* When the sender wants the Telegram handed directly to the addressee—and no one else—this special service offers just that at no charge.

- *Alternate delivery.* If there is a chance the Telegram may be undeliverable at one location (for example, if the message is apt to reach a destination office after business hours), an alternate address, at varying additional cost, may be specified.

- *Confirmation copy.* When you want a written record of a Telegram, a copy can be sent to you as a Mailgram message at a nominal charge.

- *Report delivery.* When the sender wishes confirmation that a Telegram has been delivered, whether by telephone or messenger, a Telegram or Mailgram can be sent to the originator, advising when the message was delivered. Cost for this service is the minimum prevailing rate for a full rate Telegram or base rate Mailgram.

WHEN TO CHOOSE:

- When time is the most important consideration and nothing else is fast enough.
- When you—or the recipient—need a written record for filing or followup.

FOR BEST RESULTS WITH MAILGRAM OR TELEGRAM:

- If the message is to be written out for your office message center or for delivery to a local Western Union office, use either your organization's forms or those of Western Union, as appropriate. Type, if possible. Otherwise, write clearly.

- If the message is phoned in, it will be typed by an operator and simultaneously recorded. To save time and assure accuracy, have all necessary information in front of you before phoning. This includes correct spelling of the addressee's name and company, street address, city, state, zip code, telephone number and billing information. Have the message read back to you.

- Write the message, if this is your responsibility, for clarity and economy. Write for brief, quick reading. Use active verbs. Avoid unneeded adjectives, and substitute numerals for words when possible.

- If your office doesn't have Telex or TWX but the addressee's office does, you can save time on your phone-originated message by sending it as a Telegram transmitted to the recipient's teletypewriter terminal. The Western Union Operator can obtain the addressee's office Telex or TWX number if you don't have it.

INTERNATIONAL TELEGRAM

The International Telegram (also referréd to as a cablegram) is the means by which a brief, urgent, written message can be sent to overseas points or ships at sea.

An International Telegram can be sent as quickly and easily as a domestic message. If your office has either Telex or TWX, you may already know how to send an International Telegram via teletypewriter.

International messages also can be placed through Western Union by telephone or in person. Upon receiving the message, Western Union then transmits the message to one of the five international record carriers.

Unless a particular carrier is requested, Western Union relays the message to a carrier that transmsits to the receiving country. (Not every carrier operates in all countries.) Once the international carrier receives the message, the carrier assumes all responsibility for handling and delivery.

Because of the confidential nature of some international business messages, code is sometimes used.

Two classes of service are available for international messages: full-rate International Telegram and Letter Telegram. The full-rate Telegram is the fastest international message service and charges are on a per word basis, with a 7-word minimum. The less costly Letter Telegram is accepted with the understanding that, generally, it will be delivered the day after the message is filed. Letter Telegram charges are based on a 22-word minimum, with a charge for each additional word. Letter Telegram service is available to most—but not all—countries.

TELETYPEWRITER NETWORKS

The teletypewriter is a device that transmits and receives written messages. It combines the best of two other communications methods: the *telephone*, with its speed and immediacy, and the *letter*, with its documentation and accuracy. Although basically a means of communicating, in writing, with another office equipped with a teletypewriter, it is much more. Access to a teletypewriter—which provides direct-dial communications to more than 148,000 terminals in North America and 565,000 overseas—means access to the world through Western Union's InfoMaster computer system and public message services.

The teletypewriter can be the fastest and most efficient means of communication when the need is immediate and a written record desirable. The teletypewriter, by and large, is the least expensive method–making it a popular communications tool for many business people.

Many large companies have their own internal teletypewriter systems, permitting instant written communication with their own branch offices. However, they usually have Telex and/or TWX as well.

Telex and TWX (the latter often is pronounced "twix"), the two teletypewriter networks, are operated by Western Union on an interconnected basis. Modern computer technology enables Telex and TWX subscribers to communicate with each other. But with Western Union's InfoMaster computer system—the heart of the linked teletypewriter networks—the modern business office can do more than talk "teletype-to-teletype." For instance:

- Send multiple address messages by teletypewriter, including Mailgram messages.
- Use stored texts and address lists.

Telex and TWX vary only slightly in how they work, and they're very similar in what they can do.

Major features and advantages of Telex and TWX communication are:

- Teletype communication can take place 24 hours a day, seven days a week. Messages can be received when terminals are unattended, including non-office hours—especially useful when you must reach offices in substantially different time zones.

- Both sender and receiver get an exact, permanent copy of every message—an invaluable aid as backup for oral decisions, a written record of a two-way teletypewriter "conversation," and the memory-jogging written reminder of the message sent to the recipient.

- To assure accuracy, the message can be recorded on punched paper tape on a tape punch built into the teletypewriter. Any errors on the tape can be corrected prior to sending, and then the punched tape is used to transmit the message at maximum teletypewriter speed. (Since Telex and TWX costs are based partly on transmission time, sending a message on punched tape also helps to lower costs.)

- After dialing Telex-to-Telex or TWX-to-TWX, you can get an automatic identification (also called an "answerback") assuring you've reached the desired party. This safeguards against transmitting to a wrong party. The automatic identification may be repeated at the end of the transmission, confirming the message was received.

- A Mailgram message, Telegram or international Telegram (cablegram) can be sent easily from a teletypewriter.

- If the same names and addresses are used frequently, you can save time, error and the added clerical expense of repetitive typing with RediList. This is a special address list service for Telex and TWX subscribers. One or more address lists with delivery instructions can be stored in Western Union's computer, ready at any time for immediate use.

If your organization has its own internal teletypewriter system, it's wise to familiarize yourself with the directory for it. Besides listing personnel, their terminal numbers and answerbacks, such directories also include detailed information about using the system.

WHEN TO CHOOSE:

- When an office in another time zone is closed and the addressee can act on your message immediately upon his or her arrival.
- When saving time is important and either party needs a written record.
- When making a one-way call that needs no response.
- When requesting information that otherwise would require waiting on the phone while the other party looks it up.
- When statistical details require written form for accuracy.
- When it's necessary to reach a number of people in a variety of locations with an important message.
- Prior to an important telephone call when you want the other person to prepare for the discussion.

FOR BEST RESULTS:

- If the message is to be written out for your office message center, use your organization's forms for this purpose and type, if possible, for greatest readability.
- If your organization has its own teletypewriter network as well as Telex or TWX, use the company network unless the location you need to reach is *not* on it.
- After transmitting a tape, save it at least one business day in case the message must be re-sent. For example, if Western Union's InfoMaster computer is relaying the message to an especially busy terminal, it will keep trying the number for an average of forty-five minutes and sometimes longer. (If InfoMaster still cannot get through, the sending terminal will be notified that the message must be retransmitted.)

- If you frequently send a message to the same list of people, it's smart to prepare an "address only" tape that can be used for several transmissions. Better yet, inquire about Western Union's RediList service.

INTERNATIONAL TELEX

Offices equipped with Telex or TWX equipment can dial overseas Telex stations through the facilities of Western Union and the five international telegraph carriers operating in the United States—ITT World Communications, RCA Global Communications, TRT Telecommunications, Western Union International (a company not related to Western Union), and the French Cable Company.

After getting the intercontinental area code from the Telex/TWX directory, you simply dial up the number of the international carrier of your choice and proceed with the call much the same way as you would to another point in the U.S.

International Telex provides all the same important benefits of domestic teletypewriter networks. It can be the fastest and most efficient way to send your message when the need is immediate and a written record desirable. International Telex can be less expensive than a telephone call. Also, since messages can be received when terminals are unattended—including when offices are closed—international Telex is especially helpful when trying to reach someone in a substantially later (or earlier) time zone.

● *Western Union FYI News Service, available by teletype dial-up or subscription, offers fast, concise reports on the latest developments in news, sports, weather, Congress, finance, commodities and even local ski conditions (in season) to Telex and TWX users.*

All of these reports except STOCK are available by subscription. Like to see a sample?* Dial Telex 8513 or TWX 710-988-5956 (East), TWX 910-221-2115 (Chicago and West). Pause for exchange of answerbacks. Type the desired category (for example: NEWS).

NEWS: News bulletins updated on the half-hour from 7:30 A.M. to 8:30 P.M.

SPECIAL: Big stories of the day, updated at 8 A.M., 1:30 P.M., 4:30 P.M.

CONGRESS: Daily U.S. Chamber of Commerce report on legislation affecting business, updated at 10 A.M.

SPORTS: Sports news and scores from 8 A.M.

WEATHER: Two-day forecast for 20 cities, updated at 8 A.M. and 8 P.M.

METRO: Metropolitan New York weather forecast, updated three times daily Mon.-Fri.

MARKET: Market commentary from 9 A.M. to 10:59 A.M. Stock averages from 11 A.M. to 5 P.M.

STOCK: Trade price/volume information (aged at least 15 minutes) on individual securities . . . from 10 A.M. to 11 P.M., Monday-Friday, until 4 P.M. on Saturday.

FINANCE: Business and financial news from 9 A.M. to 6:59 P.M.

CURRENCY: Foreign exchange and domestic money rates from 9 A.M.

LATIN: Latin American currency report updated at 4 P.M. Mon.-Fri.

METAL: Domestic futures of copper, silver, gold from 10:45 A.M. to 1 P.M.; 3:40 P.M. to 9:44 A.M. London metal market from 9:45 A.M. to 10:44 A.M.; 11:01 A.M. to 3:39 P.M.

GOLD: Gold futures from 10 A.M.

LIVESTOCK: Commentary 6:45 P.M. to 10:59 A.M. Cattle, live hog, pork belly and egg prices from 11 A.M.

GRAIN: Commentary from 6:45 P.M. to 10:59 A.M. Wheat, corn, oats, soybean prices from 11 A.M.

SUGAR: Sugar and coffee futures from 11 A.M.

CASH: USDA prices on 22 agricultural products updated at 4:30 P.M.

SKI:
REPORTS:
(In Season) NESKI for Vermont and New Hampshire 9 A.M. to 3 P.M.; Massachusetts, Maine and Connecticut after 3 P.M.; EASTSKI for Pennsylvania, New Jersey and New York updated at 3 P.M. daily; MIDSKI for Midwestern areas from 1:30 P.M.; WESTSKI for Western areas from 1:30 P.M.; ROCKSKI for Rocky Mountain report from 1:30 P.M.

All times Eastern Standard Time.
The first six FYI reports are available only to Telex and TWX subscribers; not for reprint or rebroadcast of any kind.

Normal low Telex/TWX usage charges apply.
Also available by subscription is News Alert, which automatically delivers to your Telex or TWX major news bulletins which might affect your company's business. News Alerts (the outbreak of combat, Presidential news conferences, strikes and other major news events) are flashed electronically from United Press International to Western Union for relay, usually within 20 minutes of UPI release.

CITIZENS BAND RADIO

Citizens Band, or CB, as it is usually referred to, is a two-way radio service licensed by the Federal Communications Commission (FCC) and intended for short distance (under 150 miles) personal and business radiocommunications.

A Citizens Band radio can be installed in your home or office, mounted in a vehicle, or carried with you wherever you go. You can use CB two-way radio in your car, truck, recreational vehicle, boat, golf cart, airplane, tractor or mobile home.

Almost everyone is familiar with their "mobile" (used in a vehicle) radio. Your fire department also uses two-way radio, as do most public utilities, many delivery services, plumbers, appliance repairmen, cab companies, towing services, gas stations . . . almost any service-related business has found that two-way radio dispatching helps them provide more efficient service to their customers in addition to saving them time and money.

Two-way Citizens Band radiocommunications are used by forestry services, ski patrols, TV technicians, surveyors, electricians, construction crews, security patrols, highway maintenance crews, business executives, truckers, farmers and salespersons. Boaters use CB for economical ship-to-shore communications. Racing teams use it to communicate between driver and pit crew.

In many areas you can use your CB radio to call ahead and make reservations at hotels, motels and restaurants as you travel along the highway in your car. You can call a CB-equipped garage or service station to obtain assistance if you're having car trouble.

There is also a national *Highway Emergency Locating Plan* (HELP) in which Citizens Band channel 9 is monitored along thousands of miles of highway by clubs, individuals, police departments, rescue units, hospitals, garages and other facilities which can provide assistance to you in the event of an emergency or if you simply need street directions.

One of the largest groups providing this worthwhile public service is *REACT* (Radio Emergency Associated Citizens Teams). REACT has volunteer teams throughout the United States and in many parts of Canada that monitor channel 9 twenty-four hours a day to provide assistance to motorists and provide local two-way radio communication in response to emergencies.

© *Radio Shack,* All About CB Two-Way Radio.

THE WALL STREET JOURNAL'S EASTERN EDITION

The Wall Street Journal's Eastern Edition is printed in four regional production facilities located in Chicopee, Mass.; South Brunswick, N.J.; White Oak, Md. and Orlando, Fla. The Orlando facility was the first newspaper production plant in the world to

*This earth station has a 33 foot antenna
and related equipment.*

operate via a communications satellite system. The edition of *The
Journal* distributed from the Orlando plant is put together at the
Chicopee production facility. A facsimile of each page is then
transmitted electronically to a satellite positioned 22,300 miles
above the equator. The satellite relays the page data to a *Journal*

plant in Orlando, Florida where it is received on page-sized photographic film. Once the facsimile data is received, the photographic film is used to make lithographic plates. These plates are then placed on a newspaper press which can turn out up to 80,000 *Journals* an hour for distribution in Florida and other parts of the Southeast.

A remote control room, shielded from the press by lead panels and double-thick panes of glass, allows the production staff to operate the press at a substantially reduced noise level. Press speed and the flow of ink and water are regulated from a console designed by Dow Jones' engineers.

A labeling system, developed jointly by Dow Jones and the Avery Label Co., individually stamps each paper—while still in stream form—with a preprinted, pressure sensitive label. By the time each paper reaches the stacker, it has been individually addressed to a subscriber and presorted by zip code.

THE DOW JONES NEWS SERVICE—THE BROADTAPE

The primary function of this unique "instant" news service is to report, quickly and accurately, financial news or general news that could affect the nation's securities markets or the world in general. To this end, a group of copyreaders and editors—all seasoned professionals—staff the Service's headquarters desk at 22 Cortlandt Street in New York City for ten hours each day that the U.S. securities markets are operating.

The copy desk of the Dow Jones News Service office is huge and horseshoe-shaped, capable of accommodating up to a dozen copyreaders at one time. At each position is a call director telephone containing 23 extensions, a typewriter and other tools of the profession. Some 15 feet away from the desk is the wire room where 25 teletypewriter, teletypesetter, telex and TWX printers bring a constant flow of news into Dow Jones newsrooms. The machines, arranged in banks for easy monitoring and under constant surveillance by a Broadtape staffer, connect New York with Dow Jones' 12 other domestic bureaus situated in large cities throughout the nation as well as four in Canada.

In addition to Dow Jones' own communications network, the wire room also contains the major circuits of the Associated Press (AP), United Press International (UPI) and various business wires, to insure that every aspect of news will be at the disposal of the Dow Jones News Service and, subsequently, to subscribers.

AP-DOW JONES—THE INTERNATIONAL NEWS SERVICE

AP-Dow Jones is a minute-to-minute global news service that ticks 24 hours a day, six days a week and links two of the world's most reputable news-gathering organizations: Dow Jones and Company and the Associated Press. This unique news service was formed in 1967; a companion service known as the AP-Dow Jones Financial Wire was formed in 1968. Members of the international financial community who are AP-DJ subscribers include: central banks and other government bodies, large commercial banks, merchant banks, trading companies, leading brokerage houses, newspapers and industrial concerns.

All news generated by reporters in the United States, Canada or abroad is channelled via computer, to an editorial control desk in New York which operates 24 hours a day. Copy is screened for accuracy by financial editors before being speedily transmitted to subscribers who receive the information on teleprinter equipment via a complex computer and satellite transmission system. In New York, editors work with the newest electronic and computer editing devices to insure accurate, fast editing and instantaneous transmission to subscribers.

The AP-DJ Economic Report is distributed and sold in 35 nations to news agencies, private business subscribers and to foreign newspapers.

The AP-DJ Economic Report also offers another dimension: three highly specific news services for decision makers who desire condensed packages of information to meet selective needs—the Bankers Report, the Eurofinancial Report and the Petroleum News Service.

By means of an electronic device attached to the teletype machine in a client's office, stories which have a special coding activate the subscriber's machine when they are transmitted. This allows the client to receive the specialized service edited to his needs.

The Bankers Report carries news appealing to money management levels at a time when markets are becoming increasingly complex and their movement rapid. Information that AP-DJ would

Dow Jones has primary editorial responsibility for the news service. The Associated Press is responsible for distribution.

The Dow Jones News Service, known on The Street as the Broad-tape or "ticker," has its headquarters in Dow Jones' New York office. Editors using both paper and pencil and cathode-ray terminals, check the copy which can go out on the wire to subscribers in the U.S. and Canada at a maximum rate of 300 words-per-minute.

send to the Bankers Report includes: corporate and government financing through capital markets; eurocurrency market prices, developments and trends; new money market regulations; new banking legislation; interest rates and currency exchange rates; and statistical data on capital markets.

The businessman subscribing to the Petroleum News Service would find the following information: government and other decisions affecting the petroleum and petrochemical industries; price changes and production statistics; drilling and exploration news; scientific developments relating to petroleum and government events likely to affect these industries.

For the European investment community, the Eurofinancial Report includes key *Wall Street Journal* columns such as *Heard on the Street* and *Abreast of the Market* plus the other early morning features run on the AP-Dow Jones Financial Wire.

The companion to the Economic Report—The Financial Wire—is specifically tailored to meet the needs of the international investment community. It operates 24 hours a day, Monday through Friday and provides information from the world's stock exchanges, the international money markets, the corporate scene, the major commodity markets and the political arena.

11

secretarial billing, banking and bookkeeping made effortless

Within today's world of electronic calculators and electric adding machines are models which perform just about any kind of mathematical function—so the mechanics of your job should be simple.

The rest becomes easy when you comprehend the procedures involved to get the end result. Once you know the "what" and "why," "how" becomes "of course."

Take, for instance, the task of simplifying your billing procedure. Each example here bypasses the non-essentials and finishes only with essentials.

An "easy to grasp" system of single entry bookkeeping is set up step by step and page by page, showing you: how to post cash received, bank deposits, checks paid out, payroll, contributions, bad checks and bad debts, how to do a statement of income, weekly, monthly and quarterly summaries, depreciation, a balance sheet; the definition of an accrual basis schedule; an efficient way to index accounts and to record accounts receivable and accounts payable.

There's nothing to organizing petty cash with an envelope especially for that purpose, with places to record paid outs.

A glossary is also included defining bookkeeping and banking terms in everyday language.

INNOVATIVE BILLING IDEAS

Kenneth R. Fehrman, Interior Design

4112 California Street • San Francisco, CA 94118 • (415) 387-7613

June 10, 19--

Mr. and Mrs. John Doe
44 Berkeley Court
San Francisco, CA

<u>STATEMENT</u>

2 custom designed wing chairs upholstered in natural linen @ $687.00 each	$1374.00
Sales Tax	89.31
Freight Charges	35.00
30 yards T-1359 special finish fabric for living room draperies @ $30.00/yd	900.00
Sales Tax	58.50
Freight Charges	13.00
Labor charge for draperies	450.00
9 x 12 100% wool Indo-Heriz carpet for reception hall	1400.00
Sales Tax	91.00
Freight Charges	31.00
Labor charge for framing 2 Japanese wood block prints	80.00
Design fee for living room elevations	100.00
TOTAL	$4621.81
Deposit Paid on Account	2500.00
BALANCE DUE	$2121.81

This is done on stationery, original size 6″ × 8″—can be cut for a short bill (using ¾ of original size). It is dark grey lettering on dove grey paper, making it either a formal letter or an informal note.

FRANKLIN, ULLMAN, KIMLER & ENTIN, P.A.
2020 NORTHEAST 163RD STREET ● SUITE 300
NORTH MIAMI BEACH, FLORIDA 33162
TELEPHONE (305) **944-9100**

DATE

STATEMENT

Please detach here and return upper portion with your remittance.

AMT. ENCLOSED $ _____

RE:

FOR LEGAL SERVICES:

COSTS ADVANCED:

FRANKLIN, ULLMAN, KIMLER & ENTIN P.A. — North Miami Beach, Florida 33162

This is an original and two copies—printed on self-copying NCR paper—needs no carbon paper—set up to fit in window envelope—top portion to be returned with check.

DERMATOLOGY   STATEMENT   Telephone: 346-5377

BERNARD I. GORDON, M.D.
2300 SUTTER STREET, SUITE 202
SAN FRANCISCO, CALIFORNIA 94115

TO: BERNARD I. GORDON, M.D.
2300 SUTTER STREET, SUITE 202
SAN FRANCISCO, CA 94115

DATE	RVS No.	DESCRIPTION	CHARGE	PAYMENT	BALANCE
4-10	1700·58	# 1 & 6	35.00		35.00
4-15	11400	# 7 on left hand	50.00		85.00
5-10	88310	# 9	20.00		105.00
6-14		Payment (Blue Shield)		85.00	20.00
7-10		Patient paid in full		20.00	—

DESCRIPTION:
1. Office Consult.-History & Exam.
2. Office Visit
3. Hospital Consultation
4. Hospital Visit
5. Intralesional Steroid Injection
6. Liquid Nitrogen Treatment
7. Surgery
8. Biopsy
9. Pathologic Examination
10. Incision & Drainage
11. Debridement of Skin or Nails
12. Culture for Fungus
13. Injections
14. Electrocautery
15. Chemocautery
16. Other

▲
PAY LAST
AMOUNT IN
THIS COLUMN

COMMENTS: *Blue Shield Insurance*

THIS IS A COPY OF YOUR ACCOUNT AS IT APPEARS ON YOUR LEDGER CARD.

THE ELEMENTS OF A CHECK

THE PAYEE'S NAME is written after "PAY TO THE ORDER OF"

THE AMOUNT IN WORDS as far to the left as possible. Finish the space with a line. That prevents the insertion of words that increase the amount.

CHECK ROUTING SYMBOL. The first two digits are Hibernia Bank's Federal Reserve District Number. The third digit is the Federal Reserve Office (Head Office or Branch) or the designation of a special collection arrangement. The fourth digit designates Hibernia Bank's state or a special collection arrangement.

Hibernia Bank's IDENTIFICATION NUMBER (numerator) over its CHECK ROUTING SYMBOL (denominator). Both parts are encoded in magnetic ink across the bottom of the check, except the first two digits of the numerator. These digits are city, state or other territorial designations needed for hand processing but not for electronic sorting. These numbers go on the deposit slip.

THE AMOUNT IN NUMBERS close to the $ sign. If these numbers do not agree with the amount in words, your bank will probably pay the amount in words, but this will take extra time.

YOUR SIGNATURE should match the one filed when you opened the account.

THE DOLLAR AMOUNT is usually encoded in magnetic ink characters by the first bank to receive the check.

YOUR CHECK NUMBER

YOUR ACCOUNT NUMBER

HIBERNIA BANK'S IDENTIFICATION NUMBER

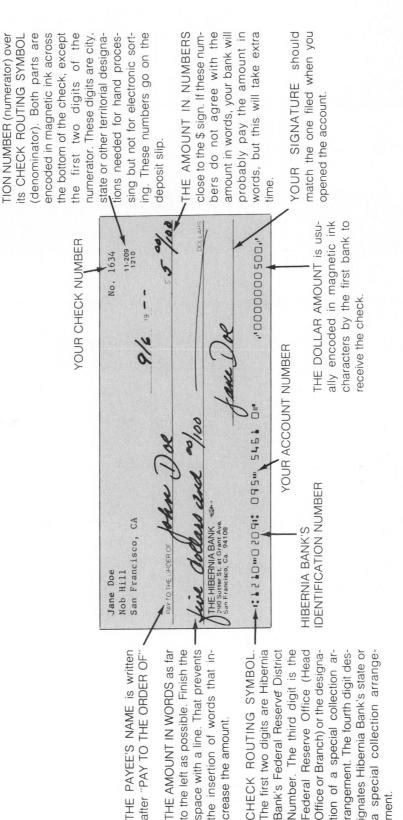

HOW TO ENDORSE A CHECK

BLANK ENDORSEMENT

John Doe

This endorsement makes the check negotiable, and anyone can cash it.

SPECIAL ENDORSEMENT

Pay to the Order of William Smith John Doe

The right to the money is transferred to someone else and only they can cash the check.

RESTRICTED ENDORSEMENT

for deposit only in Hibernia Bank Account # 093-0808-3 John Doe

This endorsement cancels any further use of the check except for collection purposes between banks. This is the safe way to mail a deposit.

CONDITIONAL ENDORSEMENT

pay Richard Smith upon the satisfactory performance of his contract John Doe

The endorser imposes a condition.

"WITHOUT RECOURSE" ENDORSEMENT

without recourse John Doe

The endorser is protected from liability.

Jane Doe
Nob Hill
San Francisco, CA

No. 1550

11-209
1210

SIGNATURE _____
RECEIVED $ _____ IN CASH
DATE _____

DEPOSITED WITH

THE HIBERNIA BANK
290 Sutter St. at Grant Ave.
San Francisco, Ca. 94108

LIST EACH CHECK SEPARATELY
SPECIFY BY NUMBER THE BANK ON WHICH EACH CHECK IS DRAWN
IF MORE THAN 3 CHECKS, LIST ON REVERSE SIDE

CURRENCY	500	00
COIN		
CHECKS 1		
2		
3		
TOTAL FROM OTHER SIDE		
SUB TOTAL IF CASH RETURNED		
LESS CASH RECEIVED		
TOTAL DEPOSIT	500	00

⑆1210⑉0209⑈ 095⑈ 5461 0⑆

When DEPOSITING CASH ONLY, list the total amount on both the Currency line and the Total line

---

Jane Doe
Nob Hill
San Francisco, CA

No. 1551

11-209
1210

SIGNATURE _____
RECEIVED $ _____ IN CASH
DATE _____

DEPOSITED WITH

THE HIBERNIA BANK
290 Sutter St. at Grant Ave.
San Francisco, Ca. 94108

LIST EACH CHECK SEPARATELY
SPECIFY BY NUMBER THE BANK ON WHICH EACH CHECK IS DRAWN
IF MORE THAN 3 CHECKS, LIST ON REVERSE SIDE

CURRENCY		
COIN		
CHECKS 1 11-209	300	00
2 11-3430	100	00
3		
TOTAL FROM OTHER SIDE		
SUB TOTAL IF CASH RETURNED		
LESS CASH RECEIVED		
TOTAL DEPOSIT	400	00

⑆1210⑉0209⑈ 095⑈ 5461 0⑆

When DEPOSITING CHECKS AND CASH TOGETHER, list the cash total on the Currency line, each check by bank number and amount, and fill in the Total line

---

Jane Doe
Nob Hill
San Francisco, CA

No. 1552

11-209
1210

SIGNATURE _____
RECEIVED $ _____ IN CASH
DATE _____

DEPOSITED WITH

THE HIBERNIA BANK
290 Sutter St. at Grant Ave.
San Francisco, Ca. 94108

LIST EACH CHECK SEPARATELY
SPECIFY BY NUMBER THE BANK ON WHICH EACH CHECK IS DRAWN
IF MORE THAN 3 CHECKS, LIST ON REVERSE SIDE

CURRENCY	200	00
COIN		
CHECKS 1 11-209	125	00
2 11-209	35	50
3		
TOTAL FROM OTHER SIDE		
SUB TOTAL IF CASH RETURNED		
LESS CASH RECEIVED		
TOTAL DEPOSIT	360	50

⑆1210⑉0209⑈ 095⑈ 5461 0⑆

When DEPOSITING CHECKS ONLY, be sure to leave Currency line blank or draw a line through it, list the checks by bank number and amount, fill in Total line

---

Jane Doe
Nob Hill
San Francisco, CA

No. 1553

11-209
1210

SIGNATURE _____
RECEIVED $ 50.00 6/22/77 IN CASH
DATE _____

DEPOSITED WITH

THE HIBERNIA BANK
290 Sutter St. at Grant Ave.
San Francisco, Ca. 94108

LIST EACH CHECK SEPARATELY
SPECIFY BY NUMBER THE BANK ON WHICH EACH CHECK IS DRAWN
IF MORE THAN 3 CHECKS, LIST ON REVERSE SIDE

CURRENCY		
COIN		
CHECKS 1 11-3430	250	00
2		
3		
TOTAL FROM OTHER SIDE		
SUB TOTAL IF CASH RETURNED	250	00
LESS CASH RECEIVED	50	00
TOTAL DEPOSIT	200	00

⑆1210⑉0209⑈ 095⑈ 5461 0⑆

When DEPOSITING ONLY A PORTION OF A CHECK (split deposit), list the check by bank number and amount, Subtotal, Less Cash Received, Total Deposit. Fill in date and amount of cash received, but SIGN FOR CASH IN FRONT OF TELLER

HOW TO RECONCILE A BANK STATEMENT

THE HIBERNIA BANK

STATEMENT OF ACCOUNT

| ACCOUNT NO. 095 5461 0 |
| STATEMENT DATE **MAY 31** 19-- |

09   JANE DOE
NOB HILL
SAN FRANCISCO CA 94108

EDP 1-

CHECKS AND OTHER DEBITS			DEPOSITS	DATE		BALANCE
		BALANCE LAST STATEMENT		04	29	319.45
			20.00	05	02	339.45
3.20	36.95			05	04	299.30
10.00	165.00		35.00	05	05	159.30
1.00				05	06	158.30
1.34	3.20	3.20		05	10	150.56
1.25	3.63			05	11	145.68
1.02				05	12	144.66
20.00	22.00	51.00	20.00	05	13	71.66
3.20	7.00			05	16	61.46
12.10				05	17	49.36
1.25	5.48	14.00	50.00	05	18	78.63
1.60				05	19	77.03
			15.00	05	23	92.03
1.28	3.89	6.88				
7.80	38.00			05	24	34.18
21.35			10.00	05	26	22.83
1.80				05	27	21.03
10.00	2.49**AC**		211.75	05	31	220.29

YOUR PREVIOUS BALANCE WAS	WE HAVE ADDED DEPOSITS		AND SUBTRACTED CHECKS TOTALING		ACTIVITY CHARGE	RESULTING IN YOUR PRESENT BALANCE OF
	NO.	AMOUNT	NO.	AMOUNT		
319.45	7	361.75	29	458.42	2.49	220.29

TRANSACTION CODES: CM = Credit Memo   DM = Debit Memo   AC = Activity Charge   CP = Credit Preauthorized   DP = Debit Preauthorized   AT = Automatic Transfer   RT = Returned Items

THIS FORM IS PROVIDED TO HELP YOU
BALANCE YOUR BANK STATEMENT

CHECKS OUTSTANDING - NOT
CHARGED TO ACCOUNT

NO	$	
1601	2	99
1616	1	50
1619	165	00
1620	8	52
1621	4	79
1622	24	00
TOTAL	$ 206	80

BANK BALANCE SHOWN
ON THIS STATEMENT $ _220.29_

ADD +
DEPOSITS NOT CREDITED
IN THIS STATEMENT
(IF ANY) $ _500.00_

TOTAL $ _720.29_

SUBTRACT -
CHECKS OUTSTANDING $ _206.80_

BALANCE $ _513.49_

SHOULD AGREE WITH YOUR CHECK BOOK BAL-
ANCE AFTER DEDUCTING SERVICE CHARGE (IF
ANY) SHOWN ON THIS STATEMENT.

IF YOUR ACCOUNT DOES NOT BALANCE CHECK THE FOLLOWING

☐ Are the amounts of all your deposits entered on your check book stubs the same as those on the statement?

☐ Have you deducted all service charges on your check book stubs?

☐ Have you written a counter check which has not been deducted on your check book stub?

☐ Have you carried the correct balance forward from one check book stub to the next?

☐ Have you entered the amounts correctly on your check book stub for each check you have written?

☐ Are all additions and subtractions correct on your check book stub?

THE HIBERNIA BANK
SAN FRANCISCO, CALIF.

There are different accounting systems for different needs. For small businesses, single entry systems are easier for the nonaccountant to understand. Sample pages from one such method are illustrated here courtesy of Dymo Visual Systems Inc., Augusta, Georgia, publishers of **ideal**™ Record and Bookkeeping Systems.

FACSIMILE PAGE ILLUSTRATING THE USE OF THIS IDEAL SYSTEM FORM 2900

CASH RECEIPTS FROM SALES & SERVICES

THE IDEAL SYSTEM, COPYRIGHT U.S. PAT. OFFICE

BANK ACCOUNT

SIMPLIFIED WEEKLY RECORD

PAYMENTS—ALL CHECKS AND CASH PAID OUT

IDEAL SYSTEM FORM 2900

	CASH RECEIVED FROM				TOTAL CASH RECEIVED	OTHER CASH RECEIVED (MEMO)	BANK DEPOSITS (MEMO)	BANK BALANCE (4+3−5)	DATE 19 MO DAY	CHECK NO.	NAME OR MEMO	PAID OUT BY CHECK	PAID OUT BY CASH	
	Dept A.	Dept B.	Dept C.	Dept D.	SALES TAX COLLECTED			Starting bank bal. 74800						
1	1000	800		400	88	2288			91288	31		Days Receipts			1
2	600	2100	1380	2720	272	7072				2		Days Receipts		7072	2
3										2	1118	Days Cash pay-outs			3
4								85099		2	1119	B. Carson Co.	11200		4
5	400	3800	1200		216	5616		5616		3		Days Receipts			5
6										3		P.B. Shares Fin. Co. (payroll)	3570		6
7										3	1120	M. Massey—insurance	900		7
8										3	1121	Core. Gas Co.	420		8
9										3	1122	R. A. Smith	4350		9
10										3	1123	Geo. Jones	3390		10
11										3	1124	M. Smith—owner	10000		11
12	4100	1490	620	248		6448		6448	69194	4		Days Receipts			12
13										4	1125	City Clerk—license	1200		13
14										4	1126	County Tax Collector	2692	70740	14
15	350	3350	800		188	4888		4888	75628	5		Days Receipts			15
16							YOU MAY USE AS MANY LINES DAILY AND AS MANY PAGES MONTHLY AS ARE NEEDED								16
17										30		Bank loan			17
18										30	1138	Collector of Int. Rev. Wthld. Tax	12243		18
19										30	1139	Collector of Int. Rev. F.O.A.B. Tax	1316		19
20	1920	2095	900	1655	259	6729	10000	4899		30		Days Receipts			20
21	1600	1100			68	2768		9497		31		Days Receipts			21
22										31	1140	State Treasurer—Un. Ins.	2526		22
23										31	1141	Bell Telephone Co.	910		23
24										31	1142	Art Craft Co.	21875		24
25										31	1143	State Treasurer—sales tax	6320		25
26										31		Days Delivery		1400	26
27										31	1144	Leonard Company	6000		27
28										31	1145	Acme Printers	690		28
29										31	1146	Wm. Langan	940		29
30															30
31															31
32															32
33	57170	17545	5760	53895	1359	35809	10000	287373 23 15					90422	8472	33

YOU MAY USE THESE COLUMNS FOR ANY BREAKDOWN OF SALES YOU WISH, TO ADAPT THIS SYSTEM TO YOUR BUSINESS. FOR EXAMPLE: WHOLESALE SALES, RETAIL SALES. SALES TAX, INCOME FROM SERVICES, DEPARTMENTAL INCOME, MISC. ETC.

ALL OF YOUR SALES AND CASH RECEIPTS AND ALL OF YOUR CASH OR CHECK PAYMENTS, PURCHASES AND EXPENSES ARE ALL ENTERED ON THIS ONE DOUBLE PAGE FORM, MAKING THIS THE EASIEST TO KEEP—COMPLETE BOOKKEEPING SYSTEM EVER DEVISED.

PETTY CASH: IF YOU DESIRE TO OBTAIN YOUR PETTY CASH POSITION, USE THE FOLLOWING:
COL 2 + COL 2-A − COL 3 = COL 6
COL 6 = PETTY CASH

BANK BALANCE: ENTER YOUR STARTING BANK BALANCE AT THE TOP OF THE COLUMN. YOU MAY ARRIVE AT YOUR CURRENT BALANCE AT ANY TIME BY ADDING YOUR BANK DEPOSITS (COL 3) TO YOUR PREVIOUS BANK BALANCE (COL 4) AND DEDUCTING THE AMOUNTS PAID OUT BY CHECK IN COL 5.

BY ENTERING EACH ITEM DIRECTLY INTO THE PROPER COLUMN AND TRANSFERRING THE TOTALS OF EACH COLUMN TO THE SUMMARY (DOMO'S 2901-2) AT THE END OF EACH PERIOD—YOU KNOW EXACTLY HOW MUCH YOU HAVE MADE, HOW MUCH YOU HAVE SPENT AND WHERE IT WENT. YOUR FIGURES ARE READY—COMPLETE, ACCURATE AND EXACT FOR ALL YOUR TAX RETURNS.

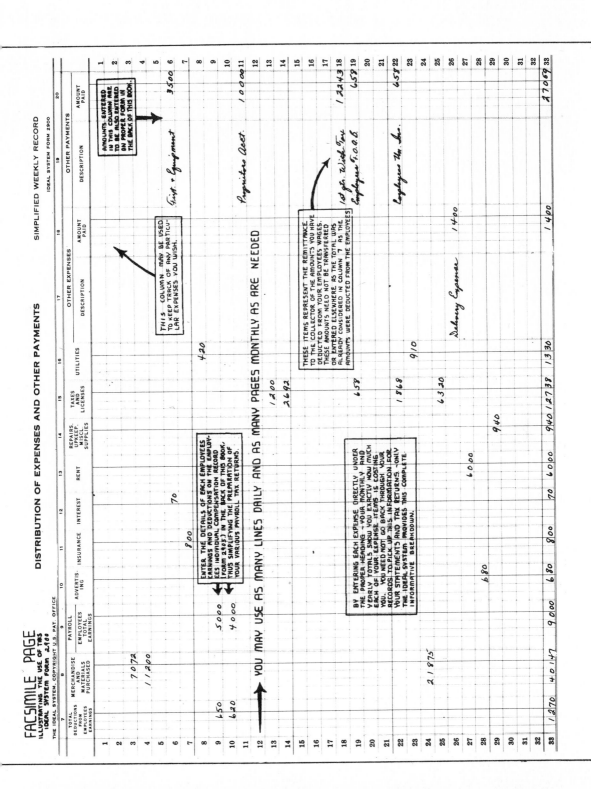

FACSIMILE PAGE
ILLUSTRATING THE USE OF THIS
IDEAL SYSTEM FORM 2900

DISTRIBUTION OF EXPENSES AND OTHER PAYMENTS

SIMPLIFIED WEEKLY RECORD

THE IDEAL SYSTEM, COPYRIGHT U.S. PAT. OFFICE

IDEAL SYSTEM FORM 2900

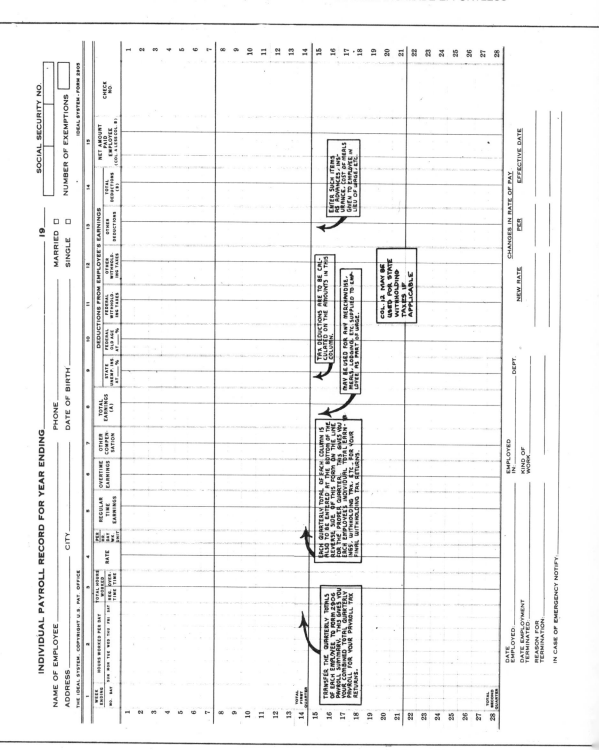

INDIVIDUAL PAYROLL RECORD FOR YEAR ENDING _____ 19 ___

NAME OF EMPLOYEE _____

ADDRESS _____ CITY _____ PHONE _____

DATE OF BIRTH _____

SOCIAL SECURITY NO.

MARRIED ☐ SINGLE ☐

NUMBER OF EXEMPTIONS

THE IDEAL SYSTEM. COPYRIGHT U.S. PAT. OFFICE
IDEAL SYSTEM - FORM 290S

1	2	3		4	5	6	7	8	DEDUCTIONS FROM EMPLOYEE'S EARNINGS					14	15
									9	10	11	12	13		
WEEK ENDING	HOURS WORKED PER DAY	TOTAL HOURS WORKED	PER HR. DAY WK. UNIT	RATE	REGULAR TIME EARNINGS	OVERTIME EARNINGS	OTHER COMPENSATION	TOTAL EARNINGS (A)	STATE UNEMP. INS. AT ___%	FEDERAL OLD AGE AT ___%	FEDERAL WITHHOLDING TAXES	OTHER WITHHOLDING TAXES	OTHER DEDUCTIONS	TOTAL DEDUCTIONS (B)	NET AMOUNT PAID EMPLOYEE (COL A LESS COL B)
MO. DAY	SUN MON TUE WED THU FRI SAT	REG. TIME OVER TIME													CHECK NO.

TAX DEDUCTIONS ARE TO BE CALCULATED ON THE AMOUNTS IN THIS COLUMN.

MAY BE USED FOR ANY MERCHANDISE, MEALS, LODGING, ETC. SUPPLIED TO EMPLOYEE AS PART OF WAGE.

COL. 12 MAY BE USED FOR STATE WITHHOLDING TAXES IF APPLICABLE.

ENTER SUCH ITEMS AS ADVANCES, INSURANCE, COST OF MEALS GIVEN TO EMPLOYEE IN LIEU OF WAGE, ETC.

EACH QUARTERLY TOTAL OF EACH COLUMN IS ALSO TO BE ENTERED AT THE BOTTOM OF THE REVERSE SIDE OF THIS FORM ON THE LINE FOR THE PROPER QUARTER. THIS GIVES YOU EACH EMPLOYEE'S INDIVIDUAL TOTAL EARNINGS, WITHHOLDING TAX, ETC., FOR YOUR FINAL WITHHOLDING TAX RETURNS.

TRANSFER THE QUARTERLY TOTALS OF EACH EMPLOYEE TO FORM 290-6 PAYROLL SUMMARY. THIS GIVES YOU YOUR COMBINED TOTAL QUARTERLY PAYROLL FOR YOUR PAYROLL TAX RETURNS.

TOTAL FIRST QUARTER

TOTAL SECOND QUARTER

DATE EMPLOYED: _____ EMPLOYED IN: _____ DEPT. _____

DATE EMPLOYMENT TERMINATED: _____ KIND OF WORK: _____

REASON FOR TERMINATION: _____

CHANGES IN RATE OF PAY

NEW RATE _____ PER _____ EFFECTIVE DATE _____

IN CASE OF EMERGENCY NOTIFY: _____

MONTHLY AND QUARTERLY SUMMARY OF BUSINESS YEAR ENDING _____ 19__

THE IDEAL SYSTEM, REG. U. S. PAT. OFFICE. MADE IN U.S.A.

IDEAL SYSTEM - FORM 2902A

MONTHLY TOTALS

	FROM FORM 2900	JANUARY	FEBRUARY	MARCH	TOTAL FIRST QUARTER	APRIL	MAY	JUNE	TOTAL SECOND QUARTER	
1 CASH RECEIPTS:	COLUMN NO.									1
2	1-A									2
3	1-B									3
4	1-C									4
5	1-D									5
6	1-E									6
7 TOTAL CASH RECEIPTS	2									7
8 PURCHASES	8									8
9 EXPENSES:										9
10 Payroll	9									10
11 Advertising	10									11
12 Insurance	11									12
13 Interest	12									13
14 Rent	13									14
15 Repairs, Upkeep, Miscel. Supplies	14									15
16 Taxes & Licenses	15									16
17 Utilities	16									17
18 Other Expenses	18									18
19 Bad Debts— Bad Checks	FROM FORM 2907									19
20 Contributions	FROM FORM 2907									20
21 Depreciation	FROM FORM 2907									21
22 Other Deductions	FROM FORM 2907A FROM FORM 2907									22
23										23
24										24
25 TOTAL EXPENSES	(Total of Lines 9 to 24 incl.)									25
26 SUMMARY										26
27 TOTAL CASH RECEIVED	(From Line 7 Above)									27
28 TOTAL PURCHASES	(From Line 8 Above)									28
29 GROSS PROFIT	(Line 27 Less Line 28)									29
30 TOTAL EXPENSES	(From Line 25 Above)									30
31 NET PROFIT	(Line 29 Less Line 30)									31
32 OTHER INCOME	(From Form No. 2912)									32
33 TOTAL NET PROFIT	(Line 31 Plus Line 32)									33

THE IDEAL SYSTEM, REG. U. S. PAT. OFFICE. MADE IN U.S.A.

IDEAL SYSTEM - FORM 2902B

MONTHLY AND QUARTERLY SUMMARY OF BUSINESS YEAR ENDING _____ 19___

MONTHLY TOTALS

	FROM FORM 2900	COLUMN NO.	JULY	AUGUST	SEPTEMBER	TOTAL THIRD QUARTER	OCTOBER	NOVEMBER	DECEMBER	TOTAL FOURTH QUARTER	
CASH RECEIPTS:											1
		1-A									2
		1-B									3
		1-C									4
		1-D									5
		1-E									6
TOTAL CASH RECEIPTS		2									7
PURCHASES		8									8
EXPENSES:											9
Payroll		9									10
Advertising		10									11
Insurance		11									12
Interest		12									13
Rent		13									14
Repairs, Upkeep, Miscel. Supplies		14									15
Taxes & Licenses		15									16
Utilities		16									17
Other Expenses		18									18
Bad Debts— Bad Checks		FROM FORM 2907									19
Contributions		FROM FORM 2907									20
Depreciation		FROM FORM 2907A									21
Other Deductions		FROM FORM 2907									22
											23
TOTAL EXPENSES	(Total of Lines 9 to 24 incl.)										24
SUMMARY											25
TOTAL CASH RECEIVED	(From Line 7) Above										26
TOTAL PURCHASES	(From Line 8) Above										27
GROSS PROFIT	(Line 27 Less Line 28)										28
TOTAL EXPENSES	(From Line 25 Above)										29
NET PROFIT	(Line 29 Less Line 30)										30
OTHER INCOME	(From No. 2912)										31
TOTAL NET PROFIT	(Line 31 Plus Line 32)										32
											33

QUARTERLY SUMMARY OF BUSINESS AND STATEMENT OF INCOME YEAR ENDING _____ 19___

THE IDEAL SYSTEM, REG. U. S. PAT. OFFICE. MADE IN U.S.A.

IDEAL SYSTEM - FORM 2903

QUARTERLY TOTALS

Line		TOTAL FIRST QUARTER	TOTAL SECOND QUARTER	TOTAL THIRD QUARTER	TOTAL FOURTH QUARTER	TOTAL FOR YEAR
1	**CASH RECEIPTS** (Sales) FORWARD QUARTERLY TOTALS FROM SAME LINES ON FORM NO. 2902					
2						
3						
4						
5						
6						
7	**TOTAL CASH RECEIPTS** (Sales)					
8	**PURCHASES**					
9	**EXPENSES:**					
10	Payroll					
11	Advertising					
12	Insurance					
13	Interest					
14	Rent					
15	Repairs, Upkeep, Misc. Sup.					
16	Taxes and Licenses					
17	Utilities					
18	Other Expenses					
19	Bad Debts—Bad Checks					
20	Contributions					
21	Depreciation					
22	Other Deductions					
25	**TOTAL EXPENSES** (Total of Lines 9 to 24 Above)					

STATEMENT OF INCOME

26	**TOTAL SALES**	(From Line 7 Above — See Footnote A)
28	**TOTAL PURCHASES**	(From Line 8 Above — See Footnote B)
29	**GROSS PROFIT**	(Line 27 Less Line 28 Above)
30	**TOTAL EXPENSES**	(Line 25 Above)
31	**NET PROFIT**	(Line 29 Less Line 30 Above)
32	**OTHER INCOME**	(From Form No. 2912)
33	**TOTAL NET PROFIT**	(Line 31 Plus Line 32)

STATEMENT OF INCOME - YEAR 19___

U. S. INCOME TAX RETURN STATEMENT

(USE FIGURES FROM COLUMN HEADED "TOTAL FOR YEAR")

1	**INCOME:**	
2	Income from Sales & Services	(From Line 7 at Left)
3	**COST OF GOODS SOLD:**	
4	Inventory at Beginning of Year	
5	Mdse. & Materials Purchased	(From Line 28 at Left)
6	**TOTAL**	(Line 4 plus Line 5)
7	LESS: Inventory at End of Year	
8	Cost of Goods Sold	(Line 6 Less Line 7)
9	**GROSS PROFIT**	(Line 2 Less Line 8)
10	**EXPENSES:**	
11	Payroll	(Line 10 at Left)
12	Advertising	(Line 11 at Left)
13	Insurance	(Line 12 at Left)
14	Interest	(Line 13 at Left)
15	Rent	(Line 14 at Left)
16	Repairs, Upkeep, etc.	(Line 15 at Left)
17	Taxes and Licenses	(Line 16 at Left)
18	Utilities	(Line 17 at Left)
19	Other Expenses	(Line 18 at Left)
20	Bad Debts—Bad Checks	(Line 19 at Left)
21	Contributions	(Line 20 at Left)
22	Depreciation	(Line 21 at Left)
23	Other Deductions	(Line 22 at Left)
24		(Line 23 at Left)
25		(Line 24 at Left)
26	**TOTAL EXPENSES**	(Line 11 to Line 25 incl.)
27	**NET PROFIT**	(Line 9 Less Line 26 Above)
28	PLUS: Other Income	(Line 32 at Left)
29	**TOTAL NET PROFIT FOR YEAR**	(Line 27 Plus Line 28 Above)

FOOTNOTES The following instructions apply only if you are on an accrual basis:

(a) Enter on line 27 at left the figures from line 5 on the opposite page (form 2903A) instead of the figures from line 7 on this page.

(b) Enter on line 28 at left the figures from line 19 on the opposite page (form 2903A) instead of the figures from line 8 on this page.

ACCRUAL BASIS SCHEDULE YEAR ENDING _____ 19____

USE THIS SCHEDULE WHEN PREPARING "STATEMENT OF INCOME" AND INCOME TAX REPORT ON ACCRUAL BASIS

(SEE INSTRUCTIONS IN FRONT PART OF BOOK)

THE IDEAL SYSTEM, REG. U. S. PAT. OFFICE, MADE IN U.S.A.

IDEAL SYSTEM - FORM 2903A

IMPORTANT NOTICE: If the production, purchase, and sale of merchandise are income producing factors in your business, then you must use the "ACCRUAL BASIS METHOD" and not the "CASH BASIS METHOD." See "ACCRUAL BASIS" schedule under instructions in front of this book.

	TOTAL FIRST QUARTER	TOTAL SECOND QUARTER	TOTAL THIRD QUARTER	TOTAL FOURTH QUARTER	TOTAL FOR YEAR
SALES—CASH AND CREDIT:					
1 Accounts and Notes Receivable due from Customers at end of Period					
2 Plus: Total Cash Received during Period (From Summary, Line 7)					
3 Total (Line 1 Plus Line 2)					
4 Less: Accounts and Notes Receivable due from Customers at Beginning of Period					
5 TOTAL CASH AND CREDIT SALES FOR PERIOD (Line 3 Minus Line 4)					
6 Enter "Total Cash and Credit Sales" from Line 5 above on Line 27 of "Monthly Statement of Income," Form 2903. On the opposite side of this page					
7 if you are on an accrual basis					
PURCHASES—CASH AND CREDIT:					
8 Amount Owing for Mdse. or Material at End of Period					
9 Plus: Total Purchases Paid for during Period (From Summary, Line 9)					
10 Total (Line 8 Plus Line 9)					
11 Less: Amount Owing for Mdse. or Material at Beginning of Period					
12 TOTAL CASH AND CREDIT PURCHASES FOR PERIOD (Line 10 Minus Line 11)					
13 Enter "Total Cash and Credit Purchases" from Line 12 above on Line 15 below					
14					
NET COST OF SALES					
15 Total Cash and Credit Purchases for Period (From Line 12 above)					
16 Plus: Inventory of Stock on Hand at Beginning of Period					
17 Total (Line 15 Plus Line 16)					
18 Less: Inventory of Stock on Hand at End of Period					
19 NET COST OF SALES (Line 17 Minus Line 18)					
20 Enter "Net Cost of Sales" from Line 19 above on Line 28 of "Monthly Statement of Income," Form 2903. On the opposite side of this page if you are on an accrual basis					
21					
OTHER ACCRUALS:					
22					
23					
24					
25					
26					
27					
28					
29					
30					
31					
32					
33					

DEDUCTIONS

CONTRIBUTIONS AND OTHER DEDUCTIONS

THE IDEAL SYSTEM, REG. U. S. PAT. OFFICE. MADE IN U.S.A.

DATE 19____	TO WHOM PAID OR DESCRIPTION	1 AMOUNT CONTRIBUTED	2 OTHER DEDUCTIONS	3
1				
2				
3				
4				
5				
6				
7				
8				
9				
10				
11				
12				
13				
14				
15				
16				
17				
18				
19				
20				
21				
22				
23				
24				
25				
26				
27				
28				
29				
30				
31				
32				
33				

BAD CHECKS CASHED – BAD DEBTS

ENTER BAD DEBT ONLY IF THE SAME SALE WAS ORIGINALLY INCLUDED IN INCOME

IDEAL SYSTEM - FORM 2907

DATE 19____	NAME, LAST ADDRESS AND REASON CHARGED OFF	1 DATE ACCOUNT CLOSED	2 AMOUNT CHARGED OFF	3 TOTALS
1				
2				
3				
4				
5				
6				
7				
8				
9				
10				
11				
12				
13				
14				
15				
16				
17				
18				
19				
20				
21				
22				
23				
24				
25				
26				
27				
28				
29				
30				
31				
32				
33				

DEDUCTIONS

DEPRECIATION (WEAR AND TEAR) OF BUSINESS PROPERTY

THE IDEAL SYSTEM, REG. U. S. PAT. OFFICE. MADE IN U.S.A.

IDEAL SYSTEM - FORM 2907A

DATE 19___	1 KIND OF PROPERTY	2 DATE ACQUIRED	3 COSTS	4 DEPRECIATION IN ALL PRIOR YEARS	5 REMAINING COST TO BE RECOVERED	6 ESTIMATED TOTAL LIFE	7 ESTIMATED REMAINING LIFE	8 DEPRECIATION ALLOWABLE THIS YEAR
1								
2								
3								
4								
5								
6								
7								
8								
9								
10								
11								
12								
13								
14								
15								
16								
17								
18								
19								
20								
21								
22								
23								
24								
25								
26								
27								
28								
29								
30								
31								
32								
33								

IDEAL SYSTEM—FORM 2904

BALANCE SHEET
YEAR 19____

ASSETS AND LIABILITIES AT BEGINNING OF YEAR

ASSETS

CURRENT ASSETS:
Cash on Hand ....
Cash in Bank ....
Notes Receivable ....
Accounts Receivable ....
Inventory Stock on Hand ....
    TOTAL ....

FIXED ASSETS:
Land ....
Buildings ....
Equipment ....
Furniture and Furnishings ....
    TOTAL ....

OTHER ASSETS:
....
....
    TOTAL ....
    TOTAL ASSETS ....

LIABILITIES

CURRENT LIABILITIES:
Notes Payable ....
Accounts Payable ....
    TOTAL ....

FIXED LIABILITIES:
Mortgages ....
    TOTAL ....
    TOTAL LIABILITIES ....

NET WORTH (Deduct Total Liabilities from Total Assets and enter the difference here) ....
    TOTAL LIABILITIES AND NET WORTH ....

ASSETS AND LIABILITIES AT END OF YEAR

ASSETS

CURRENT ASSETS:
Cash on Hand ....
Cash in Bank ....
Notes Receivable ....
Accounts Receivable ....
Inventory Stock on Hand ....
    TOTAL ....

FIXED ASSETS:
Land ....
Buildings ....
Equipment ....
Furniture and Furnishings ....
    TOTAL ....

OTHER ASSETS:
....
....
    TOTAL ....
    TOTAL ASSETS ....

LIABILITIES

CURRENT LIABILITIES:
Notes Payable ....
Accounts Payable ....
    TOTAL ....

FIXED LIABILITIES:
Mortgages ....
    TOTAL ....
    TOTAL LIABILITIES ....

NET WORTH (Deduct Total Liabilities from Total Assets and enter the difference here) ....
    TOTAL LIABILITIES AND NET WORTH ....

INDEX TO ACCOUNTS
A - L

IDEAL SYSTEM - FORM 162-A

NAME	PAGE NO.	NAME	PAGE NO.	NAME	PAGE NO.
A		**E**		**I**	
B		**F**		**J**	
C		**G**		**K**	
D		**H**		**L**	

INDEX TO ACCOUNTS
M - Z

IDEAL SYSTEM - FORM 162-M

NAME	PAGE NO.	NAME	PAGE NO.	NAME	PAGE NO.
M		**Q**		**U**	
N		**R**		**V**	
O		**S**		**W**	
P		**T**		**X Y Z**	

ACCOUNTS RECEIVABLE

NAME

ADDRESS

ACCOUNTS RECEIVABLE

IDEAL SYSTEM - FORM 804

DATE 19__	NO.	MEMO	CHARGES	CREDITS	BALANCE	
						1
						2
						3
						4
						5
						6
						7
						8
						9
						10
						11
						12
						13
						14
						15
						16
						17
						18
						19
						20
						21
						22
						23
						24
						25
						26
						27
						28
						29
						30
						31
						32
						33

NAME

ADDRESS

THE IDEAL SYSTEM. REG. U. S. PAT. OFFICE. MADE IN U.S.A.

DATE 19__	NO.	MEMO	CHARGES	CREDITS	BALANCE	
						1
						2
						3
						4
						5
						6
						7
						8
						9
						10
						11
						12
						13
						14
						15
						16
						17
						18
						19
						20
						21
						22
						23
						24
						25
						26
						27
						28
						29
						30
						31
						32
						33

THE IDEAL SYSTEM CO., LOS ANGELES
PUBLISHED BY
REG. U. S. PAT. OFFICE
THE IDEAL SYSTEM

ACCOUNTS PAYABLE

NAME

ADDRESS

PAGE NO.

NAME

ADDRESS

THE IDEAL SYSTEM, REG. U.S. PAT. OFFICE. MADE IN U.S.A.

IDEAL SYSTEM - FORM 106

DATE 19__	MEMO.	AMOUNT OF PURCHASE	DISCOUNT	AMOUNT PAID	BALANCE DUE	DATE 19__	MEMO.	AMOUNT OF PURCHASE	DISCOUNT	AMOUNT PAID	BALANCE DUE
1						1					
2						2					
3						3					
4						4					
5						5					
6						6					
7						7					
8						8					
9						9					
10						10					
11						11					
12						12					
13						13					
14						14					
15						15					
16						16					
17						17					
18						18					
19						19					
20						20					
21						21					
22						22					
23						23					
24						24					
25						25					
26						26					
27						27					
28						28					
29						29					
30						30					
31						31					
32						32					
33						33					

AN EASY WAY TO KEEP PETTY CASH

OFFICE FUND VOUCHER

Voucher No._____

From_____19____to_____19____ Paid by Check No. _____

DATE	RECEIPT NO.	TO WHOM PAID	FOR WHAT	ACCT. NO.	AMOUNT

AUDITED BY | APPROVED BY

TOTAL DISBURSED

CASH ON HAND

AMOUNT OF FUND

DISTRIBUTION

Courtesy Burroughs Corporation
Business Forms Division

*Automatic tellers are machines with built-in alarms hooked up to comput-
ers. The customer inserts an ID card, enters a security card that verifies
and identifies the user, and via instructions in the "window," presses the
proper combination of buttons for each transaction. The transaction receipt is printed in duplicate—one copy which, along with the card (as the
last step), is returned to the customer; the other to be retained for an audit
trail. In a matter of minutes it allows customers to make deposits, cash
withdrawals, loan payments, account transfers where appropriate, payments on credit cards and utility bills, and it even has a "hot card" capability that retrieves invalid cards.*

*DOCUTEL TOTAL TELLER®
Courtesy Docutel Corporation, P.O. Box 22306,
Dallas, Texas 75222*

GLOSSARY

ACCELERATION CLAUSE—mortgage or trust deed provision which makes the balance due and payable upon the happening of a certain event.

ACCOUNTS PAYABLE—money the company owes.

ACCOUNTS RECEIVABLE—the amount due from a firm's customers, usually maturing in less than one year.

AFFIDAVIT—a written statement of facts sworn to or affirmed by oath before an authorized official (usually a Notary Public).

AMORTIZE—to pay off by installment payments.

ANNUITY—the interest or dividends paid annually on an investment of money.

ASSET—items of ownership capable of being converted into cash.

ASSUMPTION (OF MORTGAGE OR TRUST DEED)—taking over the primary liability for payment of the existing mortgage or trust deed.

BALANCE SHEET—a financial statement showing assets, liabilities and net worth as of a specific date.

BALLOON PAYMENT—the final payment of a note which is more than the preceding installments.

BANK—an organization that lends, borrows, exchanges, issues or cares for money.

BENEFICIARY—the recipient of funds or other property under a trust, will, etc.

BINDER—an informal contract, with deposit, followed by formal contract.

BOND—(AN IOU)—a legal instrument wherein borrower promises to pay a stated sum to lender.

CASHIER'S CHECK—a check drawn by a bank on its own funds and signed by the cashier.

CERTIFIED CHECK—a check bearing a guarantee of payment by the bank on which it is drawn.

CHECK—a written order to a bank to pay an amount from funds on deposit.

COMMERCIAL BANK—a bank specializing in checking accounts and short term loans.

COMPOUND INTEREST—interest on the original principal of a loan plus accrued interest.

CONTRACT—a deliberate agreement between two competent parties to perform or refrain from doing a specific act.

CREDIT—(banking) an individual's power to command funds later to be repaid; (bookkeeping) an entry of payment received.

CREDITOR—one to whom money is owed.

DEBIT—(banking) a charge against a bank deposit account; (bookkeeping) a recorded item of debt.

DEBT—that which is owed.

DEBTOR—one who owes.

DEMAND DEPOSIT—a checking account (no advance withdrawal notice required).

DISCOUNT—the sale of a note for less than its face value.

DRAFT—a document for transferring money.

ENDORSEMENT—a signature on the back of a promissory note or check for the purpose of transferring ownership.

EQUITY—the interest of an owner in property over and above liens against it.

ESCROW—a written document put into the custody of a third party until certain conditions are fulfilled.

FEDERAL DEPOSIT INSURANCE CORPORATION—a public corporation, established in 1933, which insures, up to a specified amount, all demand deposits of member banks.

FEDERAL RESERVE SYSTEM—a federal banking system under the control of a Board of Governors (7 officials) which supervises 12 Reserve banks and 25 branches. These officials have the major responsibility for formulating national monetary policy.

FORECLOSE—to sell, in the event of default, the property pledged as security for a debt.

GROSS—without deductions.

INTEREST—a sum paid or charged for the use of money.

LIABILITY—money owed.

LIEN—the charges on property to pay a debt.

LOAN—the grant of the temporary use of something.

MONEY ORDER—an order for the payment of money.

MORTGAGE—the document used to make property security to pay a debt.

NEGOTIABLE—capable of being legally transferred to another.

NET—that which remains after deductions.

NOTARY PUBLIC—an official authorized to certify or attest documents, affidavits, etc., and to take depositions.

NOTE—a paper acknowledging a debt and promising payment.

OVERDRAFT—a draft of more than one's credit.

POINT—one percent of the amount of a loan paid to lender at the time the loan is made so that the loan can be obtained.

PREPAYMENT PENALTY—a clause in a note providing for a penalty in the event the note is paid off early.

PRINCIPAL—money or capital rather than interest or income.

SAVINGS AND LOAN ASSOCIATION—a cooperative savings institution, chartered and regulated by a State or the Federal Government. It receives deposits in exchange for shares of ownership and invests its funds primarily in loans secured by first mortgages on homes.

SAVINGS BANK—a bank that receives time deposits only and pays interest to its depositors.

SAVINGS BOND—a United States Government bond with principal amounts up to $10,000.

STATEMENT—a report of an account given to show the balance due.

STRAIGHT NOTE—a note wherein the principal is paid in one sum.

TIME DEPOSIT—a deposit that can be withdrawn by the depositor only after advance notice has been given or after the elapse of an agreed period of time.

TRAVELER'S CHECKS—checks·sold by a bank, etc., that can be cashed by countersigning in the presence of a payee.

TRUST ACCOUNT—wherein money is deposited by an agent for the account of a principal. The account must be kept intact and may not be co-mingled.

TRUSTEE—a person who holds the title to property for the benefit of another.

TRUST DEED—a deed by which a trustor conveys his title to the trustee as security for the payment of a debt.

12

successful reading, comprehension and memory aids

Fast reading with good comprehension and the ability to concentrate are tools which make the secretary's job easier. A few easy steps such as reading with your hand, doing eye exercises and learning to recall will improve both your reading rate and comprehension. An all important factor is word recognition. To start you out, follow commonly used prefixes and suffixes and their meanings as well as Greek and Latin roots and their meanings. Build a larger vocabulary by learning ten new words a day, doing crossword puzzles and playing word games. Words are communication, and part of communication is giving clear instructions, so a few pointers and examples are included.

It's one thing to read or see something and another to remember it. The key to remembering something is association—use lists, signs, codes, pictures and the other ideas shown here or devise something new.

Proofreading becomes easier when you apply some of your new found reading skill or use some of the tips suggested.

Just as reading is a skill, conversation is an art—the art of talking together. By applying basic principles, you can not only participate more fully, but you can guide so everyone gets the information and enjoyment.

199

HOW TO IMPROVE YOUR READING RATE, COMPREHENSION AND RECALL

1. **Always read silently.**
2. **Concentrate.**
3. **Continually improve your vocabulary. Word recognition = instant understanding.** As a start, learn the prefixes, roots and suffixes on the following pages.
4. **Do read with your hands.** Begin by moving your fingers slowly under each line. This pushes your eye.
5. Begin to look for **ideas** (Subject + Verb + "What") at a pace which **allows comprehension.**
6. Remembering that **paragraphs are built around a central theme,** guide your hand in an "S" to pick out **main ideas** at a pace which **does not sacrifice comprehension.**
7. Do **eye exercises** daily. *Consciously widen your field of vision vertically and horizontally.* Look at and digest the whole as the sum of its parts. Choose your own subjects—a street, a display case, a horizon.
8. Look for **themes** in the world around you—coordination of textures, the areas of light and dark in a landscape (squint), watch machines function, look at shapes and sizes in relation to each other.
9. Choose a scene—look away—attempt to recall all the elements and their placement until you can. Begin with a written list—then go to a mental list.
10. Using your hand and the "S", try to digest two paragraphs at a time. Look for themes, descriptions, functions, purpose. Try to "see" what the author is saying. Summarize content upon completion—beginning with a written list, then go to a mental list. Go as fast as you can **without sacrificing comprehension.**
11. Practice steps 7, 8 and 9; apply step 10 and increase paragraphs as you are able **without sacrificing comprehension.**

HOW TO ACHIEVE BETTER CONCENTRATION

Concentration depends on attention control. Distractions divide attention and take energy away from concentration. To be most productive:

1. Do detailed work in the most quiet possible.
2. Background music should be *background*.
3. Use earplugs if necessary.
4. Relax.
5. Mentally, deliberately close out any thoughts except for the project at hand.
6. Work rapidly (against a clock if you must) to maintain attention span.
7. In conversation, when taking dictation, when listening to instructions, when trying to make a decision—**focus only on the immediate topic.**

PREFIXES

a, ab: away, from
a, ac, ad, af, ag, an, ar, as, at: to (adhere)
amphi: around, on both sides
ana: against, back
ante: before
anti: against, opposite
apo: away, off
arch: ancient, chief, main
auto: alone

be: over, throughout
bene: good, well
bi: two

cata: down
cent: one hundred
circum: around
cis: on this side of
co, cog, col, com, con, cor: together, with
contra, contro, counter: against
crypto: hidden

de: down, from
demi: half
di: twice
dia: through
dis: apart

e: out
em: in, into
ep, eph, ephi, epi: upon
eu: happy, well
ex: without
extra: besides, beyond, outside

fore: before, in front of

hecto: one hundred
hemi: half
hept: seven
hex: six
holo: entirely, wholly
hyper: excessive
hypo: below, beneath, under

il, im, ir: in, into, on
in: not
inte, inter: among, between
intra, intro: on the inside
ise: to cause to resemble
iso: equal

macro: large
mal: bad, evil
mega: great, mighty
meso: intermediate
meta: across, beyond
micro: small
mili: one thousand
mis: bad, defect, error, wrong
mono: single
multi: many

neo: current
nil: nothing
non: not

ob, oc, of, op: against, toward
octo: eight
off: from
ortho: right, straight, true
out: beyond, complete
over: above, beyond

pan, panto: all, every
para: by the side of
peri: around, surrounding
post: after, behind
pre: before
pro: toward
proto: ahead, early
pseudo: false

quasi: as if

re: back, over again
retro: backward, behind

semi: half, not fully
sub, suc, suf, sug, sum, sup, sur, sus: below, beneath, under
super: above, on top of, over
syl, sym, syn: together with

trans: on the other side of
tri: three

ultra: beyond, on the other side of
uni: one

vice: in the place of another

GREEK AND LATIN ROOTS

act, ag: arrive, do
acu: sharp
agi: move
ali: other
ani: year
anthrop: man
audi: hear
auto: self

bibl: book
belli: war
bio: life

cap, cept, cip: hold, take
capit: head
ced: go, yield
chal: hot
chrom: color
chron: time
cip: to take
civ: citizen
clam: cry out
clus: shut
cogn: know
cola: filter

cord: heart, string
corpor: body
cosm: world
cour: heart
crat: authority
cycl: circle, wheel

dei: god
dem: people
dict: say
duc: lead
dyna: power

endo: within
enni: year
ev: age

fac, fect, fic: do, make
feder: trust
fense: keep off
fer: bear, bring
fi, ficci: make
fid: faith
fin: end
fluvio: river
format: form
fort: strength
fum: smoke

gast: stomach
gen: to be born
germin: grow
gest: carry
gon: angle
grad, gress: take steps, to go
graph, gram, scrib, script: write
gratulat: rejoice
gyn: woman

habilet: suitable
helio: sun
hetero: different
homo: same
hum: earth
hydro: water
hypno: sleep

jec: throw
judi: judge
junc: join
juris: law

later: side
lectu: gather knowledge
leg: law
liber: free
licit: permit
litera: letters

lith: stone
loco: place
lumin: light

magni: big
mar: sea
matr: mother
med: heal
mega: huge
mess: send
mete, metr: measure
migrat: wander
mise, mit: send, throw
miso: hate
mogre: move
monstr: show
morse: death

nat: born
neo, novel: new
no: to set in motion
nunci: declare, warn
nym: name

omni: all
oper: work
orama: view
ossi, oste: bone

pan: all
path: feeling, suffering
patr: father
ped: child, foot
pel: throw
pen: almost
phil: kind, loving
phon: sound
photo: light
pict: paint
plac: to calm
plic: bend, fold
plur: more
poly: many, much
pon: place, set
port: carry

portion: share
potent: powerful
prim: first
punct: dot, point
pyro: fire

rect, reg: rule, straight
ri: laughter
roga: ask

sati: more than enough
scop: see
sect: cut
sequ: follow
sesqui: one and one half
signi: sign
simile: like, same
sist: stand
soph: wise
spec, spect, spic: look, see
sphere: ball
spons: pledge
sta, stat: stand
stereo: solid
stow: place
stru: build
sumpt: use, waste away

techni: art
tele: far
tempor: time
ten, tent, tin: hold
tend: stretch
terra: land
thanatos: death
therm: heat
toler: endure
tort: twist
tract: drag, draw
trib: payment

ultimo: last

vac, voc: call
vale: be well

ven: come, go
veri: truth
vest: clothe
vid, vis: see
vigr: energy
vinc: conquer
vivi: alive

xantho: yellow
xeno: foreign, strange
xero: dry
xylo: wood

zoo: animal
zygo: yoke
zyme: leaven
zymo: fermentation

SUFFIXES

able, abil, ible: having the power to
acy: office, quality, state
ade: act of
age: state of
al, ial: of, like, suitable for
an, ian: belonging to, of
ana: anecdotes, sayings, writings
ance, ancy: art of, quality of
ant, ent: **adj.**—that has
      noun—a person or thing that
ar, ary, ory: **adj.**—relating to
arch: ruler
ard: one who carries action to excess
asis: a condition resembling
ate, ite: **adj.**—of or characteristic of
      noun—object of an action
ation, ition: act of or result of
ative: relating to

cian: one who
cide: kill
cracy: type of government
cule: small
cy: state of being

dom: condition, quality

ean: belonging to
ee: recipient of a special action
eer: to have to do with
en: to make
ence: degree, quality, result, state

end: that which
eous: like
er: one who, that which
ery, ry: place to
esce, escence: giving off or reflecting
    light
escent: slightly
ese: in the language or style of
esis: process of
esque: like
ess: female
et (m): added to nouns means little
etic: like
ette (f): added to nouns means little
eur: one who

hood: state of

ia: diseases, names of countries
iatric, iatry: medical treatment
ic, ical: having characteristic or nature
    of
id: a thing belonging to or connected
    with
ier: a person concerned with a spe-
    cific action or thing
ile: having to do with, of
ine: used to form commercial names,
    feminine names, nature of
ion, sion: act or condition of
ious: characterized by
ise: to cause to resemble, make

ish: belonging to, of
ism: condition of being, doctrine of
ist: a person who does, makes or
      practices
ite, ity: quality of
itis, osis: disease
ive: of, relating to, tending to
ize: to cause or make

kin: little

less: without
let: small
lite: used in names of fossils, minerals,
      rocks

ment: act, art, fact, process, result

ness: state of
nomy: law, rule

old: resemble
ology: science, study of, word
or: a person or thing that
ose, osity, ous: characterized by, full

phile: loving
phobia: fear

ship: office, position, state of
some: having

tomy: piece of, slice of
tude: condition, state of
ty: condition of, quality of

ule: little
ure: agent, instrument, scope of

y: characterized by

HOW TO GIVE CLEAR INSTRUCTIONS

      Assemble your facts
        Answer

                    Who
                    What
                    Where
                    When
                    How
                    Why
  Make up a form and fill in the blanks

CALL TO MESSENGER SERVICE
TO PICK UP AND DELIVER
FILE TO CLIENT

Who	Your company name and address
What	Large manila envelope (approximate dimensions)
Where	From your office to *name and address*

When	Day and date of pick up and delivery
How	Name of messenger service
Why	Not applicable here
Additional Info	None

RETURN OF INCORRECT ORDER FROM STATIONERY STORE

Who	Your office name
What	Note pads
Where	Your office address
When	Day and date
How	Stationery store's delivery truck
Why	Didn't order
Additional Info	Request no charge

DELEGATION OF WORK WITHIN OFFICE

Who	Ms. Roberts
What	Attached order for postage
Where	Not applicable
When	As soon as possible
How	Via màil
Why	Not applicable
Additional Info	Obtain check for amount of total made payable to U. S. Postal Service

ORDERING PRINTING FROM COPY COMPANY

Who	Your company name and address
What	100 copies of attached press release on 8½″ × 11″ paper
Where	Name and address of copy company
When	Need by time, day and date
How	Specify printing process
Why	Not applicable
Additional Info	Call Barbara when ready (phone number)

15 SUCCESSFUL MEMORY AIDS

Use any or all of these as suggested or innovate—**the important thing is to use what works for you.**

1. Daily "TO DO" lists—mark priorities, record progress, carry to next day.
2. *Errand list*—map out stops so you don't retrace your steps—try making a circle from start.
3. Post signs such as "Remember Original" on the copy machine where it can't be missed.
4. **Write** step by step routines for new tasks.
5. Establish definite places for things—automatic acts (telephone messages in slot with name) save time.
6. Use first letter codes to remember lists—the colors of the spectrum in their proper order are red, orange, yellow, green, blue, violet—Roy G. Bv.
7. *Word Association*—remember the jingle "**Chi**cken in the **car**, the can can't **go**, that's how you spell Chicago."
8. Remember to a musical beat—Miss iss ippi.
9. **Rote** learning **does** work—look at a word you are trying to learn to spell, write it, close your eyes, picture it in your mind's eye. Do this as many times as it takes for the word to become a familiar unit.
10. Easy ways to remember numbers
    Use the telephone number method technique:
    xxx-xxxx
    62183429564321396873222268977 becomes
    621 8342   956 4321   396 8732   226 8977
    or use the Social Security number method:
    09838478920938518907932 4961 becomes
    098 38 4789   209 38 5189   079 32 4961
11. *Alphabetize a list*

erasers	carbon paper
pens	erasers
pencils	minute book paper
ring binder	pencils
minute book paper	pens
reinforcements	reinforcements
carbon paper	ring binder

12. *Or organize a list according to categories*

coffee	coffee
note pads	sugar
stationery	first aid supplies
pencils	note pads
first aid supplies	stationery
sugar	pencils

13. *Or remember by making up or using common acronyms* (An acronym is a word formed from the first or first few letters of a series of words)

ABC	American Broadcasting Company
CBS	Columbia Broadcasting System
COD	Cash On Delivery
CPA	Certified Public Accountant
NBC	National Broadcasting Company
RADAR	RAdio Detecting And Ranging
SONAR	SOund Navigation And Ranging
TV	Television
US	United States

14. *Remember by word pictures*

separate becomes sep a rate

station**er**y is made of pap**er**

a princi**ple** is a r**ule**

Capit**ol** is **o**nly the building in Washington in which the United States Congress meets

the gaso**line line**

p**ea**ce is **ca**lm but a **pie**ce of **pie**

if something is **real**, it is a **fact**; but **reel** the **eel**

st**ee**l is m**eta**l, but st**ea**l a wallet

15. *Remember by "seeing" mental pictures*

"See" a room in your mind's eye, or a face, or a street, or a list, or a number—or practice until you do.

PROOFREADING SIMPLIFIED

1. Proofread by taking "word" pictures (as your reading ability increases, take "line" pictures) as you move your hand under each line.

2. For highly technical matter, read to someone else.

3. Proof continuous documents page by page as each is completed.
4. Proof **duplicate originals** by typing and proofing one, typing the second from the first, the third from the second, and so on, proofing as you type.
5. If you are retyping a page because an erasure shows or because there are a few errors only, hold finished page over the page with the problem, facing the light. Words should match perfectly except for the change(s).

GETTING THE MOST FROM A CONVERSATION

Conversation is the art of talking together; it is a verbal exchange of ideas, opinions and/or facts. To participate fully:

DO	DON'T
1. Explain instead of tell	1. React emotionally
2. Talk *with* instead of *to*	2. Demean
3. Listen intelligently	3. Antagonize
4. Question courteously	4. Wound
5. Reply candidly	5. Battle

13

talking shop

It is the "behind the scenes" knowledge that you will learn in this chapter. The tips and tricks of using your tools and supplies such as: a "see through" engineering triangle makes a fine line guide for copy typing, sharpening your scissors by cutting through sandpaper, knowing that peroxide will loosen screws and using a magnifying glass ruler.

Also included is "how to do" information for the typewriter that you will need in order to know how to center a line horizontally, how to justify right margins, how to draw vertical lines, how to fit tight column totals, how to correct pages bound at the top and how to perform similar tasks.

Described within is how to care for and clean your typewriter (did you know you should never oil your typewriter and that certain cleaning fluids may have harmful effects on the plastic parts and painted portions?) and a checklist for proper typewriter operation in case you turn it on and nothing happens.

For the secretary in today's world who is becoming more and more involved with printing, included are some fundamental graphic arts tips such as: the basic kinds of erasers available and which do what for artwork; basic information about pencils, leads and ink; and tricks to keep bottles from spilling and stacked papers from slipping. And photographs—how to mark them, how to mount them, how to uncurl them, how to handle them, how to hold them, how not to lose them and how to mail them properly.

EFFECTIVE USE OF TOOLS
AND SUPPLIES

- An excellent line guide for copy typing is a "see through" engineering triangle in soft green or yellow.
- Paint measurements on scissors blades with nailpolish.
- Write special mailing instructions on envelopes using pens with waterproof ink.
- Sharpen scissors blades by rubbing them across pumice stone or by cutting through sandpaper.
- Label keys and/or color code keys with nailpolish and/or purchase colored keys.
- Keep a small pencil sharpener at your desk for emergencies.
- Keep the first aid box well stocked.
- A kneaded eraser will clean type bar adding machines and type bar typewriters.
- If copies from the copy machine are recorded for billing, paste the chart on the top of the copier with a pencil on a string also taped to the machine.
- If stamps are charged back to a partner or division, keep charge book near postage scale.
- Type addresses directly on envelopes, omitting label.
- A magnifying glass ruler is handy.
- Black or blue ink shows up best on yellow paper.
- Pencil creates glare for typist.
- Matte carbon paper rarely smudges.
- Correction paint sometimes cracks if used on erasable paper.
- Typewriter ribbons will dry out.
- A ream of paper has 500 sheets.
- Use a backing sheet with a black horizontal line heavy enough to show through to typing page positioned as the last page line.
- Peroxide will loosen tight screws.
- A T-square and a drawing board insure straight lines.
- Always erase with the grain of the paper (eraser rule is soft eraser for soft paper, hard eraser for hard paper).

- Use carbon ribbons on a spool fitting standard electric typewriters with corresponding lift-off tabs which remove letters from paper by picking up the ink instead of covering the letter with chalk.

TYPING TIPS AND TRICKS

Pica type *has 10 digits to 1 horizontal inch.*
Elite type *has 12 digits to 1 horizontal inch.*
There are *6 lines* of typing *to one vertical inch.*
There are *85 horizontal pica spaces on a page 8½" wide.*
There are *102 horizontal elite spaces on a page 8½" wide.*
There are *66 vertical lines on a page 11" long.*

HOW TO CENTER A LINE HORIZONTALLY

1. Assume a 60 space line on a pica typewriter with margins of 12 and 72.
2. Count total digits to be centered and include punctuation and spaces (assume a total of 20).
3. Subtract 2 from 1 (answer is 40).
4. Divide answer to 3 in half (answer is 20).
5. Add answer to 4 to left hand margin in 1 (12 + 20 = 32, which is where to begin typing line to be centered).

HOW TO JUSTIFY RIGHT MARGINS

Justify your copy by using the half space lever twice for each letter to be added or removed, as follows:

- Set a right margin.
- Type as close to that margin as possible.
- For each line you type, count the number of characters short of the margin or beyond the margin that the line runs. Use the margin release lever when it is necessary to type beyond the margin.
- For each space short of the margin, add two half spaces. For each space beyond the margin, eliminate two half spaces. Write down the number of spaces you must add or subtract.

For example:
- Set margins at 30 and 60.

Justified copy looks very much like the printed material you see everyday in the newspaper or magazines that you read.	ok +1 −2	Justified copy looks very much like the printed material you see everyday in the newspaper or magazines that you read.

If you do not have a half space lever on your typewriter, either move the paper manually or move the carriage manually.

Courtesy IBM

HOW TO INSERT A LETTER

Erase the incorrect word.

Move the carriage to the space after the last letter of the word just typed.

Depress the half space lever or move the carriage or the paper manually.

Keep the half space lever depressed until you wish to insert a half space (probably at the end of the word) or move the paper or the carriage manually at the time you wish to insert the letter.

HOW TO REMOVE A LETTER

Erase the entire word.

Move the carriage to the space after the last letter of the word just typed.

Space once.

Depress the half space lever and hold it until the new word is typed or move the paper or the carriage manually.

Release the half space lever.

Depress the space bar and continue typing.

Example: "He will come." Substitute "can" for "will."
- Erase "will"—this makes it necessary to accommodate 1 space (2 half spaces).

- Add the half spaces before and after the word "can."

He will come.   He can come.

Courtesy IBM

HOW TO CREATE LIGATURES

Type the first letter.
Backspace.
Depress and hold the half space lever or move the paper or
the carriage manually.
Type the remainder of the word.

HOW TO DRAW VERTICAL LINES

Put your pen or pencil in the notch of the cardholder.
Hold pen steady, pull line finder lever forward.
Manually turn the platen.

HOW TO UNDERSCORE BACKWARDS

Hold down underscore key and backspace key at the same
time.

HOW TO TYPE LINES AT THE VERY
BOTTOM OF THE PAGE

As your backing page, use a sheet of paper longer than the
one on which you are typing. Be sure they are paper clipped at the top. (You can put a drop of rubber cement at the
lower two corners to make sure there is no slippage—when
done, the pages will pull apart and the cement will rub off.)

FIT TIGHT COLUMN TOTALS BY "STAIR
STEPPING" THEM

116,339,247	98,762,941	643,977,521	970,331,699	144,985,889	653,221
741,105,309	34,908,862	67,421,691	894,570,344	966,984,831	985,942
857,444,556					
	133,671,803				
		711,399,212			
			1,864,902,043		
				1,111,970,720	
					1,639,163

SAVE TIME USING A PARTIAL
CARRIAGE RETURN

Set tab stops.
Touch the carriage return followed by the tab key as soon as
  the carriage return has passed the tab stop.
Use for typing addresses on envelopes or for columns.

HOW TO CORRECT PAGES
BOUND AT THE TOP

Insert the whole document as if one page.
Pull paper release lever forward.
Flip to desired sheet.
Push paper release lever back.
Align, correct.

HOW TO CARE FOR AND CLEAN YOUR
TYPEWRITER

Cover the typewriter with the dust cover at the end of each
  day.
If you use a carriage machine, move the carriage to the far
  right or left when erasing so eraser particles fall *outside* the
  machine.
If you use a machine on which the carriage does not move, be
  careful not to drop jewelry, hair ornaments, pens or pencils
  in the machine.
Clean typewriter keys by using a dry bristle brush, with a
  brushing motion toward you and away from the type basket. If your type becomes caked with dirt, use a tapping
  motion with the ends of the bristles of your type cleaning
  brush. Finish the cleaning by wiping the type faces with a
  clean, dry cloth.
If you do use a cleaning fluid, moisten a cloth *slightly* and dab
  the type faces lightly.

Avoid excessive use of any fluid and do not oil your machine.
Oil used indiscriminately may contact rubber parts and cause damage.

To clean a typing element, remove it from the machine, hold and, using a dry bristle typewriter brush, brush away from you.

Type cleaners in sheet form are also available.

Certain cleaning fluids may have harmful effects on the plastic parts and painted portions of your typewriter. Use only a mild detergent.

Courtesy IBM

CHECKLIST FOR PROPER TYPEWRITER OPERATION

Be sure the electric cord is correctly plugged into the outlet.

The ON portion of the On/Off Control should be depressed.

Make certain the Ribbon/Stencil Control is not in stencil position and that the Multiple Copy Control is appropriately set.

If the carriage will not move, turn the motor OFF for a few seconds, then ON. Press the Margin Release Key or Tab Key to release the carriage then try to move the carriage by hand, but do not force it.

When erratic line spacing occurs, check to see that the line finder is engaged.

Remove the element to check for a broken tooth at the bottom. If a tooth is broken the element will have to be replaced.

On a fabric ribbon typewriter, reverse the ribbon *manually* and continue typing.

Courtesy IBM

GRAPHIC ARTS TIPS

Use an old telephone book as an aid in paste-up by using the top page as a back-up for brushing on rubber cement. Discard the page; another is ready.

Make your own rubber stamp by drawing your new image (in reverse so it will print to read from left to right) on a piece of rubber or on a soft red rubber eraser and cut away the part you do not want to print. Carefully remove the rubber from the old stamp and glue the new one to the base of the handle.

KINDS OF ERASERS AND THEIR USES

Soft pliable rubber eraser is an all purpose eraser that cleans as it erases.

Kneaded eraser for pencil, chalk, pastel and charcoal (as well as cleaning typewriter keys). It can be shaped to any convenient form and is non-abrasive.

Art gum eraser is free of grease and cannot scratch. It crumbles. It is used to remove pencil marks from inked art.

Plastic (vinyl) drafting eraser for use on tracing cloth, film or paper. It is hard and does not crumble.

Paper-wrapped erasers are pencil shaped, soft or abrasive. For use in very small areas and can be pointed.

Dry, clean pad eraser comes in a mesh bag with gum bits that sift through. It is used to clean large jobs such as signs and charts.

Fiberglass eraser is cigar-shaped. Has a fiberglass brush tip and is used for extremely difficult erasures.

Electric erasers for general use. Move them gently in a rotating manner. Nibs are soft or abrasive and are interchangeable.

OTHER KINDS OF "ERASERS"

Razor blades and knives can be used to remove heavy deposits of ink and paint. Use a gentle scraping motion. When you are near the surface of the paper, switch over to one of the other more conventional methods.

Cotton balls, swabs and small pieces of clean rags can be used with rubber cement thinner to take grease, scuff marks and other stubborn marks away. Use a gentle scrubbing action.

Erasing fluids (two bottles—one hypochlorite and the other an acid) can be used successively on the mark and removed with a blotter.

Special abrasive powders are made for use in airbrushes for extremely difficult situations when all other erasing methods have failed.

INFORMATION ABOUT PENCILS

Pencils are graded from 9H (hardest) to 6B (softest). The lead is thinnest in hard pencils and large in soft.

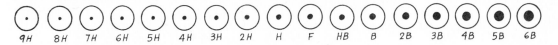

Always sharpen this end of a wood clenched pencil—the end away from the marking.

A pencil extender can be used for small pencils and will save money. The extender gives continued balance.

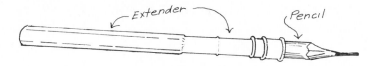

Stabilo pencils come in many grades and colors and are used for marking on glass, acetate, plastic, metal and glossy surfaces.

From Studio Tips for Artists and Graphic Designers *by Bill Gray,* © *1976 by Litten Educational Publishing, Inc. Reprinted by permission of Van Nostrand Reinhold Company.*

Mechanical pencils are most economical. When needed, leads are easily replaced and can be purchased in all grades which are inter-changeable in the same pencil.

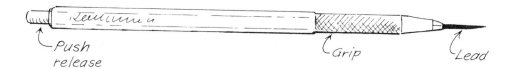

Push release   *Grip*   *Lead*

If you use many grades of lead in mechanical pencils, it is a good idea to use one pencil for each grade and to mark the grade on the side of the pencil.

If you are using a wood clenched pencil and are in a hurry to complete a project, *sharpen both ends. One* end can have a *chisel edge*, the *other a point*.

FOR INK

Mark your bottles with the dates on which you receive them as ink can dry out.

Touch the tip of a ball point pen (which has ink in it and does not write, or which is new) with something hot (a flame or the end of a cigarette) to make it work.

HOW TO PREVENT INK OR ANY OTHER BOTTLE
FROM TIPPING OVER

Cut a strip of paper about 6″ × 1″ and cut a slit in the paper, as shown.

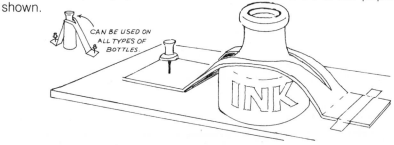

CAN BE USED ON ALL TYPES OF BOTTLES

INK

From Studio Tips for Artists and Graphic Designers *by Bill Gray,* © *1976 by Litten Educational Publishing, Inc. Reprinted by permission of Van Nostrand Reinhold Company.*

HOW TO PREVENT STACKED PIECES FROM SLIDING

Cut a stiff card and fold as shown.

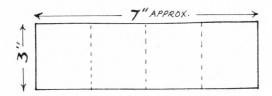

Shape a "stopper" and secure to table top or floor with tape or pins.

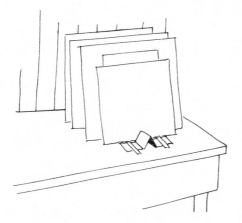

From Studio Tips for Artists and Graphic Designers *by Bill Gray,* © *1976 by Litten Educational Publishing, Inc. Reprinted by permission of Van Nostrand Reinhold Company.*

HOW TO WORK WITH PHOTOGRAPHS

Never write instructions on the back of a photograph—especially not with a hard ball-point pen . . . or a marker pen. The ink of a marker pen may bleed through and stain the photo on the other side. A stabilo pencil is made especially for writing on glossy surfaces.

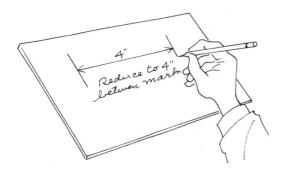

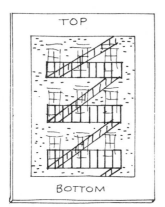

Always mark TOP and BOTTOM on all photos, particularly on photos in which the subject is not easily recognized.

Always ask for margins on photos where you can mark instructions.

---

5 WAYS TO FLATTEN A CURLED PRINT

1. A curled print is carefully uncurled in the direction opposite the curl on a cardboard tube, fastened at the ends with tape, and left for a few days.

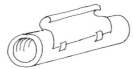

2. If the print is nonglossy the back of the print can be worked back and forth against a smooth corner.

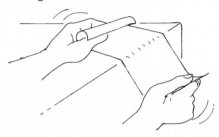

3. First soak the print, if it is unretouched, in water for 5 or 10 minutes. Then hang the wet print on a clothesline and weight it at the bottom.

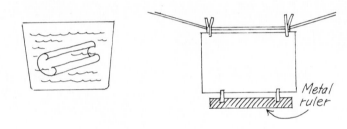

Metal ruler

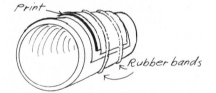

Print

Rubber bands

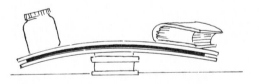

4. You can wrap thin cards around the print and then wrap it on a cardboard tube as in (1) above. This method is for extremely fragile prints.

5. The print can be inserted between cards, as shown, and bent in the opposite direction of the curl by weights on both sides.

HANDLING ARTWORK

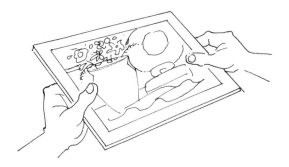 

Keep thumbs off the artwork. Never talk, cough or sneeze over art, especially when the art is flat, airbrushed and unflapped.

Always hold art by the sides, as shown. Never lay anything on top of flat artwork even if it does have a flap to protect it.

Minimize the loss of your artwork by labeling every piece of artwork belonging to you with your name and address on the back.

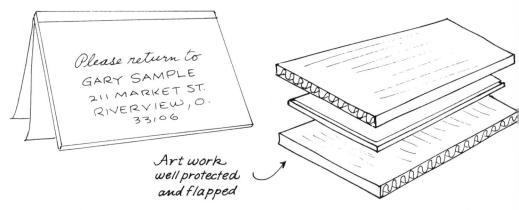

Please return to
GARY SAMPLE
211 MARKET ST.
RIVERVIEW, O.
33106

*Art work
well protected
and flapped*

Properly mail artwork by laying two oversized pieces of corrugated boards (bigger than the artwork) over the art, as shown. The corrugated boards are at right angles to each other to minimize the possibility of your package getting bent. For extra protection you can double the pieces, always at right angles to each other. Wrap well and put addresses on both sides of the package. Insure and send.

TYPE FACES IN COMMON USE

TEXT FACES

Baskerville
ABCDEFGHIJKLMNOPQRSTUVWXYZabcdefghijklmnopqrstuvwxyz1234567890
ABCDEFGHIJKLMNOPQRSTUVWXYZabcdefghijklmnopqrstuvwxyz1234567890

Bodoni
ABCDEFGHIJKLMNOPQRSTUVWXYZabcdefghijklmnopqrstuvwxyz1234567890
ABCDEFGHIJKLMNOPQRSTUVWXYZabcdefghijklmnopqrstuvwxyz1234567890

Caledonia
ABCDEFGHIJKLMNOPQRSTUVWXYZabcdefghijklmnopqrstuvwxyz1234567890
ABCDEFGHIJKLMNOPQRSTUVWXYZabcdefghijklmnopqrstuvwxyz1234567890

Century Schoolbook
ABCDEFGHIJKLMNOPQRSTUVWXYZabcdefghijklmnopqrstuvwxyz1234567890
ABCDEFGHIJKLMNOPQRSTUVWXYZabcdefghijklmnopqrstuvwxyz1234567890

Garamond
ABCDEFGHIJKLMNOPQRSTUVWXYZabcdefghijklmnopqrstuvwxyz1234567890
ABCDEFGHIJKLMNOPQRSTUVWXYZabcdefghijklmnopqrstuvwxyz1234567890

News Gothic Condensed
ABCDEFGHIJKLMNOPQRSTUVWXYZabcdefghijklmnopqrstuvwxyz1234567890

Primer
ABCDEFGHIJKLMNOPQRSTUVWXYZabcdefghijklmnopqrstuvwxyz1234567890
ABCDEFGHIJKLMNOPQRSTUVWXYZabcdefghijklmnopqrstuvwxyz1234567890

Times Roman
ABCDEFGHIJKLMNOPQRSTUVWXYZabcdefghijklmnopqrstuvwxyz1234567890
ABCDEFGHIJKLMNOPQRSTUVWXYZabcdefghijklmnopqrstuvwxyz1234567890

By courtesy of the publisher from the Random House Dictionary of the English Language. Copyright © 1966, 1973 by Random House, Inc.

DISPLAY FACES

Albertus
ABCDEFGHIJKLMNOPQRSTUVWXYZabcdefghijklmnopqrstuvwxyz1234567890

Bank Script
ABCDEFGHIJKLMNOPQRSTUVWXYZabcdefghijklmnopqrstuvwxyz1234567890

Barnum
ABCDEFGHIJKLMNOPQRSTUVWXYZabcdefghijklmnopqrstuvwxyz1234567890

Bodoni Bold
ABCDEFGHIJKLMNOPQRSTUVWXYZabcdefghijklmnopqrstuvwxyz1234567890
ABCDEFGHIJKLMNOPQRSTUVWXYZabcdefghijklmnopqrstuvwxyz1234567890

Bodoni Ultra
ABCDEFGHIJKLMNOPQRSTUVWXYZabcdefghijklmnopqrstuvvw
ABCDEFGHIJKLMNOPQRSTUVWXYZabcdefghijklmnopqrstuv

Bulmer
ABCDEFGHIJKLMNOPQRSTUVWXYZabcdefghijklmnopqrstuvwxyz1234567890
ABCDEFGHIJKLMNOPQRSTUVWXYZabcdefghijklmnopqrstuvwxyz1234567890

Lydian
ABCDEFGHIJKLMNOPQRSTUVWXYZabcdefghijklmnopqrstuvwxyz1234567890

Lydian Cursive
ABCDEFGHIJKLMNOPQRSTUVWXYZabcdefghijklmnopqrstuvwxyz1234567890

Microgramma Bold
ABCDEFGHIJKLMNOPQRSTUVWXYZ1234567890

Palatino
ABCDEFGHIJKLMNOPQRSTUVWXYZabcdefghijklmnopqrstuvwxyz1234567890
ABCDEFGHIJKLMNOPQRSTUVWXYZabcdefghijklmnopqrstuvwxyz1234567890

Peignot Medium
ABCDEFGHIJKLMNOPQRSTUVWXYZabcdefghijklmnopqrstuvwxyz1234567890

Stymie Medium
ABCDEFGHIJKLMNOPQRSTUVWXYZabcdefghijklmnopqrstuvwxyz1234567890
ABCDEFGHIJKLMNOPQRSTUVWXYZabcdefghijklmnopqrstuvwxyz123456789

14

how to apply knowledge to everyday situations

The purpose of this chapter is to *deliberately give*, in *"broad generalizations*," enough abstracts so you have *theory* to apply *as a basis for making a judgment*. No two situations are *exactly* the same, so no two processes of thought used to arrive at an end result will be exactly the same—but there are guideposts.

These questions are for you to ask yourself—they are the "middle"—the context must come first (that is your situation) and the solution must be uniquely yours.

You might say that some of the ideas *seem* to be duplicated—note that the *context is different*, making it, in fact, a different situation.

These ideas can be used as "food for thought." A good mental exercise is to construct hypothetical situations, apply the ideas and determine an answer (thus forcing yourself to think ahead). Then, when you *must* make a choice "on the spot," you will have had the practice.

Another way to use these guides is to make up additional questions—or set down additional ideas under each category as you think of something different, or as something happens.

The important thing is to make this chapter work for you. Whether you have to do it by practice ahead of time, by reference at the time of choice, by making lists or by discussion has no bearing upon the fact that the important thing is to *use the ideas*.

HOW TO THINK ON YOUR FEET

Say you don't know if you don't know; then say you'll find out; then
 find out.
Keep an open mind.
Keep a pencil handy.
Ask:

Who (does)	when told a department or a person doesn't handle, know, do or have something.
What	premise was the basis for this conclusion and are both correct?
	. . . do I do to achieve a certain end result?
	. . . procedure is to be followed?
	. . . did I do wrong?
	. . . is company policy?
	. . . value will this purchase be?
	. . . is causing such and such?
Where	do I find an answer?
	. . . in the classified section of the telephone book?
When	will such and such be ready (exactly)?
	. . . will this item be available?
	. . . will payment be made?
	. . . *must* you have the information?
	. . . *must* I mail it to get it there by_____?
How	do I do this?
	. . . do I make something better?
	. . . do I find an answer?
Why	does this function take five steps; can it be done in less?
	. . . did such and such happen—is the end result what was originally wanted?
	. . . was this idea chosen above that?
	. . . should (or shouldn't) I allow this person without an appointment to see the boss?
	. . . is there a communication problem?
	. . . is this particular product being used when there is another which would do the job better?

. . . is this answer incorrect?
. . . didn't I think of that?

IT'S EASY TO DO MANY THINGS AT ONCE

Never go emptyhanded—get into the habit of asking yourself:
    where you are going,
    what and who you will pass along the way,
    if there are things you can do or
    stops you can make along the way.
Set the copy machine for multiple copies:
    then type the letter,
    then pick up the copies.
Call the delivery service:
    then type the letter.
Use a shoulder rest on the telephone so you can:
    type *or*
    file *or*
    sort the mail while waiting.
Or leave a message and take the "waiting" time to:
    do something requiring total concentration.
Concentrate on the task at hand, but "program" the outer limits of
    your field of vision to register who comes and goes—hand
    them messages, papers, reminders as they pass.
Or point to a bulletin board.
Or alert them to clients.
Keep things in the same place—reaching for a pencil, a paper clip,
    the stapler or the phone book becomes automatic and can be
    done automatically while the brain works elsewhere.
Establish patterns—walk the same way to the copier, the file
    room, the supply room—the act of walking will become au-
    tomatic and you can be solving a problem along the way.

ALWAYS HAVE AN ALTERNATE SOLUTION

Bank by mail.
Know a second printer, copy machine, messenger service, taxi
    company, typewriter repair shop, stationer, notary public.
Use a broom if the vacuum breaks.
Send packages inter- and intra-state by bus, train or courier.

3 × 5 cards make good postcards.

Enclose a letter which you don't want creased (or a photo) in a file folder if you don't have cardboard and then package for mailing.

Rent a typewriter that does special things.

Rent an adding machine.

Use temporary help for peak periods.

HOW TO PLAN AHEAD

Keep flashlight with batteries,
    light bulbs,
    needle and thread,
    safety pins,
    straight pins,
    spot remover.

Know the location of fuse boxes and keep extra fuses.

Know the phone number of, and/or how, when and where to locate building management.

Know your bank's hours.

Make a master list of credit cards and include numbers and expiration dates.

Keep charge accounts current.

Be on suppliers' mailing lists to know about sales.

Know the location of the reference materials, the departmental phone numbers of public and private libraries, hours of availability, borrowing fees and/or have or know the requirements for a card.

Keep a Chron File (a file folder containing, in chronological order, a copy of all outgoing correspondence).

Read, keep and know machine manuals and instruction books.

Keep an idea file.

Make and keep appointments.

Set deadlines (a day ahead).

Know more than one outside secretarial service where work can be done on their machines in their offices—know:
    their hours;
    if they will give same day service;
    the type of equipment they have;
    in what condition they will accept work;
    how much notice you must give them that work will be coming;

> if they have a pickup and delivery arrangement;
> whether they have charge accounts, will accept credit
> cards, checks, or if terms are cash only.

Have change for automatic stamp machines.

Use a rubber stamp for return address on blank envelopes.

"Executive size" stationery is 7¼″ × 10½″—use a paper cutter.

Lightly iron bond paper on back if it accidentally creases.

Put the phone on answering service if you have a rush job.

Magnets quickly pick up tacks, nails, clips, pins.

Pieces of cellophane tape or masking tape clean lint.

HOW TO USE OLD SOLUTIONS FOR NEW PROBLEMS

If you keep an appointment book (or a telephone log or a copy
charge sheet) for two people, color code it.

If you mail to certain people over and over, pre-address by running
address labels on the copier. Use one label for the rolidex
card, another for the inside left front of the file folder—all you
have to write are the phone numbers and the names of particular persons.

Take the list of denominations of stamps you need with you to the
post office—the clerk will stamp it with the official post office
stamp and that is your receipt.

Continually redesign forms and form letters.

Instruct the paper boy to put the newspaper through the mail slot
in the door rather than leaving it on the hall floor.

Keep small packets of sugar (or a small box), powdered milk or
cream substitute for visitors.

Keep a supply of paper towels in your desk.

THE VALUE OF DISCUSSING A PROBLEM PROJECT

Time is saved.

Knowledge is shared.

Possible unexplored hypotheses and solutions develop.

Errors can be pinpointed and eliminated.

The responsibility of responding and participating forces alert
thinking.

Emotions are triggered—the mind expands—the "on the spot"
reaction occurs—new ideas are born.

The attention span is directed.

Information and knowledge, buried and forgotten in the depths of
the mind, are awakened by the stimulus of activity.
The creative process becomes more active.

HOW TO MAKE DECISIONS

Ask:

Who   was first in line?

... must make a deadline?

... needs just a draft?

... will do the best job?

What   work *must* be done today?

... firm should I choose and why?

... is the unit price?

... is the bulk price?

... kind of performance can I reasonably expect from this
product?

... company repairs this item and/or carries parts?

... kind of guarantee or warranty comes with this product?

... are the capabilities of this item?

... qualifications does this applicant have?

... time *must* the document be ready?

... obligations will be incurred?

... are the terms of payment?

... are the terms of the contract?

... are the dimensions of the room, new machine, new
piece of furniture, floor space to be covered, window?

... is the percentage of commission?

... credentials are held?

Where   shall I place my supplies so they are easiest to reach?

... have supplies been purchased in the past?

... is last year's report for reference?

... can I put "closed" files so they are accessible but out of
the way?

... will you be staying?

... will the ship dock, plane land?

... is this credit card valid?

... is identification accepted?

When   is the payment due?

. . . does the insurance come up for renewal?

. . . is interest posted?

. . . are commissions paid?

. . . are tax deadlines?

. . . do penalty charges begin?

. . . are the sales?

How   is interest calculated?

. . . much more value is the time than the money (or the money than the time)?

. . . will you get there?

. . . did you do that?

. . . much is the *total* debt?

. . . do I make a room look smaller (larger)?

Why   should I choose this product over that product?

. . . should I hire this person?

. . . am I getting this result?

. . . do I want to do it another way?

. . . should I do business with this firm?

. . . should this fact be included in (or excluded from) the report?

. . . should this page be set up this way?

15

how the secretary can help the executive accomplish more

This chapter describes various methods through which you can assist your boss.

Your job is to get things done. Perhaps a memory typewriter could handle some of the work, or perhaps a secretarial service with a memory typewriter is the answer for overload or specials. So here we have basic information and illustrations of some of the projects in general business and law that can be handled efficiently this way—statistical typing, lists, forms, changed documents.

The best way to do your job is to be sure that the work coming your way is done as efficiently as possible. To this end, included here is a list of **10 Ways to Make Machine Dictation Easy** and a fill-in-the-blanks form **(Instructions to Secretary)** the executive can give you with each batch of work.

Once the work is done, what about putting it where it can be picked up quickly and efficiently? Organizing the office for fingertip availability of file folders used over and over during the day? Making files accessible without spending two persons' time unnecessarily (yours to get it and your boss's to ask for and wait for it)? A place to put magazines or follow ups? Look at the page showing ideas using a new kind of file.

Did you know there is a financial planning calendar which

gives money due dates, the most used 30-day time periods, the closing of lending institutions enabling you to collect more interest before withdrawal, and more? Your boss might not know either.

This chapter also shows how efficient it is to use appointment books for the desk or pocket showing the day, week and month (some tabbed for telephone numbers and addresses); a book to keep automobile operating and maintenance expenses; or an expense and tax record book.

How should you tell your boss? Leave this book open to the appropriate page.

MEMORY TYPEWRITER PROJECTS

STATISTICAL TYPING

With the IBM Memory 100 Typewriter, your secretary can type statistical material, such as the Closed File Summary, shown here, with increased speed and accuracy. An automatic decimal tabulation capability aligns columns of figures electronically. In addition to reducing keystrokes, decimal tabulation enables your secretary to concentrate on the accuracy of the information being typed rather than worrying about proper column alignment.

This typewriter incorporates advanced typing capabilities including the IBM correction system, automatic formatting with memory and electronic information storage. Yet, it requires no specialized secretarial skills, and is designed for convenient desk-top operation.

The IBM Memory 100 Typewriter provides a productive tool for handling the wide range of legal typing requirements. From routine correspondence to forms typing, statistical tables, list updates, document revision and standard document preparation.

December 31, 19—

MEMORANDUM TO MR. R. V. SMITH

COFFEE DISTRIBUTION IN THE UNITED STATES DURING
JANUARY - DECEMBER 20, 19—, 19—, AND 19—

The U.S. Department of Agriculture reported the coffee distribution from January 1 to December 20, 19—, 19— and 19— as follows:

Month	(000) In Short Tons, Raw Value			19— As % of	19— As % of	19— As % of
	19—	19—	19—	19—	19—	19—
January	760	511	957	148.7 %	79.4 %	53.4 %
February	774	549	865	141.0	89.5	63.5
March	970	684	921	141.8	105.3	74.3

PERSONNEL

Manpower Reports
Wage and Salary Reports

MARKETING

Sales Performance
Marketing Statistics
Price Schedules

FINANCE AND ACCOUNTING

Balance Sheets
Budget Reports
Ledgers
Remittance Statements

19— CLOSED FILE SUMMARY

	TYPE	FEE	HOURS	AVERAGE HOURLY RATE
SUBROGATION	Fire	$ 25,653.59	450.3	$56.97
	Auto	38,901.46	1238.9	31.40
	Other	5,999.23	140.3	42.76
	TOTAL	$ 70,554.28	1829.5	$38.56
DEFENSE	Auto	$ 130,556.58	2351.1	$55.53
	Dram Shop	100,131.09	1899.3	52.72
	Products Liability	28,956.57	411.9	70.30
	Comp. Gen. & H.	19,973.23	350.9	56.92
	Aviation	9,975.41	150.3	66.37
	Admiralty	12,821.88	230.9	55.53
	Workmen's Comp.	5,732.50	125.0	45.86

Closed File Summaries
Open File Summaries
Billing Statements

MEMORY TYPEWRITER PROJECTS

LISTS

The IBM Memory 100 Typewriter gives you the typing power to maintain personnel, product and other lists, accurate and up-to-date.

Lists, such as your Client Phone Directory and the departmental roster shown here, can be maintained electronically. Changing or deleting information is accomplished simply by typing new information or deleting out-of-date material electronically. The memory will then play out the revised list, error-free, incorporating all your changes automatically.

```
                         UNITED SERVICES GROUP
                         DEPARTMENTAL HEADCOUNT
                            JANUARY, 1977
```

Dept. 205	Dept. 215	Dept. 700	Dept. 701	Dept. 702	Dept. 703	Dept. 704
K. Carsey	M. de sa Pereira	G. Baker	C. Clark	W. Anthony	S. Hancox	L. Beeson
M. Cerra	J. Freeborn	N. Carayas	N. Coleman	P. Bartlett		D. Kutner
B. Ezzolo	D. Hamilton	R. Pontier	P. Connolly	R. Bruderman		G. Schreiner
T. Keehn	J. McComas	L. Walker	T. Daniels	W. Clark		E. Tutun
N. Langevin	M. Smith		S. Kacin	N. Cotter		
D. Parisi	W. Wilson		M. Leaf	B. Ethridge		
B. Peabody	R. Zuniga		A. Lehmann	R. Forsaith		
R. Rowe			L. Levine	J. Ghuzzi		
J. Scheu			C. Lynch	J. Healy		
A. Semple			M. Magid	W. Hickey		
M. Stone			M. Michael	V. Kunz		
			K. Scargill	P. Lin		
			J. Stiene	A. Ling		

PERSONNEL

Benefits
Absentee Lists
Promotion Lists
Skills Inventories
Overtime Schedules
Seniority Lists

PURCHASING

Supplies
Inventory
Vendors

MARKETING

Product Listings
Price Schedules
Labels

```
                        CLIENT PHONE DIRECTORY


    CLIENT                       TELEPHONE        RESPONSIBLE ATTORNEY

    ABG Company                  769-3000         D. N. Bauer

    Brian, Cindy W.              329-6001         C. R. Smith

    Bridges, Betty K.            322-1222         A. G. Reed

    Dayton Enterprises           727-3500         C. R. Smith

    Dalton Construction          386-2700         C. R. Smith

    Ernst, Mary R.               389-2501         P. L. Moore

    Foley, Cathy L.              386-6160         P. L. Moore

    Gardner, Michael L.          522-8888         P. L. Moore
```

Client Listings
Open Cases
Opposing Attorneys
Will/Trust Listings

MEMORY TYPEWRITER PROJECTS

FORMS

You can also prerecord the positioning of variable information on frequently used forms, such as the requisition and the Real Estate Closing form below.

AJAX COMPANY REQUISITION FORM

REQUISITION NO.

ACK REQ	RECEIPT REQ
X	

ORIGIN CODE	PREFIX CODE		SUBORDER	ORIGINAL REQUISITION	REQUISITION CHANGE	LTR
B13	B13A		☐	X	☐	

PAGE	CONFIRMING	SUPPLIER REPRESENTATIVE	ISSUE DATE	PURCHASE ORDER NO.
1 of 1	M. Johnson	B. Riley	3/1/—	C5616

Centennial Corporation
32 Lilac Lane
Lindsayville, N. Y.   ZIP CODE 32744

FOB (CITY)	VIA	PREPAID COLLECT	AREA CODE	AWARD CODE	TERMS
Robertsville	Concord Freight	X ☐	862	F	2/10 Net 30

Then, instead of manually tabbing, indexing and spacing, your secretary automatically plays out the format to the exact point where information is to be typed in—saving keystrokes, reducing the possibility for errors, and substantially reducing typing time.

CLOSING STATEMENT

Property Address: 30 Winthrop Drive, Prestbury, Webster Grove, Ill.
Sellers: Robert J. & Kathleen M. Sanders
Buyers: John M. & Marian M. Barron
Closing Date: June 15, 19— - Local S & L

	Buyers' Credits	Sellers' Credits
Purchase Price		$70,000.00
Earnest Money (Dep w/ Jones)	$3,000.00	
General Taxes 19—	1,318.42	
General Tax Proration		
for 1/1/ — to 6/15/ —	604.25	
Rents:		
Miscellaneous		

PERSONNEL

Personnel Forms
Health Forms
Insurance Forms

PURCHASING

Purchase Orders
Requisitions
Bills of Lading

FINANCE AND ACCOUNTING

Invoices
Freight Bills
Claim Vouchers
Schedules
Tax Forms
Petty Cash Forms
Real Estate Closings
Waivers of Divorce
Warranty Deeds
Joint Ownership Agreements
Releases of Easements
Income Tax Forms

MEMORY TYPEWRITER PROJECTS

CHANGED DOCUMENTS

Complex documents like budget reports, that normally require several drafts and Articles of Incorporation can now be revised faster and with greater efficiency. Using the IBM Memory 100 Typewriter can help you meet tight deadlines for revised documents, such as Articles of Incorporation. As information is initially typed, it is stored in the typewriter's electronic memory. With the information held in storage, your secretary can add or delete a word, a sentence, a paragraph or more. Then, only new information need be typed.

The IBM Memory 100 Typewriter incorporates the revisions into the unchanged material, playing out completed documents automatically.

```
                                               January 6, 19—

    MEMORANDUM TO MR. C. A. MYERS


                          CENTENNIAL
                   MONTHLY OPERATING REPORT
                        DECEMBER 1976


  a revised        Centennial net income was $435,000 in December compared
                        $24,000                        $411,000.
            to budget of $20,000 for a favorable variance of $415,000.

            For the January/December period, Centennial earned $1,233,000,
  a revised            $1,033,000
            over budget by $1,037,000 and ahead of 19— by $1,050,000.
```

PERSONNEL	MARKETING	FINANCE AND ACCOUNTING
Procedure Manuals	Proposals	Budget Reports
Job Descriptions	Presentations	Finance Memoranda
Personnel Reports	Feasibility Studies	
	Market Analyses	
	Planning Reports	
	Sales Plans	
	Sales Manuals	

```
                    ARTICLES OF INCORPORATION
                              OF
                      Worldwide Charities

    We, the undersigned, incorporators, hereby associate ourselves
together to establish a corporation -for profit- under the laws of
the State of Kansas.                     ⌐ non-profit in purpose

    FIRST.    The Name of this Corporation is Worldwide Charities.

    SECOND.   The location of its Principal Place of Business in
this State is 2029 North Woodlawn, Wichita, Kansas.

    THIRD.    The location of its Registered Office in this State
is 3629 East Main Street, Topeka, Kansas.

    FOURTH.   The Name and Address of its Resident Agent in Kansas
is Mr. Steven E. Johnson, 4356 South Arrow, Wichita, Kansas.

    FIFTH.    This Corporation is -organized for profit- and the
nature of its business is:          ⌐ non-profit
```

Legal Briefs	Judgments
Articles of Incorporation	Contracts
Petitions	Negotiations

FREQUENTLY USED DOCUMENTS

If your office is like most, your secretary is completely retyping the same information in correspondence, like this employee benefits letter, or Wills and Trusts that rarely change but that your secretary presently retypes with each use—can be handled with a dramatic savings in time using the IBM Memory 100 Typewriter. With it, you can have prerecorded documents, which require typing only the variable fill-ins for final copy. And you can assemble entire documents from standard sentences and paragraphs. Up to 100 or more pages of typed material can be stored, with any page accessible in seconds through the twist of a dial.

 Global Industries, Inc.

```
January 30, 19—

Ms. Consuelo Rodriguez
2124 Hancock Drive
Austin, Texas  72580

Dear Consuelo,

     On behalf of the Employee Benefits Department, I would
like to invite Jose and you to a meeting at the plant
cafeteria on Friday, February 3, 19—, at 8:00 pm.

     We plan to review the new Employee Benefit Plan and dis-
```

```
                    LAST WILL AND TESTAMENT
                         PREPARED FOR

                    ___John Jones___

         .    I, John Jones, being of sound and disposing
    mind and memory, and considering the uncertainty of this
    life, do hereby make, publish and declare this to be my last
    will and testament, hereby revoking any and all other former
    wills or codicils made by me at any time.

            .    I direct that all of my debts and funeral expenses
    be paid.

            .    I give, bequeath and devise all of the rest, resi-
    due and remainder of my estate, real, personal or mixed, of
    whatever kind, nature or description, and wherever situated
    of which I may die seized or possessed or in which I may have
    any power of appointment or testamentary disposition, to
    my son, John Jones, Jr.
```

PERSONNEL	PURCHASING	MARKETING
Appraisal Letters	Requests for Quotes	Mass Mail
Benefits Letters	Contracts	Sales Bulletins
Recruiting Letters		Price Quotations
Confirmation Letters		Inquiry Letters
		Price Change Letters
		Interrogatories
		Employment Contracts
		Security Agreements
		Wills
		By-laws
		Resolutions
		Collection Letters

10 WAYS TO MAKE MACHINE DICTATION EASY

1. Keep a "Key" sheet for information about each document and give it to typist with dictated material.
2. Begin dictation by telling typist:
   a. the type of finished product needed (final letter, draft, original for printer—white paint acceptable, etc.);
   b. the number of copies;
   c. other special instructions (wider or narrower than usual margins, etc.);
   or by noting this information after document #1 on "Key" sheet.

INSTRUCTIONS TO SECRETARY:

NAME: _____ LOCATION: _____

PHONE/EXTN: _____ TIME SUBMITTED: _____ AM PM

DATE SUBMITTED: _____ TIME REQUIRED: _____ AM PM

DATE REQUIRED: _____ ACTIVITY NO: _____

JOB NO: _____ SUB NO: _____ SPECIAL—SPECIFY: _____

MARGINS: _____ OTHER—SPECIFY: _____

PAPER: _____ NUMBER OF COPIES: _____

SPACING: _____ TYPEFACE: _____

PURPOSE: DRAFT REVISION FINAL

SPECIAL INSTRUCTIONS:

Designed by Phiroze Wadia, 11 Catskill Court, San Anselmo, California 94960

3. If the machine has a device for gauging length of line, it will show on a strip of paper the number at which the dictation begins and at which it ends for each document dictated. This must be given to the typist as the means of indicating spacing and length on the page, and it is best to attach it to the "Key" sheet. If no device is on the machine, use the numbers on the cassettes where one reel winds to the other and indicate it next to the proper document number on the "Key" sheet. If no numbers are available, indicate on the "Key" sheet: short, medium, long.

4. Unless pages showing unusually spelled names, addresses and/or statistical material are given to typist with dictation, spell anything questionable and enunciate numbers *very* clearly.

5. If there is a correction or omission in a letter, cue the typist to it on the "Key" sheet next to the proper document.

6. Unless the typist is expected to totally punctuate the material, *say* "comma," "semicolon," etc. instead of assuming voice inflection does the job.

7. Speak clearly at a pace slower than normal conversation. Play it back.
8. Backtrack one phrase as the first thing on a new side or new tape or belt to be certain nothing is lost in the changeover.
9. **Always erase tapes—old phrases will drain through.**
10. **Label tapes.**

FINANCIAL PLANNING DESK CALENDAR

Calmanac.

DETERMINES AT A GLANCE the exact due date of loans at any time within a year's time, regardless of length.

PLENTY OF NOTE SPACE— almost 1/3 page for each day.

DAYS AHEAD TABLE gives instant due dates for the most commonly used pending periods.

WEEKS AHEAD TABLE gives the day of the week corresponding to the current day, but a specified number of weeks ahead.

CALL LOAN TABLE gives days ago from the current day. By determining when the date due notes were written, the lender can determine what notes are due on the current day.

SHOWS DAYS, weeks and months ahead of the current day's date.

HIGHLIGHTS the most used 30-day time periods.

WEEKEND DAYS shaded to warn of possible closing of lending institutions, thus ensuring collection of 2 extra days' interest.

FEDERAL HOLIDAYS designated to ensure collection of additional day's interest.

STATE HOLIDAY guide given in front of pad.

THE DAYS PAST and days remaining in the current year shown at bottom of each page.

A unique Anglo/metric converter, the CALCUMETRIC, that shows the Anglo/metric measurement side by side so that you can convert in seconds, without complicated mathematical formulas

A unique perpetual calendar, the PERPETUCAL, that spans 400 years—1700 through 2100—and lists traditional holidays, religious days and other commemorative occasions.

"Calmanac". Pad size: 4½" × 7⅞" (11.4 × 19.7 cm)

THESE ARE A FEW OF THE AT • A • GLANCE® BOOKS

70-800
Desk Day
AT • A • GLANCE®
Appointment Book—
8" × 4⅞" quarter hour
appointments
8 A.M.—9 P.M.

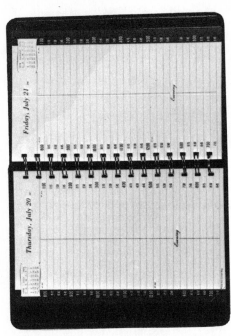

70-100
Desk Week
AT • A • GLANCE®
Appointment Book—
8" × 4⅞". Hourly ap-
pointments 7 A.M. to
6 P.M. Tab-indexed
Tel./Address section.

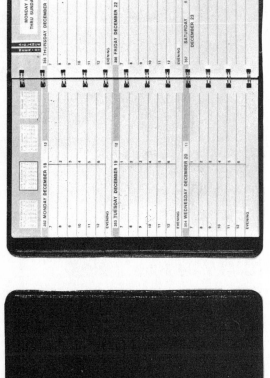

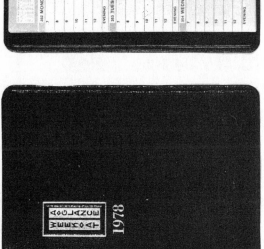

Courtesy Sheaffer Eaton Division of Textron, Inc.,
75 South Church Street, Pittsfield, Mass. 01201

70-120
Desk Month
AT • A • GLANCE®
Appointment Book—
8¾" × 6⅞". Monthly
calendar appoint-
ment section with
additional perforated
Memo section, 2
yearly planning pages
3-year calendar, and
Tel./Address Direc-
tory with area code
map.

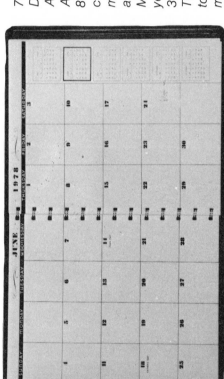

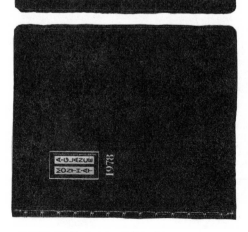

70-064
Pocket Month
AT • A • GLANCE®
Appointment Book—
6½" × 3½". Monthly
calendar appoint-
ment section with
separate tab-indexed
Tel./Address section
and Memo Pad sec-
tion.

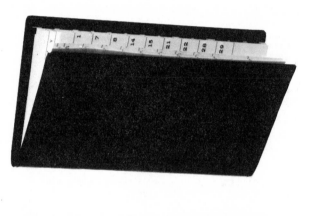

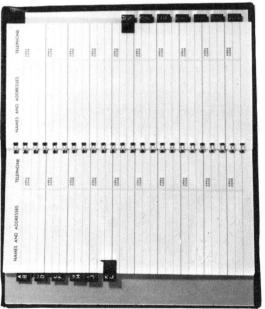

80-135
Auto Record Book—
6⅛" × 3¾". For recording automobile operating and maintenance expenses. Useful as a record of tax-deductible expenses for persons using their cars for business. Tab-indexed sections include gas and oil consumption, lubrication record, repairs and accessories, tire mileage, and trip diary. Extra pages for names, numbers and memos.

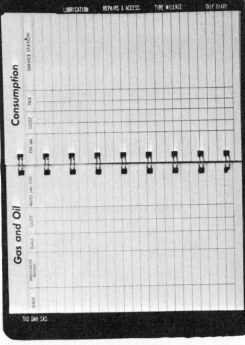

80-151
Expense & Tax Record Book—6⅛"×3¾". Planned for simplified, accurate listing of personal or business travel expenses. May be started at any time. Full week appears on double page spread. Also features monthly recap section, cash record, and pages for tax-ductible expenses.

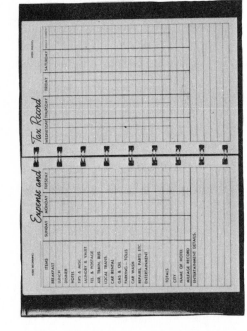

Courtesy Sheaffer Eaton Division of Textron Inc.,
75 South Church Street, Pittsfield, Mass 01201

16

quick and easy grammar review

Sometimes you need quick information. With the following "at-a-glance" charts, you will not only be able to find the answers to these and other points of grammar, you'll be able to quickly and easily learn the rule governing the answer.

Included is information such as:

- The parts of a sentence.
- Whether to capitalize a proper noun.
- How to show possession when a word ends in *s*.
- How and when to use who, which and that.
- How to use the progressive tense, the simple tense, the future tense.
- Whether to use most easy or easiest, an hour or a hour, neither . . . nor or neither . . . or.
- When a word is hyphenated, when *i* comes before *e*, if it is picnicing or picknicking, the plural of half, if it is Attorneys General or Attorney Generals.
- How to indicate a footnote, if the punctuation goes before or after the quotation mark, when to use a comma, when to use ellipses.
- The abbreviation for assistant, document, Justice of the Peace, municipal, Pacific.
- The meaning of avg., fin., i.e., N.B., orig., Q.E.D., sic.

	Function	Example	Additional Information
SENTENCE	conveys complete thought	Gene walks	
subject	tells who, whom or what	Gene	
predicate	tells what subject does	walks walks to the store walks slowly walks the dog	

	Function	Example	Additional Information
NOUN	name word	names person, place, thing, abstract	
common	names general class	girl, city, museum	
proper	names specifics	Kip, Washington, Smithsonian	Initial Caps
possessive	shows ownership	John's office	add 's if noun does not end in s
	shows authorship	Dickens'	add ' if word ends in s
	shows origin	bass' or bass's sound	personal preference prevails

	Function
PRONOUN	takes place of noun

Singular	Possessive	Plural	Possessive
I	my, mine	WE	our, ours
YOU	your, yours	YOU	your, yours
HE, SHE, IT	his, hers, its	THEY	their, theirs

1st person—person speaking
2nd person—person talking

who—refers to person
which—refers to thing or animal
that—refers to person, thing, animal

VERBS

	Function	Example	Additional Information
Linking	joins parts of sentence	It seems cold.	Can always be replaced with form of TO BE for same meaning
Action	shows action	He ran.	
Progressive Tense	shows unfinished action	I am arranging the papers now.	simple verb adds *ing* and is always preceded by form of TO BE

Past

Simple Tense	finished action	I went skiing Sunday.	

Present

Simple Tense	actions going on at present time	She is here.	
	continued or habitual	I see him each day.	
	general truth	Lemons are sour.	

Future

Simple Tense	for events which will take place	I will be there Friday.	

Perfect Tense

	Past	Present	Future
Perfect Tense	action completed before another past event	action completed in past but part of series of actions that continue up to present	action that will be completed by a specific time in the future
	I had rented the store by the time they arrived.	She has written only one play so far.	By this time Saturday he will have left.

ADVERBS—tell, how, when, where or how much—*always* and *only* used with action verbs

How to Form	Adjective	Adverb	Adjective	Adverb
add *ly* to whole adjective	swift, like	swiftly, likely	due, true, whole	duly, truly, wholly
when adjective ends in *y*, change *y* to *i* and add *ly*	busy, happy	busily, happily		

ADJECTIVES—describe nouns or pronouns and are used with linking verbs

	Function	Example	To Form	Some Irregulars					
simple	describes single item or single group	fine portrait difficult game		bad	far	far			
				good	late	late			
				little	many	much			
comparative	compares two things	finer portrait more difficult game	add *er*, or if over two syllables, use more in front	worse	farther	further			
				better	later	latter			
				less	more	more			
superlative	compares three or more	finest portrait most difficult game	add *est*, or if over two syllables, use most in front	worst	farthest	furthest			
				best	latest	last			
				least	most	most			

ARTICLES—*A, An* are indefinite articles; *The* is definite article

A	connotes thing not previously noted or recognized	before words beginning with a consonant sound or a sounded *h*	a book, a chair, a happy person
An	connotes thing not previously noted or recognized	before vowel (*a,e,i,o,u*) sound or mute *h*	an apple, an egg, an hour
The	connotes thing previously noted or recognized	before initial vowels and initial consonants	the apple, the hour, the happy person

---

PREPOSITIONS—connect noun or pronoun with description

about, above, across, after, against, along, amid, among, around, as, at, because of, before, behind, below, beneath, beside, between, beyond, but, by, concerning, down, during, except, for, from, in, into, like, of, off, on, over, regarding, respecting, since, through, throughout, till, under, underneath, until, up, upon

Example—as adjective	*Example—as adverb*
The girl in the tweed coat is next.	They stood by the sign.
I own the building on the right.	They walked behind her.

CONJUNCTIONS

accordingly, and, as soon as, because, besides, but, consequently, hence, in as much as, in order that, moreover, notwithstanding, or, otherwise, more than, supposing, therefore, though, thus, until, whereas

	Example	*Pairs Used Together*
	We will deliver the carpet as soon as we receive your check.	both . . . and, whether . . . or, either . . . or, neither . . . nor, not only . . . but also

PREFIXES

Hyphenate	*To Prevent Confusion*	*To Prevent Mispronunciation*	*When Capital Letter Follows Prefix*	*When Prefix is A Single Letter*	*After ex, quasi, self*
	re-cover, recovery	co-worker, co-op	Pro-American	T-Square, U-Turn	ex-wife quasi-free, self-made

These prefixes usually are not hyphenated

ante, anti, bi, circum, co, extra, fore, hyper, infra, inter, meta, micro, mono, multi, neo, non, over, para, poly, post, pre, pro, pseudo, semi, sub, super, trans, tri, ultra, under

SUFFIXES

Retain e
- when root ends in ce or ge — changeable, damageable, outrageous
- when suffix begins with consonant — achievement, definitely

Drop e
- when suffix begins with vowel — arguing, changing, dividing, excusing

Add k
- when word ends in c before suffix beginning with e, i, y — frolicking, mimicked, panicked, picnicked

Always Change ie to y
dying, lying, relying, trying, tying, vying

Retain y
- when root ends in y preceded by vowel — surveying, surveyor, delaying, playing

Change y to i
- when root ends in y preceded by consonant — embodied, relied
- excepting — relying

Double Final Consonant
- when preceded by single vowel — mapping
- when last syllable is accented due to addition of suffix — acquitted

Do Not Double Final Consonant
- when addition of suffix shifts accent to preceding syllable — reference
- when final consonant is preceded by two vowels — toiling
- when final consonant is preceded by consonant — folding

PLURALS

Rule	Example	Some Exceptions
add s		
most nouns	pencils, books, pens,	
nouns ending in *y* preceded by vowel	attorneys, days	
single words ending in *ful*	cupfuls, pocketfuls, spoonfuls	
add es		
nouns ending in *o* preceded by a consonant	heroes, tomatoes cargoes, potatoes	solos, banjos, pianos, zeros, sopranos
nouns ending in *y* preceded by consonant change *y* to *i* and add *es*	babies, companies, ladies, stories, worries	
nouns ending in *f* change *f* to *v* and add *es*	halves, knives, wives, leaves, selves	chiefs, proofs, roofs, gulfs, beliefs, chefs
nouns ending in *ch, sh, x, s* or *z*	churches, wishes, boxes, dresses,	
proper names ending in *s* or sound of *s*	Burnses, Joneses	
add 's		
letters	M's, b's, s's, z's	
numbers	2's, 9's, 50's, 100's	
or only *s* if clear	CPAs	

always appear singular

aeronautics, civics, economics, mathematics, measles, milk, music, news

always appear plural

goods, means, pants, proceeds, remains, riches, scissors, seasons, thanks

same for singular and plural

Chinese, corps, deer, gladiolus, Japanese, Portuguese, salmon, series, sheep, species, vermin, wheat

COMPOUNDS

Two separate words	*Written as one word*
Pluralize most important:	Pluralize last part:
Attorneys General	classmates
Notaries Public	grandchildren
Brothers-in-Law	workmen

PUNCTUATION

Mark	Rule	Example
.	end of sentence	I think you made a wise choice.
	after abbreviation	Mrs., Ave.
	separate dollars and cents	$432.10
?	only after a question	Where is he?
!	only after an exclamation	Hooray!
,	items in a series	I have red, black, green and grey yarn.
	parenthetic phrases	Her son, Mark, is smart.
	before conjunction introducing independent clause	The bundle is very heavy, but I can manage it.
	set off name of person directly addressed	Lewis, may I borrow a book?
	when question is added to statement	Pretty coat, isn't it?
	to set off opposing idea which begins with not	I want pens, not pencils.
	to set off short quotation	Pete said, "Please sign here."
	to separate two complete ideas connected by and, but, or	Joan will attend, but she may be late.
	after initial dependent clause	When Ruth arrives, we'll go.
	numbers by three	198,594,477
	date	September 6, 1940
	address	San Francisco, California
	complimentary close of letter	Sincerely yours,

PUNCTUATION

Mark	Rule	Example

:	after business letter salutation
	to introduce long, formal
	quotation
		Dear Mr. Davis:
		He said: "I know you have had the
		  faith to vote for me before, and
		  I ask that you renew it now."

	to separate minutes from hours long list	4:30 p.m. Ship invoice numbers: 135, 429, 458, 559, 627, 864 and 991.

;	to separate thoughts
	  not connected by conjunction
		Please have a seat; Mr. Adams will
		  be right with you.

...	to show omission in beginning or
	  middle of sentence
	to change mood
		". . . with $2.7 million allotted
		  for the building fund."
		"Let's go to . . . oh, never mind."

....	to show end of sentence omission	"Savings account # 1357 in the sum of $985,221.00. . . ."
{	to show relationship of items	sale items are { paper clips pens carbon paper

( )	to set off supplemental,
	  explanatory or incidental
	  thought
	to enclose definitive terms
	  and abbreviations
	to indicate alternate terms
	to set off items in a series
	to enclose figures when
	  double form is used
		Jack (the other partner) was not as
		  active in the business.
		
		The Department of Health, Education,
		  and Welfare (HEW)
		abbreviation(s)
		Copy the (a) bill (b) check (c) lease.
		Please send five (5) copies with your
		  check.

[ ]	enclose comment within quotation
	  by someone besides author
	instead of parenthesis within
	  parenthesis
		"The President, Mr. Jones. [applause]."
		
		(Chapter 4 [section 3b])

PUNCTUATION

Mark	Rule	Example
*	footnote	May 6, 1939*
'	form possession of nouns indicate omission in contraction	Josephine's car wouldn't, he'll, won't, can't
" " **,—, or** **Italics**	around direct quotation around titles of books, magazines, articles around colloquial expressions	Dr. Green said, "Bring me the chart." Buy two copies of "How to Type." I own that issue of *Typing*. She is "sharp."

' '	around quotation inside a
	   quotation
		Bill replied, "She testified 'I was
		   there.' "

	Placement of Punctuation with Quotation Mark	

	INSIDE—final **.** or **,**
	
	   when whole quotation
	   asks question
		"Give her a week," she replied, "and
		   she will pay the bill."
		She asked, "What time is the
		   appointment?"

	OUTSIDE—when whole sentence asks question, and quotation is less important but associated	Who has read "Errorless Typing"?

-	to divide word at syllable at end
	   of line
	compound words *directly pre-
	   ceding* modifier
		When you have finished, please sepa-
		   rate the bills from the letters.
		well-known person

—	unfinished or omitted thought in
	   quoted material
	to break thought
		He said, "I don't give a—!"
		
		This machine—the newest model—is
		   best.

ABBREVIATIONS

A: acre(s); Answer (Court); area; Army
A-1: First Class
abbr., abbrev.: abbreviate,-ed,-ion
abs.: absent; absolute; abstract
A.C.: Alternating Current
ack.: acknowledge,-ment
ad: advertisement
A.D.: in the year of our Lord (L. Anno Domini)
ad fin.: to the end (L. ad finem)
ad inf.: to infinity (L. ad infinitum)
ad init.: at the beginning (L. ad initium)
ad int., a.i.: meanwhile (L. ad interim)
adj.: adjacent; adjective
ad lib.: improvise (L. ad libitum)
ad loc.: at or to the place (L. ad locum)
adv.: adverb
ad val.: according to value (L. ad valorem)
afft.: affidavit
agcy.: agency
agr., ag., agri.: agriculture,-al
aka.: also known as
a.m., A.M.: before noon (L. ante meridian)
amt.: amount
ans.: answer,-ed
A.P.: accounts payable
app.: apparatus; appendix; applied
approx.: approximate,-ly
appt.; appoint,-ed,-ment
apt.: apartment
ar., arr.: arrange; arrive
A.R.: accounts receivable
asgd.: assigned
assn., ass'n.: association
assoc.: associate,-ed
asst.: assistant
att.: attach,-ed
attn., atten.: attention
atty.: attorney
auth.: author,-ized

aux.: auxiliary
Ave.: avenue
avg., av.: average

b.: born
bal.: balance,-ing
bar.: barometer
bbl.: barrel(s)
B.C.: before Christ
bd.: board; bond; bound
bdl.: bundle
bet.: between
bf.: boldface
biog.: biography,-er,-ical
biol.: biology,-ical,-ist
bk.: bank; black; book
bldg.: building
bldr.: builder
Blvd.: Boulevard
bros.: brothers
BTU: British Thermal Unit
bu.: bushel
bul.: bulletin
bur.: bureau
bus.: business
bx.: box

c.: carat; cycle
C.: Celsius; Centigrade; Congress
©: copyright
canc.: cancel,-ation,-ed
cap.: capital,-ize; capacity
caps.: capital letters
cat.: catalog; category
cc: carbon copy
cert., ct., ctf.: certificate, certified
CH.: Court House; Custom House
chap., chapt., ch., C (with number): chapter
chg.: change; charge
cir.: circle; circular; circumference
cit.: citation; citizen
civ.: civil; civilian

ck.: check
cl.: class,-ification,-ified; clause
clk.: clerk
clr.: clear; color
coll.: collect,-ed,-ion; collateral
com, comm.: commerce;
    commission,-er; committee;
    communication
coml., cml.: commercial
cons.: consign,-ed,-ment;
    consolidate,-ed
const.: constant; construction
Const.: Constitution
cont.: contents; continue,-ed,-ation
Corp.: Corporation
corr.: correct,-ed; correspond,-ing
cp.: coupon
cr.: credit
Ct.: Court
CT: Central Time
ctr.: center; counter
cur.: currency; current
cust.: customer
cwt.: hundredweight

d.: date; density; died; distance
D.: Democrat; diameter
D.A.: District Attorney
db: decibel (unit of sound)
deb.: debenture
dec.: decease,-ed; decimal;
    decrease,-ed
def.: defense; definition
del.: deliver,-y
dept.: department
dia., diam.: diameter
diag.: diagonal; diagram
do.: ditto
doc.: document
doz.: dozen
dwg.: drawing
dwt.: pennyweight

E.: east
ea.: each
ed.: edit,-ion,-or; education

EDT: Eastern Daylight Time
educ.: educate,-ion,-al
e.g.: for example (L. exempli gratia)
elec.: electric,-al,-ian,-ity
enc., encl.: enclosure
end.: endorse,-ed,-ment
ENE: east-northeast
eng.: engine,-er; engrave
E.&O.E.: errors and omissions
    excepted
equip., eqpt.: equipment
ESE: east-southeast
esp.: especially
Esq.: Esquire
est.: establish,-ed,-ment; estate;
    estimate
EST: Eastern Standard Time
et al.: and others (L. et alii)
etc.: and so forth (L. et cetera)
et seq.: and the following (L. et
    sequens)
et ux: and wife (L. et uxor)
et vir: and husband (L.)
ex.: out of; without; example; extra
exam.: examine,-ed
exch.: exchange,-ed
exec.: executive
exp.: expense; export; express
exr.: executor

F.: Fahrenheit
f., ff.: and following page(s)
fac.: facsimile
Fed.: Federal; Federation
fem.: female; feminine
Fid.: Fidelity; Fiduciary
fig.: figure
fin.: finance,-ial; finish
fl.: fluid; floor; fuel
fm.: fathom; form; from
fn., ftnt.: footnote
fol.: folio; follow,-ed,-ing
for.: foreign; forestry; forward
frt.: freight
ft.: feet; foot
furn.: furnish,-ed,-ing; furniture

fwd.: forward
F.Y.I.: for your information

g.: gauge; gold; gravity; gulf
gds.: goods
gen.: general; generator
GNP: Gross National Product
GOP: Republican Party
Gov.: Governor
govt.: government
gr.: grain; great; gross
grad.: graduate,-ed,-ion
guar.: guarantee,-ed

h.a.: this year (L. hoc anno)
hd.: head
hdqrs.: headquarters
hist.: history,-ian,-ical
hosp.: hospital
hp.: horsepower
hr.: hour
ht.: heat; height
Hwy., Hy.: Highway

I.: Island(s); Isle(s)
ib., ibid.: in the same place (footnote)
    (L. ibidem)
id.: the same (L. idem)
ID: identification
i.e.: that is (L. id est)
ill., illus.: illustrate,-ed,-ion
imp.: imperial; implement; import;
    improve
in., ": inches
Inc.: Incorporated
inc.: income,-ing; increase,-ing
incl.: include,-ing; inclusive
incog.: incognito; in secret
ind.: independent; index; industry,-ial
inf.: inferior; below (L. infra)
init.: initial
in loc.: in the proper place (L. in loco)
ins.: inspector; insurance
inst.: install,-ment; instant; instrument
Inst.: Institute,-ion
in trans.: on the way (L. in transitu)

int.: interest; interior
intl., intnatl.: international
inv.: invent,-or,-ion; invest,-ment;
    invoice
IOU: I owe you
I.Q.: Intelligent Quotient
IR: Internal Revenue
iss.: issue
ital.: italic(s)

J.: Judge; Justice
JJ: Justices
jour.: journal
J.P.: Justice of the Peace
Jr.: Junior
jt.: joint
junc., jct.: junction

K: karat (gold measure)
kn.: knot

l.: left; length; line
L.: Latin; law(s)
lab.: labor; laboratory
lang.: language
lb.: pound(s)
lbr.: lumber
lc.: lowercase
l.c.: in the place cited (see Loc.cit)
L/C: letter of credit
leg.: legal
legis.: legislature; legislation
lf.: lightface
lge.: large
lib.: liberal; library
liq.: liquid; liquor
lit.: literally; literature
ln.: lien; line; loan
loc.: local; location
loc. cit.: in the place cited (L. loco
    citato)
log.: logarithm
long.: longitude
L.S.: place of the seal (L. locus Sigilli)
lt.: left; light
ltr.: letter
lv.: leave

m.: male; married; masculine; minutes; noon

M: Master (degree); Monsieur (pl. MM)

mach.: machine,-ery

mag.: magazine; magnitude

maj.: majority

man.: manager; manual

mar.: maritime; market; married

mat.: matinee; maturity

math.: mathematics,-cal,-ian

max.: maximum

mdse.: merchandise

meas.: measure,-ment

mech.: mechanic,-al,-s

med.: medical; medicine; medium

mem.: member

memo.: memorandum

Messrs., MM: Misters (Messieurs)

met.: metal; metropolitan

mfg.: manufacturing

mfr.: manufacture,-er

mgr.: manager

mid., mdnt.: midnight

mil.: mileage; military; million

min.: minimum; minister; minority

misc.: miscellaneous

mkt.: market

Mlle.: Mademoiselle (Miss)

Mme.: Madame

mo.: month

m.o.: mail order; money order

mot.: motor

m.p.: melting point

Mr.: Mister

Mrs.: Mistress or Madam (pl. Mmes.)

MS., MSS: manuscript

Ms.: Miss or Mrs.

msg.: message

Msgr., msgr.: Monsignor; messenger

MST: Mountain Standard Time

Mt.: Mount; Mountain

mtg.: meeting; mortgage

mun.: municipal

mus.: museum; music; musical

m.v.: market value

n.: net; news; note

N.: Navy; north

n/a: not applicable; not available

nat., natl.: national

naut.: nautical

nav.: naval; navigation

n.b., N.B.: note well; take notice (L. nota bene)

NB: northbound

NE: northeast

neg.: negative,-ly

nem. con.: no one contradicting (L. nemine contradicente)

neut., n.: neuter

N. Lat.: north latitude

n/m: no mark; no message

NNE: north-northeast

NNW: north-northwest

No.(s): number(s)

N., No.: North; northern

nom.: nominal

non seq.: it does not follow (L. non sequitur)

n.o.p.: not otherwise provided for

N.P.: Notary Public

nr.: near

n/s: not specified; not sufficient

N.S.F.: not sufficient funds (banking)

nth: indefinite

nt. wt.: net weight

NW: northwest

o.: old; order; oxygen

ob.: died (L. obiit)

obit.: obituary

obs.: obsolete; observatory

ob.s.p.: died without issue (L. obiit sine prole)

oc.: ocean; overcharge

off.: office; officer; official

opp.: opposite

op. cit.: in the work cited (L. opere citato)

oppor.: opportunity

opr.: operate,-ing,-ion(s)

opt.: optician; optional

ord.: order; ordinance; ordinary
org.: organic; organization
orig.: original,-ly
oz.: ounce(s)

p.: page (pl.pp); parallel; per; population
Pac.: Pacific
p. ae.: equal parts (L. partes aequales)
pam: pamphlet
paren.: parenthesis
part.: particular
pat. pend.: patent pending
payt.: payment
pc.: piece
P/C: Petty Cash
p.c.: post card
pcl.: pencil
pct.: percent
pd.: paid; passed; period
per an.: by the year (L. per annum)
Per Pro., P.P.: on behalf of; by proxy (L. per procurationem)
pert.: pertaining
pet., petr.: petroleum
petn.: petition
pfd.: preferred
pharm.: pharmacist; pharmacy
pk.: pack,-ing; park; peck
pkg.: package (pl. pkgs.); parking
Pkwy.: Parkway
pl.: place; plate; plural
p.m.: afternoon
pm., prem.: premium
P.O.D.: payable on death; pay on delivery
pol.: policy; political; politics
pop.: population
pos.: position; positive
pot.: potential
pow.: power
pp.: pages
P.P.: Parcel Post
ppd.: post paid; prepaid
pr.: pair; price; printed

pref., pf.: preface; preference; prefix
prem.: premium
prep.: preparation; preposition
Pres.: President
prin.: principal
prob.: problem
prod.: produce,-ed,-tion; product
pron.: pronoun; pronounced; pronunciation
prop.: property; proposition
pro tem.: for the time being (L. pro tempre)
prox.: of the next month; proximo
P.S.: postscript
psgr, pass.: passenger
PST: Pacific Standard Time
pt.: part; pint; point; port
PT: Pacific Time
ptg.: printing
pub.: public,-ation; publish,-ed,-er,-ing
pur.: purchase,-er,-ing
Pvt.: Private
pwt.: pennyweight
PX: post exchange

q.: quart; query; question; quick; quire
Q.E.D.: which was to be proved (L. quod erat demonstrandum)
Q.E.F.: which was to be done (L. quod erat faciendum)
Q.E.I.: which was to be ascertained (L. quod erat inveniendum)
qly.: quality
qt.: quart
qtr.: quarter
qty.: quantity
quad.: quadrangle; quadrant
ques.: question(s)
q.v.: which see (pl. qq.v) (L. quod vide)
qy.: query

r.: right; road; rule
R.: radius; river
®*:* Registered in U.S. Patent Office

radar: radio detection and ranging
R. & D.: research and development
rcd.: record
rd.: road; rod; round
R.D.: rural delivery
re.: in regard to
R.E.: real estate
rec.: receipt; recipe; record
recd.: received
ref.: referee; reference; referred
refd.: refund
reg.: register,-ed; regular; regulation
rep.: repair; repeat; report
Rep.: Republic; Representative
req.: require,-ed; requisition
res.: reserve; residence; resolution; resort
ret.: retired; return
Rev.: Reverend
rev.: revenue; review; revise,-ed,-ion; revolution
rm.: ream; rooms
Rom.: Roman
ROP: run of paper
r.p.m.: revolutions per minute
RR: railroad
R.S.V.P.: please reply (F. respondez s'il vous plait)
Rte., Rt.: Route

s.: shilling; silver; son; stock
S.: south
sav.: saving(s)
SB: southbound
s.c.: small capital letters; same case (legal)
sc., scil.: namely, to wit (see ss)
sch.: schedule; school
sci.: science
SE: southeast
sec.: second
sect.: section
secy.: secretary
sel.: select,-ed,-ion
Sen.: Senate; Senator

sep.: separate
seq.: the following; in sequence (pl. seqq.)
serv.: service
sess.: session
Sgt.: Sergeant
sh.: share
sic.: thus (Latin; no period)
sig.: signature
sm.: small
So., S.: south,-ern
soc.: society
sol.: solicitor(s); soluble; solution
sonar: sound, navigation and ranging
SOP: standard operating procedure
SOS: Help! (distress signal)
sp.: special; species; spelling
s.p.s.: without surviving issue (L. sine prole superstite; law)
sq.: square
sq.: the following (L. sequens) (pl. sqq.)
Sq.: Square (in address)
Sr.: Senior; Señor; Sister
ss.: namely (L. scilicet; law)
SSE: south-southeast
SSW: south-southwest
St., Ste.: Saint, Sainte (pl. SS)
St.: State, Store; strait; Street
sta.: station
stat.: statistics; status; statutes
std.: standard
stet: let it stand (L.)
stg.: sterling
stge.: storage
Stk. Ex.: Stock Exchange
Stk. Mkt.: Stock Market
sub.: subscribe,-er; subscription
subj.: subject
subs.: subsidiary
sup.: above (L. supra); superior; supply
supp.: supplement
supt.: superintendent
surg.: surgeon; surgery; surgical

svc.: service
SW: southwest
syll.: syllable(s)
syn.: synonym,-ous
synd.: syndicate
sys., syst.: system

t.: temperature; time; town
T., Tp.: township
tab.: table(s); tabulation(s)
tbsp., tbs., T.: tablespoon(s)
tech.: technical
tel.: telegram; telegraph; telephone
temp.: temporary
Ter.: terrace; Territory,-ial
thou.: thousand
tr.: trace; translate,-or,-ion; trustee
trans.: transfer
transp.: transportation
Treas., Tr.: Treasurer; Treasury
tsp., t.: teaspoon(s)
TWX: teletypewriter exchange
tx.: tax(es); text

U., Univ.: University
uc., u.c.: uppercase
u.d., ut dict.: as directed (L. ut dictum)
u.i.: as below (L. ut infra)
ult.: last month (L. ultimo); ultimate
Un.: Union; United
unl.: unlimited
u.s.: as above (L. ut supra)
util.: utility,-ies

v.: verb; versus; volt; volume
vac.: vacant; vacuum
val.: value,-ation
var.: variant; variation; variety
vel.: velocity
v.i.: see below (L. vide infra)
vid.: see (L. vide)
viz.: namely (L. videlicet)
vol.: volume; volunteer
vs.: verse; versus
v.s.: see above (L. vide supra)
v.v.: vice versa

w.: watt; week; width
W: west
WB: waybill; westbound
whf: wharf
whge: wharfage
whs: warehouse
whsle.: wholesale
wk.: work
WSW: west-southwest
wt.: weight

x: box(es); by (2x3); cross (X-walk); extra(X-lge.); without
Xch.: exchange

y., yr.: year; your

z.: zero; zone
zool: zoology,-ical

DAYS

Sunday	Sun. or S.
Monday	Mon. or M.
Tuesday	Tues. or T.
Wednesday	Wed. or W.
Thursday	Thurs. or Th.
Friday	Fri. or F.
Saturday	Sat.

MONTHS

January	Jan.
February	Feb.
March	Mar.
April	Apr.
May	May
June	June
July	July
August	Aug.
September	Sept.
October	Oct.
November	Nov.
December	Dec.

17

fingertip guide to reference sources

There will be times when, during your secretarial career, you will have to find answers outside your frame of reference. If you have a working knowledge of some of the sources available, your search will be easier.

Note that public libraries will give information over the phone, but did you know you can borrow magazines, records, framed pictures and sometimes even pets? Did you know that some reference books can be used only at the library, that back issues of newspapers are kept on microfilm and are available for viewing, or that some libraries keep current daily and/or Sunday issues of large out of town newspapers? Most public libraries also keep telephone directories of major United States cities. Speaking of telephone directories, the index will tell you where to look for certain headings and some even have local zip code maps and bus routes.

Other sources are also included—clerks of the different courts will give detailed filing information as well as procedures involved in certain types of actions. Records of property owners and the holders of fictitious names are public information and are available at city government offices. Officers and directors of corporations can be obtained from the Commissioner of Corporations of the state in which the corporation was formed. Universities will send catalogs upon request and the Public Relations Department of most companies will be glad to send a brochure or two.

ACCOUNTING

Accountant's Digest, Burlington, Vt., L. L. Briggs.
Accountant's Handbook, New York, Ronald.
Accountant's Index, New York, American Institute of Certified Public Accountants.
Dictionary for Accountants, Fifth Ed., Englewood Cliffs, N. J., Prentice-Hall.
Encyclopedia of Accounting Systems, Rev. and Enlarged, Englewood Cliffs, N. J., Prentice-Hall.

AGRICULTURE

Biological and Agricultural Index, New York, Wilson.
Literature of Agricultural Research, Berkeley, California, University of California Press.
Yearbook of Agriculture, Washington, D.C., U.S. Department of Agriculture.

ALMANACS

Europa Year Book, London, Europa Publications.
Facts on File, New York, Facts on File, Inc.
Famous First Facts, New York, Wilson.
Guiness Book of World Records, New York, Sterling.
Information Please Almanac, New York, Simon & Schuster.
Negro Almanac, New York, Bellweather.
New York Times Encyclopedic Almanac, New York, The New York Times Company.
Reader's Digest Almanac and Yearbook, Pleasantville, N. Y., Reader's Digest Association.
World Almanac and Book of Facts, New York, Newspaper Enterprise Association, Inc.

ARCHITECTURE AND ART

Art Index, New York, Wilson.
Avery Index to Architectural Periodicals, Boston, G. K. Hall.

Dictionary of Antiques and the Decorative Arts, New York, Scribner.

Dictionary of Costume, New York, Scribner.

Encyclopedia of World Art, New York, McGraw-Hill.

Guide to Art Reference Books, Chicago, American Library Association.

How to Find Out About the Arts: A Guide to Sources of Information, Oxford, Pergamon Press.

The Pelican History of Art, Baltimore, Penguin Books.

World Architecture, New York, McGraw-Hill.

ATLASES

Columbia Lippincott Gazetteer of the World, New York, Columbia University Press.

Goode's World Atlas, Chicago, Rand McNally.

Hammond Medallion World Atlas, Maplewood, N. J., C. S. Hammond & Co.

National Geographic Atlas of the World, Washington, D. C., National Geographic Society.

Rand McNally Commercial Atlas, Chicago, Rand McNally.

Rand McNally Pocket World Atlas, New York, Pocket Books.

Times Atlas of the World, Boston, Houghton Mifflin.

BANKING

Bankers Almanac and Year Book, London, Skinner.

Encyclopedia of Banking and Finance, Boston, Bankers Publishing Company.

Polk's Bank Directory, Nashville, Tenn., R. C. Polk & Co.

BIBLIOGRAPHIES

Best Books, London, Routledge.

Bibliographic Index, New York, Wilson.

Books in Print, New York, Bowker.

Cumulative Book Index, New York, Wilson.

Literary Market Place, New York, Bowker.

Paperbound Books in Print, New York, Bowker.

Publisher's Trade List Annual, New York, Publisher's Weekly.

Subject Guide to Books in Print, New York, Bowker.

BIOGRAPHIES

Biographical Dictionaries and Related Works, Detroit, Gale.
Biography Index, New York, Wilson.
Concise Dictionary of American Biography, New York, Scribner.
Current Biography, New York, Wilson.
International Who's Who, London, Europa.
New York Times Index, New York, The New York Times
    Company.
Who's Who, London, Black.
Who's Who in America, Chicago, Marquis.
Who's Who in the East, Chicago, Marquis.
Who's Who in the World, Chicago, Marquis.
Who's Who of American Women, Chicago, Marquis.
*Who Knows-And What, Among Authorities, Experts and the Spe-
    cially Informed*, Chicago, Marquis.

BIOLOGY

Encyclopedia of the Biological Sciences, New York, Reinhold.
The Use of Biological Literature, Hamden, Conn., Archon.

BUSINESS

Business Periodicals Index, New York, Wilson.
Encyclopedic Dictionary of Business and Finance, Englewood
    Cliffs, N.J., Prentice-Hall.
*How to Use the Business Library, with Sources of Business In-
    formation*, Cincinnati, Southwestern Publishing Company.
Management Information Guide Series, Detroit, Gale Research.
Prentice-Hall Executive's Lifetime Ideas Library, Englewood
    Cliffs, N. J., Prentice-Hall.
Thomas' Register of American Manufacturers, New York,
    Thomas.
Sources of Business Information, Englewood Cliffs, N. J.,
    Prentice-Hall.

CREDIT

Dun and Bradstreet Ratings and Reports, New York City and
    local offices.

DICTIONARIES—ABRIDGED

A Dictionary of Modern English Usage, New York, University Press.

American Heritage Dictionary of the English Language, Boston, American Heritage and Houghton Mifflin.

Thorndike-Barnhard Comprehensive Desk Dictionary, New York, Doubleday.

Webster's Concise Dictionary, Springfield, Mass., Merriam.

Webster's New World Dictionary, Cleveland, Collins and World.

Webster's New Collegiate Dictionary, Springfield, Mass., Merriam.

DICTIONARIES—UNABRIDGED

Funk & Wagnalls New Standard Dictionary of the English Language, New York, Funk & Wagnalls.

Random House Dictionary of the English Language, New York Random House.

Webster's Third New International Dictionary, Springfield, Mass., Merriam.

DIRECTORIES

American Business Directories, Washington, D. C., U. S. Department of Commerce.

American Register of Exporters and Importers, New York, American Register of Exporters and Importers, Inc.

Encyclopedia of Associations, Detroit, Gale Research.

Haines Criss Cross Directories, N. Canton, Ohio, Haines (individual cities indexed by address, by phone).

Kelly's Directories of Merchants, Manufacturers and Shippers, London, Kelly's Directories, Ltd.

MacRae's Blue Book, Chicago, MacRae's Blue Book Company.

Polk's City Directories, Detroit, R. L. Polk (individual cities indexed by name, by address, by phone number).

Poor's Register of Directors and Executives, New York, Standard and Poor's Corporation.

ECONOMICS

Commodity Year Book, New York, Commodity Research Bureau.

Economic Almanac, New York, National Industrial Conference Board.

Economic Indicator, Washington, D.C., Government Printing Office.

Index of Economic Journals, Homewood, Ill., American Economic Association.

Survey of Current Business, Washington, D. C., U. S. Bureau of Foreign and Domestic Commerce.

EDUCATION

Education Index, New York, Wilson.

Lovejoy's Career and Vocational School Guide, New York, Simon and Schuster.

Patterson's American Educational Directory, Mount Prospect, Ill., Educational Directories Inc.

ENCYCLOPEDIAS

Collier's Encyclopedia, New York, Crowell-Collier.

Columbia Encyclopedia, New York, Columbia University Press.

Compton's Encyclopedia and Fact Index, Chicago, F. E. Compton.

Encyclopedia Americana, New York, Americana Corporation.

Encyclopedia Britanica, Chicago, Encyclopedia Britanica.

Lincoln Library of Essential Information, Buffalo, N. Y., Frontier Press.

World Book Encyclopedia, Chicago, Field Enterprises.

ENGINEERING

Engineering Index, New York, American Society of Mechanical Engineers.

Industrial Arts Index, New York, Wilson.

Harper Encyclopedia of Science, New York, Harper.

Science and Engineering Reference Sources, New York, Libraries Unlimited.

ENTERTAINMENT

Complete Book of American Musical Theater, New York, Holt.
Dance Encyclopedia, New York, Simon and Schuster.
Guide to Great Plays, Washington, D. C., Public Affairs Press.
International Motion Picture Almanac, New York, Quigley.
International Television Almanac, New York, Quigley.
Kobbe's Complete Opera Book, New York, Putnam.
The Oxford Companion to the Theater, New York, Oxford.

GOVERNMENT

Congressional Quarterly Weekly Report, Washington, D. C. Congressional Quarterly Inc.
Guide to U. S. Government Serials and Periodicals, McLean, Va., Documents Index.
Government Publications and Their Use, Washington, D. C. The Brookings Institution.
Manual of Government Publications: United States and Foreign, New York, Appleton-Century-Croft.
Monthly Catalog of U. S. Government Publications, Washington D. C., Superintendent of Documents.
United States Department of Commerce Publications, Washington, D. C., Government Printing Office.
United States Government Publications, New York, Wilson.

HISTORY

Dictionary of American History, New York, Scribner.
Encyclopedia of World History, Boston, Houghton Mifflin.

INFORMATION

Bulletin of the Public Affairs Information Service, New York, Public Affairs Information Service.
New York Times Index, New York, The New York Times Company.
Subject Collections, New York, Bowker.

Sweet's Catalog Service, New York, F. W. Dodge.

Winchell's Guide to Reference Books, Chicago, American Library Association, Revised by E. P. Sheehy.

INSURANCE

Best's Insurance Reports, New York, Alfred Best.

Best's Rate Book, New York, Alfred Best.

Insurance Almanac, New York, Underwriter Printing and Publishing Company.

LAW

Black's Law Dictionary, St. Paul, Minn. , West.

Congressional Record, Washington, D. C., Government Printing Office.

How Our Laws Are Made, Washington, D. C., Government Printing Office.

U. S. Laws, Statutes, etc. United States Code, Washington, D. C., Government Printing Office.

LIBRARIES

Public libraries will give telephone information on almost any facts they have, including: out of area telephone directories, reverse directories, rules of grammar, foreign phrases, geographical locations and their spellings.

LITERATURE

Cyclopedia of Literary Characters, New York, Salem Press.

Cyclopedia of World Authors, New York, Harper.

Granger's Index to Poetry, New York, Columbia University Press.

Index to Fairy Tales, Myths and Legends, Boston, Faxon.

Reader's Encyclopedia to American Literature, New York, Crowell.

MAILING LISTS

Dartnell Direct Mail and Mail Order Handbook, Chicago, Dartnell.

Guide to American Directories for Compiling Mailing Lists, New York, B. Klein.

MARKETING INFORMATION

Current Sources of Marketing Information, Chicago, American Marketing Association.

Marketing Maps of the United States, Washington, D. C., U. S. Library of Congress, Map Division.

MATHEMATICS

Guide to the Literature of Mathematics and Physics, New York, Dover.

International Dictionary of Applied Mathematics, Princeton, Van Nostrand.

Universal Encyclopedia of Mathematics, New York, Simon and Schuster.

MEDICINE

Cumulative Index of Hospital Literature, Chicago, American Hospital Association.

Dorlan's Illustrated Medical Dictionary, Philadelphia, W. B. Saunders.

Index Medicus, Washington, D. C., National Library of Medicine

MUSIC

Book of World Famous Music, New York, Crown.

Grove's Dictionary of Music and Musicians, New York, St. Martin's Press.

Music Index, Detroit, Information Service, Inc.

Music Reference and Research Materials, An Annotated Bibliography, New York, Free Press of Glencoe.
Song Index, New York, Wilson.

NEWSPAPERS AND MAGAZINES

Directory of Newspapers and Periodicals, Philadelphia, N. W. Ayer & Sons.
Editor and Publisher International Yearbook, New York, Editor and Publisher.
New York Times Index, New York, The New York Times Company.
Poole's Index to Periodical Literature, New York, Wilson.
Reader's Guide to Periodical Literature, New York, Wilson.
Standard Rate and Data Service, Skokie, Ill., Standard Rate and Data Service.
Ulrich's International Periodicals Directory, New York, Bowker.

PHILOSOPHY

Encyclopedia of Philosophy, New York, Macmillan.
The Philosopher's Index, Bowling Green, Ohio, Bowling Green University.

POLITICAL SCIENCE

Dictionary of Political Science, New York, Philosophical Library.
International Bibliography of Political Science, Chicago, Aldine.
The Literature of Political Science, New York, Bowker.
Who's Who in American Politics, New York, Bowker.
Yearbook of the United Nations, New York, United Nations Office of Public Information.

PUBLICITY AND ADVERTISING

Dartnell Advertising Manager's Handbook, Chicago, Dartnell.
Dartnell Public Relations Handbook, Chicago, Dartnell.
Encyclopedia of Advertising, New York, Fairchild.

QUOTATIONS

Dictionary of Quotations, New York, Delacorte Press.
Familiar Quotations, Boston, Little Brown.

REAL ESTATE

Questions and Answers on Real Estate, Ninth Ed., Englewood
    Cliffs, N. J., Prentice-Hall.
Real Estate Principles and Practices, Eighth Ed., Englewood
    Cliffs, N. J., Prentice-Hall.

RELIGION

Encyclopedia of Religion and Ethics, New York, Scribner.
Handbook of Denominations in the United States, Nashville,
    Tenn., Abingdon Press.

REPORTING SERVICES

Bureau of National Affairs, Washington, D. C. (labor relations,
    trade, etc.; list available upon request).
Commerce Clearing House, Chicago, Ill., (banking government
    contracts, stock, etc.; list available upon request).
Prentice-Hall, Englewood Cliffs, N. J., (insurance, law, secretarial
    publications, taxes, etc.; list available upon request).

SALES

Sales Manager's Handbook, Chicago, Dartnell.
Sales Promotion Handbook, Chicago, Dartnell.

SCIENCE

Basic Dictionary of Science, New York, Macmillan.
Encyclopedia of Science and Technology, New York, McGraw-
    Hill.
Science Reference Sources, Cambridge, Mass., M.I.T., Press.

SPACE AND ASTRONOMY

Concise Encyclopedia of Astronomy, Chicago, Collins.
Guide to Information Sources in Space Science and Technology,
    New York, Interscience.
McGraw-Hill Encyclopedia of Space, New York, McGraw-Hill.

SPORTS AND GAMES

Encyclopedia of Sports, New York, A. S. Barnes.
Foster's Complete Hoyle, Philadelphia, Lippincott.

SOCIOLOGY

Encyclopedia of Social Work, New York, National Association of
    Social Workers.
International Bibliography of Sociology, Chicago, Aldine.
Social Science and Humanities Index, New York, Wilson.

STATISTICS

Catalog of United States Census Publications, Washington, D. C.
    Government Printing Office.
Demographic Yearbook of the United Nations, New York, United
    Nations.
Guide to U. S. Government Statistics, Arlington, Va., Documents
    Index.
Statesman's Yearbook, New York, St. Martin's Press.
Statistical Yearbook of the United Nations, New York, United
    Nations.
Survey of Current Business, Washington, D. C., Superintendent
    of Documents.

STYLE

Elements of Style, New York, Macmillan.
Style Book of the New York Times, New York, The New York
    Times Company (style related to newspapers).
Style Manual of the Government Printing Office, Washington,
    D. C., Government Printing Office.
Words Into Type, Englewood Cliffs, N. J., Prentice-Hall.

THESAURI

Roget's International Thesaurus of English Words and Phrases,
    New York, Thomas Y. Crowell Company.
Roget's Thesaurus in Dictionary Form, New York, Putnam.
Roget's Pocket Thesaurus, New York, Pocket Books.
Webster's New Dictionary of Synonyms, Springfield, Mass.,
    Merriam.

TRAVEL

Baedeker's Guide Books, New York, Scribner.
Encyclopedia of World Travel, Garden City, N. Y., Doubleday.
Guide to America, Washington, D. C., Public Affairs Press.
Hotel and Motel Red Book and Directory, New York, American
    Hotel Association.
Official Airlines Guide, Oak Park, Ill., Reuben H. Donnelly
    Corporation.
Reference Guide for Travelers, New York, Bowker.
The Blue Guides, Chicago, Rand McNally.

18

charts of handy information

It is the unexpected situation that usually needs an on-the-spot answer, so here are charts of handy information including one of proofreader's marks that shows which are used in text and which in the margin, along with a sample paragraph showing you how to correct proofs. The chapter also contains charts that describe the signs and symbols for mathematical calculations; physics and electricity; moons and planets; astrology; medicine and pharmacy; and weather. There is also a table of weights and measures from common to metric for linear, square, cubic, chain, surveyor's (square), nautical, dry, liquid, apothecaries' fluid, circular (angular), avoirdupois, troy and apothecaries' measure; and from metric to common for linear, square, land, volume and weight—as well as a table of numbers showing cardinal (Arabic and Roman) and ordinal numbers, and fractional and decimal number equivalents.

In addition, there are Centigrade and Fahrenheit conversions, with a thermometer to make it easy; a map of the time zones of the world; the forms of address for persons of rank and public office such as president of the United States, cabinet officers, the bench, members of Congress, officers of the armed forces, ambassador, governor, mayor, the clergy and royalty and nobility; and commonly used phrases in English, French, Italian, Spanish, German, Swedish, Portuguese, Dutch, Chinese and Japanese.

PROOFREADER'S MARKS

⊙	Insert period	*Caps.*	Caps—used in margin
⋀	Insert comma	≡	Caps—used in text
:	Insert colon	*C + ʃc*	Caps & small caps—used in margin
;	Insert semicolon	≡	Caps & small caps—used in text
?	Insert question mark	*l.c.*	Lowercase—used in margin
!	Insert exclamation mark	/	Used in text to show deletion or substitution
=/	Insert hyphen	*w.f.*	Wrong font
⌄	Insert apostrophe	⌒	Close up
⟨⟨ ⟩⟩	Insert quotation marks	⸰	Delete
⊥	Insert 1-en dash	⸰	Close up and delete
⊥	Insert 1-em dash	⟳	Correct the position
#	Insert space	⸥	Move right
ld>	Insert lead	⸤	Move left
shill	Insert virgule	⊓	Move up
∨	Superior	⊔	Move down
∧	Inferior	‖	Aline vertically
(/)	Parentheses	=	Aline horizontally
[/]	Brackets	⸥⸤	Center horizontally
☐	Indent 1 em	⊔⊓	Center vertically
☐☐	Indent 2 ems	⌣	Push down space
¶	Paragraph	⌒	Use ligature
no ¶	No paragraph	*eq.#*	Equalize space—used in margin
tr	Transpose [1]—used in margin	⌄⌄⌄	Equalize space—used in text
∼	Transpose [2]—used in text	*stet.*	Let it stand—used in margin
sp	Spell out	....	Let it stand—used in text
ital	Italic—used in margin	⊗	Dirty or broken letter
____	Italic—used in text	*run over*	Carry over to next line
b.f.	Boldface—used in margin	*run back*	Carry back to preceding line
∼∼∼	Boldface—used in text	*out, see copy*	Something omitted—see copy
s.c.	Small caps—used in margin	*ʃ/?*	Question to author to delete [3]
≡	Small caps—used in text	∧	Caret—General indicator used to mark exact position of error in text.
rom.	Roman type		

[1] In lieu of the traditional mark "tr" used to indicate letter or number transpositions, the striking out of the incorrect letters or numbers and the placement of the correct matter in the margin of the proof is the preferred method of indicating transposition corrections.

[2] Corrections involving more than two characters should be marked by striking out the entire word or number and placing the correct form in the margin. This mark should be reserved to show transposition of words.

[3] The form of any query carried should be such that an answer may be given simply by crossing out the complete query if a negative decision is made or the right-hand (question mark) portion to indicate an affirmative answer.

From U. S. Government Printing Office Style Manual

HOW TO CORRECT PROOFS

It does not appear that the earliest printers had any method of correcting errors before the form was on the press. The learned ~~The learned~~ correctors of the first two centuries of printing were not proof readers in our sense; they were rather what we should term office editors. Their labors were chiefly to see that the proof corresponded to the copy, but that the printed page was correct in its latinity, ~~that the words were~~ there, and that the sense was right. They cared ~~but~~ little about orthography, bad letters, or purely printers errors, and when the text seemed to them wrong they consulted fresh authorities or altered it on their own responsibility. Good proofs, in the modern sense, were ~~im~~ possible until professional readers were employed, men who had first a printer's education, and then spent many years in the correction of proof. The orthography of English, which for the past century has undergone little change, was very fluctuating until after the publication of Johnson's Dictionary, and capitals, which have been used with considerable regularity for the past 80 years, were previously used on the miss or hit plan. The approach to regularity, so far as we have, may be attributed to the growth of a class of professional proof readers, and it is to them that we owe the correctness of modern printing. More errors have been found in the Bible than in any other one work. For many generations it was frequently the case that Bibles were brought out stealthily, from fear of governmental interference. They were frequently printed from imperfect texts, and were often modified to meet the views of those who publised them. The story is related that a certain woman in Germany, ~~who was~~ the wife of a printer, ~~and~~ had become disgusted with the continual assertions of the superiority of man over woman which she had heard, hurried into the composing room while her husband was at supper and altered a sentence in the Bible, which he was printing, so that it read Narr instead of Herr, thus making the verse read "And he shall be thy fool" instead of "And he shall be thy lord." The word not was omitted by Barker, the King's printer in England in 1632, in printing the seventh commandment. He was fined £3,000 on this account.

NOTE—The system of marking proofs can be made easier by the use of an imaginary vertical line through the center of the type area. The placement of corrections in the left-hand margin for those errors found in the left-hand portion of the proof and in the right-hand margin for right-side errors prevents overcrowding of marks and facilitates corrections.

From U. S. Government Printing Office Style Manual

SIGNS AND SYMBOLS

+ plus
− minus
± plus or minus
∓ minus or plus
× multiplied by
÷ divided by
= equal to
≠ or ≠ not equal to
≈ or ≐ nearly equal to
≡ identical with
≢ not identical with
⇔ equivalent
∼ difference
≅ congruent to
> greater than
≯ not greater than
< less than
≮ not less than
≧ or ≥ greater than or equal to
≦ or ≤ less than or equal to
| | absolute value
∪ logical sum or union
∩ logical product or intersection
⊂ is contained in
ε is a member of; dielectric constant; mean error
: is to; ratio
:: as; proportion
≑ approaches
→ approaches limit of
∝ varies as
‖ parallel
⊥ perpendicular
∠ angle
∟ right angle
△ triangle
□ square
▭ rectangle
▱ parallelogram
○ circle
⌒ arc of circle
⟂ equilateral
⧍ equiangular
√ radical; root; square root
∛ cube root
∜ fourth root
Σ sum
! or ⌐ factorial product
∞ infinity
∫ integral
ƒ function
∂ or δ differential; variation
π pi
∴ therefore
∵ because
‾ vinculum (above letter)
( ) parentheses

[ ] brackets
{ } braces
° degree
′ minute
″ second
HP horsepower
Δ increment
ω ohm
Ω microhm
MΩ megohm
Φ magnetic flux; farad
Ψ dielectric flux; electrostatic flux
ρ resistivity
γ conductivity
Λ equivalent conductivity
ℜ reluctance
→ direction of flow
⇆ electrical current
⬡ benzene ring
→ yields
⇌ reversible reaction
↓ precipitate
↑ gas
‰ salinity
☉ or ⊙ Sun
● or ⬤ New Moon
☽ First Quarter
○ or ⊕ Full Moon
☾ Last Quarter
☿ Mercury
♀ Venus
⊖ or ⊕ Earth
♂ Mars
♃ Jupiter
♄ Saturn
♅ Uranus
♆ or Ψ Neptune
♇ Pluto
♈ Aries
♉ Taurus
♊ Gemini
♋ Cancer
♌ Leo
♍ Virgo
♎ Libra
♏ Scorpio
♐ Sagittarius
♑ Capricornus
♒ Aquarius
♓ Pisces
♂ conjunction
♊ opposition
△ trine
□ quadrature
✳ sextile
☊ dragon's head, ascending node
☋ dragon's tail, descending node
① Ceres
② Pallas
③ Juno
④ Vesta

⊕ rain
✳ snow
⊠ snow on ground
← floating ice crystals
▲ hail
△ sleet
∨ frostwork
⊔ hoarfrost
≡ fog
∞ haze; dust haze
⊤ thunder
< sheet lightning
① solar corona
⊕ solar halo
⌂ thunderstorm
↖ direction
○ or ☉ or ① annual
☉☉ or ② biennial
♃ perennial
♂ or ♂ male
♀ female
□ male, in charts
○ female, in charts
℞ take (from Latin *Recipe*)
ĀĀ or Ā or āā of each (doctor's prescription)
℔ pound
℥ ounce
ʒ dram
℈ scruple
O pint
ƒʒ fluid ounce
ƒʒ fluid dram
♏ minim
& or & and; ampersand
℔ per
number
/ virgule; solidus; separatrix; shilling
% percent
© copyright
℅ care of
℀ account of
@ at
¢ cent
* asterisk
† dagger
‡ double dagger
§ section
☞ index
́ acute
̀ grave
∼ tilde
̂ circumflex
̄ macron
̆ breve
·· dieresis
̧ cedilla
∧ caret

From U. S. Government Printing Office Style Manual

TABLES OF WEIGHTS AND MEASURES

Linear Measure

1 mil = 0.001 inch	=	0.0254 millimeter
1 inch = 1,000 mils	=	2.54 centimeters
12 inches = 1 foot	=	0.3048 meter
3 feet = 1 yard	=	0.9144 meter
5½ yards or 16½ feet = 1 rod (or pole or perch)	=	5.029 meters
40 rods = 1 furlong	=	201.168 meters
8 furlongs or 1,760 yards or 5,280 feet = 1 (statute) mile	=	1.6093 kilometers
3 miles = 1 (land) league	=	4.83 kilometers

Square Measure

1 square inch	=	6.452 square centimeters
144 square inches = 1 square foot	=	929.03 square centimeters
9 square feet = 1 square yard	=	0.8361 square meter
30¼ square yards = 1 square rod (or square pole or square perch)	=	25.292 square meters
160 square rods or 4,840 square yards or 43,560 square feet = 1 acre	=	0.4047 hectare
640 acres = 1 square mile	=	259.00 hectares or 2.590 square kilometers

Cubic Measure

1 cubic inch =	16.387 cubic centimeters
1,728 cubic inches = 1 cubic foot =	0.0283 cubic meter
27 cubic feet = 1 cubic yard =	0.7646 cubic meter
(in units for cordwood, etc.)	
16 cubic feet = 1 cord foot =	0.453 cubic meter
128 cubic feet or 8 cord feet = 1 cord =	3.625 cubic meters

Chain Measure

(for Gunter's, or surveyor's, chain)

7.92 inches = 1 link =	20.12 centimeters
100 links or 66 feet = 1 chain =	20.12 meters
10 chains or 220 yards = 1 furlong =	201.17 meters
80 chains = 1 mile =	1.6093 kilometers

(for engineer's chain)

1 foot = 1 link =	0.3048 meter
100 feet = 1 chain =	30.48 meters
52.8 chains = 1 mile =	1,609.3 meters

Surveyor's (Square) Measure

625 square links = 1 square pole	=	25.29 square meters
16 square poles = 1 square chain	=	404.7 square meters
10 square chains = 1 acre	=	0.4047 hectare
640 acres = 1 square mile or 1 section	=	259.00 hectares or 2.59 square kilometers
36 square miles = 1 township	=	9,324.0 hectares or 93.24 square kilometers

Nautical Measure

6 feet = 1 fathom	= 1.829 meters
100 fathoms = 1 cable's length (ordinary) (In the U.S. Navy 120 fathoms or 720 feet, or 219.456 meters, = 1 cable's length; in the British Navy, 608 feet, or 185.319 meters, = 1 cable's length.)	
10 cables' length = 1 international nautical mile (6,076.11549 feet, by international agreement)	= 1.852 kilometers (exactly)
1 international nautical mile = 1.150779 statute miles (the length of a minute of longitude at the equator)	
3 nautical miles = 1 marine league (3.45 statute miles)	= 5.56 kilometers
60 nautical miles = 1 degree of a great circle of the earth = 69.047 statute miles	

Dry Measure

1 pint =	33.60 cubic inches =	0.5506 liter
2 pints = 1 quart =	67.20 cubic inches =	1.1012 liters
8 quarts = 1 peck =	537.61 cubic inches =	8.8098 liters
4 pecks = 1 bushel =	2,150.42 cubic inches =	35.2390 liters

According to United States government standards, the following are the weights avoirdupois for single bushels of the specified grains: for wheat, 60 pounds; for barley, 48 pounds; for oats, 32 pounds; for rye, 56 pounds; for shelled corn, 56 pounds. Some States have specifications varying from these.
The British dry quart = 1.032 U.S. dry quarts

Liquid Measure

1 gill = 4 fluid ounces =	7.219 cubic inches =	0.1183 liter
(see next table)		
4 gills = 1 pint =	28.875 cubic inches =	0.4732 liter
2 pints = 1 quart =	57.75 cubic inches =	0.9464 liter
4 quarts = 1 gallon =	231 cubic inches =	3.7854 liters

The British imperial gallon (4 imperial quarts) = 277.42 cubic inches = 4.546 liters. The barrel in Great Britain equals 36 imperial gallons, in the United States, usually 31½ gallons.

With permission from Webster's New World Dictionary, Second College Edition.
Copyright © 1976 by William Collins and World Publishing Co., Inc.

Apothecaries' Fluid Measure

	1 minim	=	0.0038	cubic inch	=	0.0616	milliliter
60 minims	= 1 fluid dram	=	0.2256	cubic inch	=	3.6966	milliliters
8 fluid drams	= 1 fluid ounce	=	1.8047	cubic inches	=	0.0296	liter
16 fluid ounces	= 1 pint	=	28.875	cubic inches	=	0.4732	liter

See table immediately preceding for quart and gallon equivalents.
The British pint = 20 fluid ounces.

Circular (or Angular) Measure

60 seconds ('')	=	1 minute (')
60 minutes	=	1 degree (°)
90 degrees	=	1 quadrant or 1 right angle
180 degrees	=	2 quadrants or 1 straight angle
4 quadrants or 360 degrees	=	1 circle

Avoirdupois Weight

(The grain, equal to 0.0648 gram, is the same in all three tables of weight.)

1 dram or 27.34 grains			=	1.772	grams
16 drams or 437.5 grains	=	1 ounce	=	28.3495	grams
16 ounces or 7,000 grains	=	1 pound	=	453.59	grams
100 pounds	=	1 hundredweight	=	45.36	kilograms
2,000 pounds	=	1 ton	=	907.18	kilograms

In Great Britain, 14 pounds (6.35 kilograms) = 1 stone, 112 pounds (50.80 kilograms) = 1 hundredweight, and 2,240 pounds (1,016.05 kilograms) = 1 long ton.

Troy Weight

(The grain, equal to 0.0648 gram, is the same in all three tables of weight.)

3.086 grains	=	1 carat	=	200.00	milligrams
24 grains	=	1 pennyweight	=	1.5552	grams
20 pennyweights or 480 grains	=	1 ounce	=	31.1035	grams
12 ounces or 5,760 grains	=	1 pound	=	373.24	grams

Apothecaries' Weight

(The grain, equal to 0.0648 gram, is the same in all three tables of weight.)

20 grains	=	1 scruple	=	1.296	grams
3 scruples	=	1 dram	=	3.888	grams
8 drams or 480 grains	=	1 ounce	=	31.1035	grams
12 ounces or 5,760 grains	=	1 pound	=	373.24	grams

THE METRIC SYSTEM

Linear Measure

	1 millimeter	=	0.03937	inch
10 millimeters	= 1 centimeter	=	0.3937	inch
10 centimeters	= 1 decimeter	=	3.937	inches
10 decimeters	= 1 meter	=	39.37	inches or 3.2808 feet
10 meters	= 1 decameter	=	393.7	inches
10 decameters	= 1 hectometer	=	328.08	feet
10 hectometers	= 1 kilometer	=	0.621	mile or 3,280.8 feet
10 kilometers	= 1 myriameter	=	6.21	miles

Square Measure

	1 square millimeter	=	0.00155	square inch
100 square millimeters	= 1 square centimeter	=	0.15499	square inch
100 square centimeters	= 1 square decimeter	=	15.499	square inches
100 square decimeters	= 1 square meter	=	1,549.9	square inches or 1.196 square yards
100 square meters	= 1 square decameter	=	119.6	square yards
100 square decameters	= 1 square hectometer	=	2.471	acres
100 square hectometers	= 1 square kilometer	=	0.386	square mile or 247.1 acres

Land Measure

1 square meter	=	1 centiare	=	1,549.9	square inches
100 centiares	=	1 are	=	119.6	square yards
100 ares	=	1 hectare	=	2.471	acres
100 hectares	=	1 square kilometer	=	0.386	square mile or 247.1 acres

Volume Measure

1,000 cubic millimeters	=	1 cubic centimeter	=	0.06102	cubic inch
1,000 cubic centimeters	=	1 cubic decimeter	=	61.023	cubic inches or 0.0353 cubic foot
1,000 cubic decimeters	=	1 cubic meter	=	35.314	cubic feet or 1.308 cubic yards

(the unit is called a *stere* in measuring firewood)

Capacity Measure

10 milliliters	=	1 centiliter	=	0.338	fluid ounce
10 centiliters	=	1 deciliter	=	3.38	fluid ounces or 0.1057 liquid quart
10 deciliters	=	1 liter	=	1.0567	liquid quarts or 0.9081 dry quart
10 liters	=	1 decaliter	=	2.64	gallons or 0.284 bushel
10 decaliters	=	1 hectoliter	=	26.418	gallons or 2.838 bushels
10 hectoliters	=	1 kiloliter	=	264.18	gallons or 35.315 cubic feet

Weights

10 milligrams	=	1 centigram	=	0.1543	grain or 0.000353 ounce (avdp.)
10 centigrams	=	1 decigram	=	1.5432	grains
10 decigrams	=	1 gram	=	15.432	grains or 0.035274 ounce (avdp.)
10 grams	=	1 decagram	=	0.3527	ounce
10 decagrams	=	1 hectogram	=	3.5274	ounces
10 hectograms	=	1 kilogram	=	2.2046	pounds
10 kilograms	=	1 myriagram	=	22.046	pounds
10 myriagrams	=	1 quintal	=	220.46	pounds
10 quintals	=	1 metric ton	=	2,204.6	pounds

TABLE OF NUMBERS

CARDINAL NUMBERS[1]			ORDINAL NUMBERS[4]	
NAME[2]	**SYMBOL**		**NAME**[5]	**SYMBOL**[6]
	Arabic	*Roman*[3]		
zero *or* naught *or* cipher	0		first	1st
one	1	I	second	2d *or* 2nd
two	2	II	third	3d *or* 3rd
three	3	III	fourth	4th
four	4	IV	fifth	5th
five	5	V	sixth	6th
six	6	VI	seventh	7th
seven	7	VII	eighth	8th
eight	8	VIII	ninth	9th
nine	9	IX	tenth	10th
ten	10	X	eleventh	11th
eleven	11	XI	twelfth	12th
twelve	12	XII	thirteenth	13th
thirteen	13	XIII	fourteenth	14th
fourteen	14	XIV	fifteenth	15th
fifteen	15	XV	sixteenth	16th
sixteen	16	XVI	seventeenth	17th
seventeen	17	XVII	eighteenth	18th
eighteen	18	XVIII	nineteenth	19th
nineteen	19	XIX	twentieth	20th
twenty	20	XX	twenty-first	21st
twenty-one	21	XXI	twenty-second	22d *or* 22nd
twenty-two	22	XXII	twenty-third	23d *or* 23rd
twenty-three	23	XXIII	twenty-fourth	24th
twenty-four	24	XXIV	twenty-fifth	25th
twenty-five	25	XXV	twenty-sixth	26th
twenty-six	26	XXVI	twenty-seventh	27th
twenty-seven	27	XXVII	twenty-eighth	28th
twenty-eight	28	XXVIII	twenty-ninth	29th
twenty-nine	29	XXIX	thirtieth	30th
thirty	30	XXX	thirty-first	31st
thirty-one	31	XXXI	thirty-second *etc*	32d *or* 32nd
thirty-two *etc*	32	XXXII	fortieth	40th
forty	40	XL	forty-first	41st
forty-one *etc*	41	XLI	forty-second *etc*	42d *or* 42nd
fifty	50	L	fiftieth	50th
sixty	60	LX	sixtieth	60th
seventy	70	LXX	seventieth	70th
eighty	80	LXXX	eightieth	80th
ninety	90	XC	ninetieth	90th
one hundred	100	C	hundredth *or* one hundredth	100th
one hundred and one *or* one hundred one	101	CI	hundred and first *or* one hundred and first	101st
one hundred and two *etc*	102	CII	hundred and second *etc*	102d *or* 102nd
two hundred	200	CC	two hundredth	200th
three hundred	300	CCC	three hundredth	300th
four hundred	400	CD	four hundredth	400th
five hundred	500	D	five hundredth	500th
six hundred	600	DC	six hundredth	600th
seven hundred	700	DCC	seven hundredth	700th
eight hundred	800	DCCC	eight hundredth	800th
nine hundred	900	CM	nine hundredth	900th
one thousand *or* ten hundred *etc*	1,000	M	thousandth *or* one thousandth	1,000th
two thousand *etc*	2,000	MM	two thousandth *etc*	2,000th
five thousand	5,000	$\overline{\mathrm{V}}$	ten thousandth	10,000th
ten thousand	10,000	$\overline{\mathrm{X}}$	hundred thousandth *or* one hundred thousandth	100,000th
one hundred thousand	100,000	$\overline{\mathrm{C}}$	millionth *or* one millionth	1,000,000th
one million	1,000,000	$\overline{\mathrm{M}}$		

[1] The cardinal numbers are used in simple counting or in answer to "how many?" The words for these numbers may be used as nouns (he counted to *twelve*), as pronouns (*twelve* were found), or as adjectives (*twelve* boys).

[2] In formal contexts the numbers one to one hundred and in less formal contexts the numbers one to nine are commonly written out, while larger numbers are given in numerals. In nearly all contexts a number occurring at the beginning of a sentence is usually written out. Except in very formal contexts numerals are invariably used for dates. Arabic numerals from 1,000 to 9,999 are often written without commas (1000, 9999). Year numbers are always written without commas (1783).

[3] The Roman numerals are written either in capitals or in lowercase letters.

[4] The ordinal numbers are used to show the order or succession in which such items as names, objects, and periods of time are considered (the *twelfth* month; the *fourth* row of seats; the *18th* century).

[5] Each of the terms for the ordinal numbers excepting *first* and *second* is used in designating one of a number of parts into which a whole may be divided (a *fourth*; a *sixth*; a *tenth*) and as the denominator in fractions designating the number of such parts constituting a certain portion of a whole (one *fourth*; three *fifths*). When used as nouns the fractions are usually written as two words, although they are regularly hyphenated as adjectives (a *two-thirds* majority). When fractions are written in numerals, the cardinal symbols are used ($^1/_4$, $^3/_5$, $^5/_6$).

[6] The Arabic symbols for the cardinal numbers may be read as ordinals in certain contexts (January 1 = January first; 2 Samuel = Second Samuel). The Roman numerals are sometimes read as ordinals (Henry IV = Henry the Fourth); sometimes they are written with the ordinal suffixes (XIXth Dynasty).

By permission from Webster's New Collegiate Dictionary © *1977 by G. and C. Merriam Co., publishers of the Merriam-Webster dictionaries.*

DECIMALS AND FRACTIONS

	3rds	4ths	5ths	6ths	7ths	8ths	9ths	11ths	12ths	13ths	14ths	15ths	16ths
1	.3333	.2500	.2000	.1667	.1429	.1250	.1111	.0909	.0833	.0769	.0714	.0667	.0625
2	.6667	.5000	.4000	.3333	.2857	.2500	.2222	.1818	.1667	.1538	.1429	.1333	.1250
3		.7500	.6000	.5000	.4296	.3750	.3333	.2727	.2500	.3208	.2143	.2000	.1875
4			.8000	.6667	.5714	.5000	.4444	.3636	.3333	.3977	.2857	.2667	.2500
5				.8333	.7143	.6250	.5556	.4545	.4167	.3846	.3571	.3333	.3125
6					.8571	.7500	.6667	.5455	.5000	.4615	.4286	.4000	.3750
7						.8750	.7778	.6364	.5833	.5385	.5000	.4667	.4375
8							.8889	.7273	.6667	.6154	.5714	.5333	.5000
9								.8182	.7500	.6923	.6429	.6000	.5626
10								.9091	.8333	.7692	.7143	.6667	.6250
11									.9167	.8462	.7857	.7333	.6875
12										.9231	.8571	.8000	.7500
13											.9286	.8667	.8125
14												.9333	.8750
15													.9375

WORLD TIME ZONES

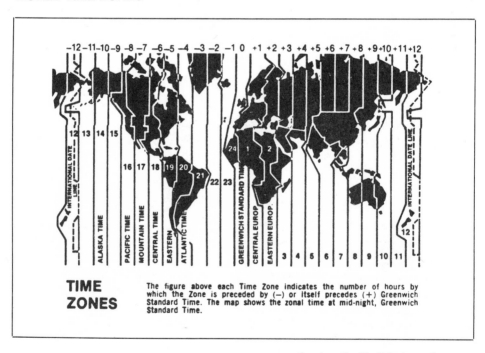

TIME ZONES

The figure above each Time Zone indicates the number of hours by which the Zone is preceded by (−) or itself precedes (+) Greenwich Standard Time. The map shows the zonal time at mid-night, Greenwich Standard Time.

Courtesy Pacific Telephone Company
San Francisco, California

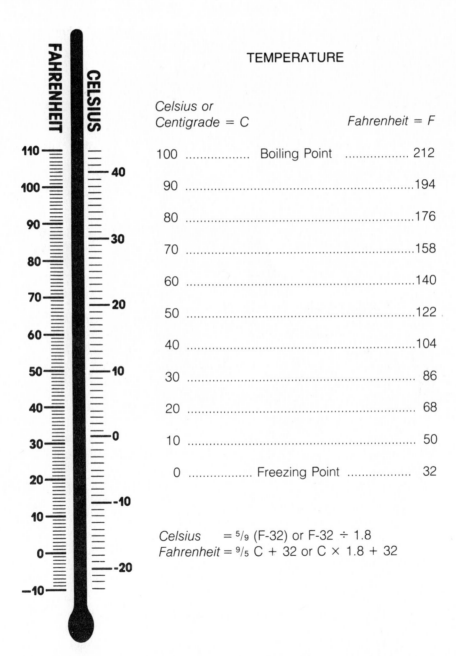

TEMPERATURE

Celsius or
Centigrade = C   *Fahrenheit = F*

100	Boiling Point	212
90		194
80		176
70		158
60		140
50		122
40		104
30		86
20		68
10		50
0	Freezing Point	32

Celsius = $\frac{5}{9}$ (F-32) or F-32 ÷ 1.8
Fahrenheit = $\frac{9}{5}$ C + 32 or C × 1.8 + 32

Thermometer Courtesy Joel Bartlett, Meteorologist, KPIX TV, CBS, Channel 5, San Francisco, California

FORMS OF ADDRESS FOR PERSONS OF
RANK AND PUBLIC OFFICE

In these examples John Smith is used as a representative American name. The salutation Dear Sir is always permissible when addressing a person not known to the writer.

President of the United States

Address: The President, The White House, Washington, D.C. 20500. Also, The President and Mrs. ——.

Salutation: Dear Sir or Mr. President or Dear Mr. President. More intimately: My dear Mr. President. Also: Dear Mr. President and Mrs. ————
The vice president takes the same forms.

Cabinet Officers

Address: Mr. John Smith, Secretary of State, Washington, D.C. or The Hon. John Smith. Similar addresses for other members of the cabinet. Also: Secretary and Mrs. John Smith.

Salutation: Dear Sir, or Dear Mr. Secretary. Also: Dear Mr. and Mrs. Smith.

The Bench

Address: The Hon. John Smith, Chief Justice of the United States. The Hon. John Smith, Associate Justice of the Supreme Court of the United States. The Hon. John Smith, Associate Judge, U. S. District Court.

Salutation: Dear Sir, or Dear Mr. Chief Justice. Dear Mr. Justice. Dear Judge Smith.

Members of Congress

Address: The Hon. John Smith, United States Senate, Washington, D.C. 20510, or Sen. John Smith, etc. Also The Hon. John Smith, House of Representatives, Washington, D.C. 20515, or Rep. John Smith, etc.

Salutation: Dear Mr. Senator or Dear Mr. Smith; for Representative, Dear Mr. Smith.

Officers of Armed Forces

Address: Careful attention should be given to the precise rank, thus: General of the Army John Smith, Fleet Admiral John Smith. The rules for Air Force are same as Army.

Salutation: Dear Sir, or Dear General. All general officers, whatever rank, are entitled to be addressed as generals. Likewise a lieutenant colonel is addressed as colonel and first and second lieutenants are addressed as lieutenant.
Warrant officers and flight officers are addressed as Mister. Chaplains are addressed as Chaplain. A Catholic chaplain may be addressed as Father. Cadets of the United States Military Academy and Air Force Academy are addressed as Cadet. Noncommissioned officers are addressed by their titles. In the U. S.

Navy all men from midshipman at Annapolis up to and including lieutenant commander are addressed as Mister.

Ambassador, Governor, Mayor

Address: The Hon. John Smith, followed by his title. He can be addressed either at his embassy, or at the Department of State, Washington, D.C. An ambassador from a foreign nation may be addressed as His Excellency. An American is not to be so addressed.

Salutation: Dear Mr. Ambassador. An ambassador from a foreign nation may be called Your Excellency.

Governors and mayors are often addressed as The Hon. John Smith, Governor of _____ ; or The Hon. John Smith, Mayor of_____; also Governor John Smith, State House, Albany, N.Y., or Mayor John Smith, City Hall, Erie, Pa.

The Clergy

Address: His Holiness, the Pope, or His Holiness Pope (name), State of Vatican City, Italy.

Salutation: Your Holiness or Most Holy Father.

Also: His Eminence, John, Cardinal Smith; salutation: Your Eminence. An archbishop or a bishop is addressed The Most Reverend, and the salutation is Your Excellency. A monsignor who is a papal chamberlain is The Very Reverend Monsignor and

the salutation is Dear Sir or Very Reverend Monsignor; a monsignor who is a domestic prelate is The Right Reverend Monsignor and salutation is Right Reverend Monsignor. A priest is addressed Reverend John Smith. A brother of an order is addressed Brother —. A sister takes the same form.

A bishop of the Protestant Episcopal Church is The Right Reverend John Smith; salutation is Right Reverend Sir, or Dear Bishop Smith. If a clergyman is a doctor of divinity, he is addressed: The Reverend John Smith, D.D., and the salutation is Reverend Sir, or Dear Dr. Smith. When a clergyman does not have the degree the salutation is Dear Mr. Smith.

A bishop of the Methodist Church is addressed Bishop John Smith with titles following.

Royalty and Nobility

An emperor is to be addressed in a letter as Sir, or Your Imperial Majesty.

A king or queen is addressed as His Majesty (Name), King of (Name), or Her Majesty (Name), Queen of (Name). Salutation: Sir, or Madam, or May it please Your Majesty.

Princes and princesses and other persons of royal blood are addressed as His (or Her) Royal Highness, and saluted with May it please Your Royal Highness.

A duke or marquis is My Lord Duke (or Marquis), a duke is His (or Your) Grace.

WORD TRANSLATIONS

ENGLISH	FRENCH	ITALIAN	SPANISH	GERMAN
1. Do you speak English?	1. Parlez-vous anglais?	1. Parla inglese?	1. ¿Habia usted ingles?	1. Sprechen Sie englisch?
2. I do not understand	2. Je ne comprends pas	2. Non capisco	2. No entiendo	2. Ich verstehe nicht
3. Yes/No	3. Qui/Non	3. Si/No	3. Si/No	3. Ja/Nein
4. Your name?	4. Votre nom?	4. Il Suo nome?	4. ¿Su nombre?	4. Ihr Name?
5. I, you, he, she	5. Je, vous, il, elle	5. Io, Lei, egli, ella	5. Yo, usted, el, ella	5. Ich, Sie, er, sie
6. Good morning	6. Bonjour	6. Buon giorno	6. Buenos dias	6. Guten Morgen
7. Good evening	7. Bonsoir	7. Buona sera	7. Buenas noches	7. Guten Abend
8. Good night	8. Bonne nuit	8. Bonna notte	8. Buenas noches	8. Gute Nacht
9. Good-bye	9. Au revoir	9. ArrivederLa	9. Adios	9. Auf Wiedersehen
10. How are you?	10. Comment allez-vous?	10. Come sta?	10. ¿Cómo está usted?	10. Wie ghet es Ihnen?
11. How far?	11. A quelle distance?	11. Quant e lontano?	11. ¿Hasta dónde?	11. Wie weit?
12. How much is it?	12. Combien est-ce?	12. Quanto costa?	12. ¿Cuánto vale?	12. Wieviel kostet es?
13. Too much	13. Trop cher	13. Troppo caro	13. Demasiado	13. Zu teuer
14. Very Well	14. Tres bien	14. Benissimo	14. Muy bien	14. Sehr gut
15. Thank you	15. Merci	15. Grazie	15. Gracias	15. Danke
16. You are welcome	16. Je vous en prie	16. Prego	16. De nada	16. Nichts zu danken
17. Excuse me	17. Exusez-moi	17. Scusi	17. Dispénseme	17. Entschuldigen Sie
18. I am sorry	18. Je regrette	18. Mi spiace	18. Lo siento mucho	18. Es tut mir leid
19. Please	19. S'il vous plait	19. Per piacere	19. Por favor	19. Bitte
20. I want	20. Je veux	20. Vorrei	20. Yo quiero	20. Ich mochte
21. Airport	21. Aeroport	21. Aeroporto	21. Aeropuerto	21. Flugplatz/Flughafen
22. Automobile/car	22. Auto/voiture	22. Automobile/macchina	22. Automóvil/coche	22. Auto/Wagen
23. Bank	23. Banque	23. Banca	23. Banco	23. Bank
24. Barber	24. Coiffeur	24. Barbiere	24. Barbero	24. Friseur
25. Beauty salon/parlor	25. Salon de beaute	25. Salone di bellezza	25. Salón de belleza	25. Frisiersalon
26. Breakfast	26. Petit dejeuner	26. Prima colazione	26. Desayuno	26. Fruhstuck
27. Bus	27. Autobus	27. Autobus	27. Autobus	27. Bus
28. Change (money)	28. Change	28. Cambio	28. Cambio	28. Geldwechsel
29. Check (bill)	29. Addition	29. Conto	29. Cuenta	29. Rechnung
30. Church	30. Eglise	30. Chiesa	30. Iglesia	30. Kirche
31. Dentist	31. Dentiste	31. Dentista	31. Dentista	31. Zahnarzt
32. Dinner	32. Diner	32. Cena	32. Cena	32. Abendessen
33. Doctor	33. Docteur	33. Dottore	33. Médico	33. Arzt
34. Flat tire	34. Pneu a plat	34. Pneumatico forato	34. Neumatico reventado	34. Reifenpanne
35. Gasoline/petrol	35. Essence	35. Benzina	35. Gasolina	35. Benzin
36. Hospital	36. Hopital	36. Ospedale	36. Hospital	36. Krankenhaus
37. Information	37. Renseignements	37. Informazione	37. Información	37. Auskunft
38. Lavatory (toilet)	38. Toilettes (WC)	38. Gabinetto	38. Retrete/excusado	38. Toilette (W.C.)
39. Lunch	39. Dejeuner	39. Colazione/pranzo	39. Almuerzo	39. Mittagessen
40. Men (gentlemen)	40. Messieurs	40. Signori/uomini	40. Señores/caballeros	40. Manner/Herren
41. Occupied (sign)	41. Occupe	41. Occupato	41. Ocupado	41. Besetzt
42. Pharmacy	42. Pharmacie	42. Farmacia	42. Farmacia	42. Apotheke
43. Post Office	43. Bureau de Poste	43. Ufficio postale	43. Oficina de correos	43. Postamt
44. Registered (letter)	44. Recommande	44. Raccomandata	44. Certificado	44. Einschrieben
45. Room (hotel)	45. Chambre	45. Camera	45. Habitación	45. Zimmer
46. Shop (store)	46. Boutique	46. Negozio	46. Tienda	46. Geschaft
47. Sick	47. Malade	47. Ammalato	47. Enfermo	47. Krank
48. Soap	48. Savon	48. Sapone	48. Jabón	48. Seife
49. Stamp (postage)	49. Timbre-poste	49. Francobollo	49. Sello/estampilla	49. Briefmarke
50. Station (railroad)	50. Gare	50. Stazione	50. Estación	50. Bahnhof
51. Suitcase	51. Valise	51. Valigia	51. Maleta	51. Koffer
52. Telephone	52. Telephone	52. Telefono	52. Teléfono	52. Telefon
53. Ticket (travel)	53. Billet	53. Biglietto	53. Billete	53. Fahrkarte
54. Time (of day)	54. Heure	54. Ora	54. Hora	54. Uhrzeit
55. Today	55. Aujourd'hui	55. Oggi	55. Hoy	55. Heute
56. Tomorrow	56. Demain	56. Domani	56. Mañana	56. Morgen
57. Towel	57. Serviette	57. Asciugamano	57. Toalla	57. Handtuch
58. Train	58. Train	58. Treno	58. Tren	58. Zug
59. Waiter	59. Garcon	59. Cameriere	59. Camerero	59. Kellner
60. Water (drinking)	60. Eau potable	60. Acqua potabile	60. Aqua potable	60. Trinkwasser
61. Women/ladies	61. Dames	61. Signore/donne	61. Señoras/damas	61. Frauen/Damen

SWEDISH	PORTUGUESE	DUTCH	CHINESE	JAPANESE
1. Talar Ni engelska?	1. Você fala inglês?	1. Spreekt U Engels?	1. Na Sic Gong Yin Mon	1. Eigo Hanashimasu Ka?
2. Jag forstar inte	2. Não compreendo	2. Ik begrijp U niet	2. Or But May Bach	2. Wakarimasen
3. Ja/Nej	3. Sim/Não	3. Ja/Nee	3. Si But See	3. Hai/Tie
4. Ert namn?	4. Seu nome?	4. Hoe heet U?	4. Na Men	4. Onamae Wa?
5. Jag, Ni, han, hon	5. Eu, você, êle, ela	5. Ik, jiji, hij, zij	5. Knou; Nea; Ha; Coy	5. Watakushi, Anata (proper names)
6. God morgon	6. Bom dia	6. Goeden Morgen	6. Jo Sun	6. Ohayoo Gozaimasu
7. God afton	7. Boa tarde	7. Goeden avond	7. Mon-On	7. Konban Wa
8. God natt	8. Boa noite	8. Goeden acht	8. Mon On	8. Sayonara
9. Adjo	9. Adeus	9. Goeden dag	9. Joy-Gen	9. Sayoonara
10. Hur star det till?	10. Como vai você?	10. Hoe gaat het met U?	10. Na Ho Ma	10. Ogenki Desu Ka?
11. Hur langt?	11. A que distância?	11. Hoe ver is het?	11. Ga Yeun	11. Dono Kurai Arimasu Ka?
12. Hur mycket?	12. Quanto custa?	12. Hoeveel kost het?	12. Ga Dor Chan	12. Ikura Desu Ka?
13. For dyrt	13. Demasiado	13. Dat is teveel (Dat is te duur)	13. Ho Dor	13. Takai Desu
14. Mycket bra	14. Muito bem	14. Heel goed	14. Oh Ho	14. Hai, Shoochi Shimashita
15. Tack	15. Obrigado	15. Dank U wel	15. Dor Jea	15. Doomo Arigatoo Gozaimasu
16. Ingen orsak	16. De nada	16. Tot Uw dienst	16. Min Say Hawk-Hay	16. Doo Itashimashite
17. Ursakta	17. Desculpe	17. Pardon	17. Ger-Ger	17. Gomen Kudasai
18. Jag beklagar	18. Perdão	18. Het spijt mij zeer	18. Yu Leung	18. Doomo Sumimasen
19. Var god	19. Por favor	19. Alst U blief	19. Ching (Um Goy)	19. Doozo
20. Jag skulle vilja ha	20. Eu quero	20. Ik wil	20. Know Surn	20. Itadakimasen Ka?
21. Flygplats	21. Aeroporto	21. Vliegveld	21. Fay Ga Chon	21. Hikoojo
22. Automobil/bil	22. Automóvel/carro	22. Auto	22. Chea	22. Jidoosha
23. Bank	23. Banco	23. Bank	23. Ong Hong	23. Ginkoo
24. Barberare	24. Barbeiro	24. Herenkapper	24. La Fax See	24. Rihatsuten
25. Damfrisering	25. Salão de beleza	25. Dameskapper	25. Dean Fax Deem	25. Byooin
26. Frukost	26. Café da manhã	26. Ontbijt	26. Jo Chon	26. Asagohan
27. Buss	27. Ônibus	27. Bus	27. Guy-Che	27. Basu
28. Vaxel	28. Trôco	28. Kleingeld	28. San Ong	28. Komakai Mono
29. Rakning	29. Conta	29. Rekening	29. Don	29. Okanjo
30. Kyrka	30. Igreja	30. Kerk	30. Li By Tong	30. Kyookai
31. Tandlakare	31. Dentista	31. Tandarts	31. Knaw-Yee	31. Haisha
32. Middag	32. Jantar	32. Avondeten (Diner)	32. Man-Chon	32. Gohan
33. Lakare	33. Doutor	33. Dokter (Arts)	33. Ye San	33. Isha
34. Punktering	34. Pneu furado	34. Lekke band	34. Che Leung Mo Hay	34. Taiya Ga Panku Shimashita
35. Bensin	35. Gasolina	35. Benzine	35. Hay Yo	35. Gasorin
36. Sjukhus	36. Hospital	36. Ziekenhuis (hospitaal)	36. Yu Yuen	36. Byoin
37. Upplysningar/information	37. Informação	37. Informatie	37. Su Sic	37. Uketsuke
38. Toalett	38. Banheiro	38. Toilet (W.C.)	38. Se Sar	38. Oterai
39. Lunch	39. Almôço	39. Middageten (Lunch)	39. Ang-Jo	39. Obentoo
40. Herrar/man	40. Homens	40. Mannen/Heren	40. Nam Yun	40. Otoko, in speech proper name
41. Upptaget	41. Ocupado	41. Bezet	41. Yo Yung Jo Chu	41. Kore Wa Shiyochu
42. Apotek	42. Farmácia	42. Apotheek	42. Yuk Fon	42. Yakkyoku
43. Postkontor	43. Correio	43. Postkantoor	43. Yo-Jin Gu	43. Yuubinkyoku
44. Rekommenderat	44. Registrado (carta)	44. Aangetekend	44. Dom Bo	44. Kakitome
45. Rum	45. Quarto	45. Kamer	45. Fon	45. Heya
46. Affar	46. Loja	46. Winkel	46. Po Tow	46. Omise
47. Sjuk	47. Doente	47. Ziek	47. Been	47. Byooki
48. Tval	48. Sabão/sabonete	48. Zeep	48. Fon Gon	48. Sekken
49. Frimarke	49. Sêlo	49. Postzegel	49. Yo Peel	49. Ishi
50. Station	50. Estação	50. Station	50. Jarm	50. Eki
51. Kappsack/resvaska	51. Valise/mala	51. Koffer	51. Pay doy (pa Kep)	51. Kaban
52. Telefon	52. Telefone	52. Telefoon	52. Din Wah (Hom Sin)	52. Denwa
53. Biljett	53. Bilhete	53. Kaartje	53. Peel	53. Kippu
54. Tid	54. Tempo	54. Tijd	54. Sea Gan	54. Jikan
55. Idag	55. Hoje	55. Vandaag	55. Gum Yet	55. Kyoo
56. I morgon	56. Amanhã	56. Morgen	56. Ting Yet	56. Ashita
57. Handduk	57. Toalha	57. Handdoek	57. Mo Gun	57. Tenugui
58. Tag	58. Trem	58. Trein	58. For Che	58. Kisha
59. Kyparen	59. Garçom	59. Kelner	59. Kay Toy	59. Kyuuji
60. Dricksvatten	60. Agua	60. Water	60. Sher (Shir)	60. Omizu
61. Damar	61. Mulheres/senhoras	61. Vrouwen/dames	61. Nu Yeung	61. Gofujin/Onna

This is only *one* of
many dialects.

Translation, courtesy
Mayumi Yamamoto
San Francisco, California.

Courtesy Pacific Telephone Company San Francisco, California.

index

q